Rethinking Educational Research

edited by W. B. Dockrell and David Hamilton

Rethinking Educational Research

HODDER AND STOUGHTON

LONDON SYDNEY AUCKLAND TORONTO

British Library Cataloguing in Publication Data
Rethinking educational research.
1. Educational research
I. Dockrell, William Bryan
II. Hamilton, David, *b.1943*
370'.78 LB1028

ISBN 0-340-20548-2

Printed in Great Britain for
Hodder and Stoughton Educational,
a division of Hodder and Stoughton Ltd,
Mill Road, Dunton Green, Sevenoaks, Kent, by
Richard Clay (The Chaucer Press) Ltd, Bungay, Suffolk

Contents

The contributors

R. A. Becher
Professor, Education Area, University of Sussex

Basil Bernstein
Professor, University of London Institute of Education

Jerome Bruner
Watts Professor of Psychology, University of Oxford

Kevin Connolly
Professor of Psychology, University of Sheffield

W. B. Dockrell
Director, Scottish Council for Research in Education

David Hamilton
Lecturer, Department of Education, University of Glasgow

Daniel Kallós
Lecturer, Department of Education, University of Lund, Sweden

Margaret Martlew
Lecturer, Department of Psychology, University of Sheffield

John Nisbet
Professor of Education, University of Aberdeen

Peter K. Smith
Lecturer, Department of Psychology, University of Sheffield

Robert E. Stake
Director, Center for Instructional Research and Curriculum Evaluation, University of Illinois at Urbana-Champaign

Rob Walker
Lecturer, Centre for Applied Research in Education, University of East Anglia

Ian Westbury
Professor, Department of Secondary Education, University of Illinois at Urbana-Champaign

Introduction

This volume provides an overview of recent thinking in educational research. Our original intention was to prepare a volume on educational research in Europe. It soon became clear, however, that such a book would be repetitive and, moreover, would fail to capture the intellectual doubts and unease felt by much of the research community. The volume was therefore recast to include papers which were representative of new thinking, irrespective of where it was taking place.

The contributions do not fall into any neat pattern—we have deliberately eschewed the traditional divisions of educational research. Nevertheless, each author adopts an educational perspective; and most share a concern for the analysis of pedagogy.

Nor are the papers conventional reviews of research. We are concerned not to survey findings over recent years, but to raise questions and focus attention on general issues. The authors of the invited papers were asked to present their own positions rather than to fit into a pre-conceived structure.

For many years the advancement of educational research has been widely regarded as a technological problem. The papers in this volume, however, reject a narrow methodological concern and, explicitly or implicitly, seek out new standards, new roles, new concepts. Indeed, in certain cases they imply a fundamental recasting of educational research. They address issues concerning the purposes of educational enquiry, the relationship between researchers and researched, the processes of data handling, the generation of theory and, not least, the presentation of research results. All these areas are the object of critical scrutiny.

The preparation of this book has taken longer than planned. Consequently, the authors were invited to revise their contributions. Some felt that their original contributions were an adequate representation of their point of view, others have taken the opportunity to incorporate their more recent thinking. The authors speak for themselves but, in combination, they address ideas and issues that, in the editors' view, are likely to continue to feature prominently in the future.

John Nisbet

1. Educational Research: The State of the Art

This attempt to review the present state of educational research in Britain is presented under three headings: growth, trends and structure. I would have found it easier to deal with the subject in a course of ten lectures—after all, the Open University course E 341 on educational research required nineteen booklets, eleven radio programmes, eight television programmes, eight assignments and one project, just to provide an introduction to the topic—but I shall do my best within the limits allowed me.

The growth of educational research

The fact that I have a problem of compressing the subject is itself evidence of my first point, the growth of educational research in recent years. When I began teaching the topic in university in 1949, the text-books I inherited were Vernon's *The Measurement of Abilities* (1940), Burt's *Mental and Scholastic Tests* (1921), Rusk's *Introduction to Experimental Education* (1913) and Whipple's *Manual of Mental and Physical Tests* (1912). Being very up-to-date, I introduced Charlotte Fleming's *Research and the Basic Curriculum* (1946), which was the first example in Britain of a compendium of research which offered something more than just psychometrics. Nearly twenty years passed before we began to see the present flow of really useful books summarising research findings in a general way, like Thouless's *Map of Educational Research* (1969) and Butcher and Pont's series, *Educational Research in Britain* (1968, 1970, 1973). In the meantime, we had to rely on American books, journals and encyclopaedias of educational research, and it is only in the last ten years that educational research has established itself in Britain as a topic in its own right.

The setting up of the British Educational Research Association in 1974 was another evidence of the growth of educational research. Other writers —particularly, Wall, Taylor and Vernon Ward—have calculated how the national expenditure on educational research multiplied ten-fold between 1963 and 1974. Whereas then only 0·01 per cent of all educational expenditure was devoted to research, the figure is now about 0·1 per cent—or, for every pound spent on education, one-tenth of a penny goes to development, research and evaluation. In 1974, for the first time ever, the number of SSRC postgraduate studentships in education reached three figures—100 exactly. If that sounds a small number, remember that in 1968 there were just fourteen SSRC studentships in education; and even in 1972 there were only sixty-five.

There has been a very substantial increase all round; but one has only to see the present position in context to acknowledge that there is still a long way to go. The figures merely demonstrate that, until very recently, educational research was a spare-time amateur activity for gentlemen of leisure.

A more important form of growth has been the widening range of types of research which can be reckoned as coming within the scope of educational research. For many years in the past, educational research was almost exclusively concerned with educational psychology and testing; and though there were eminent pioneers in the fields of the history of education, the philosophy of education and comparative education, these aspects of the subject were isolated and quite unsupported by formal associations of scholars. Recent years have seen a remarkable growth of interest in these areas, and there are now flourishing societies for each of the three aspects. The emergence of curriculum development as an area of study and research has been the largest single element in the growth of recent years, thanks to the work of the Schools Council. But each of us has his own choice of factors which have led to the multiplication of aspects of educational research: sociology, educational technology, classroom observation, participant observation, administration and management of schools, and so on—a whole range of specialist disciplines.

The emergence of these specialisms, however, also carries with it the danger that the study of education may split up into less and less meaningful sub-divisions. There was a time in Aberdeen University, in 1960, when I taught everything in the Department of Education, alone—from Aristotle and comparative education to statistics and testing. (Needless to say, the teaching was not of a uniformly high standard.) Now in the Aberdeen Department, the number of staff is in double figures, though it is still a relatively small department. But now we have to have special meetings to ensure that there is some link between the various aspects, and we require every member of staff to do some tutorial work across all the boundaries. This is a common problem in all disciplines, nowadays. In educational research, in my view, it is particularly important that the different aspects should not develop in isolation: the empirical social scientist needs to draw on history, comparative studies and philosophy. When Noel Entwistle and I wrote our report on transfer from primary to secondary education (1966, 1969), we had a section on theoretical aspects, a historical section, a chapter on comparative studies, an empirical follow-up study, and a small piece of action research. Perhaps the correct solution is to build up a research team which brings the different aspects together. But I would argue strongly against the fissiparous trend in current educational research.

Trends in educational research

Among the various sub-divisions I have been discussing, one of the most vigorous in its growth is the sociological. For many years, educational research was dominated by psychology: it aspired to scientific precision in research design and hypothesis construction and was preoccupied with measurement and statistical analysis. There has undoubtedly been a swing away from this style of research, not unconnected with hostility to examinations and testing and the selective and classificatory function of education. Some of the enthusiasts for sociological styles of research have moved in on the back of this anti-scientific and anti-measurement wave. Of course they are right to be sceptical about precision in the behavioural sciences. Sometimes important aspects are ignored merely because they are difficult to measure. Often the hypothetico-deductive method is a way of reinforcing our assumptions, for we all make assumptions which provide our orientation to the world and define it for us, and direct our attention so that we see only what we are looking for; and we ought instead to start by trying to see the situation as the other person sees it. Perhaps we are witnessing a change in educational research, like the change in music and art from a classical era to a modern one. But I don't see this trend as dispensing with the need for rigour and precision. On the contrary, there is a place for both styles, and certainly students should be responsive to the merits of both, so that they can recognise excellence and spot the flaws, whatever the style.

Rather than see this as a confrontation, I suggest that the trend of the past fifteen years has been the emergence of a range of styles, which have added greatly to the power of educational research methods. I used the word 'range', but perhaps it is better described as a 'spectrum'—

1	2	3	4	5
Experimental method	*Exploratory survey*	*Curriculum development*	*Action research*	*Open-ended inquiry*
Empirical Educational science	Fact-finding as a basis for decision making	New syllabus content and method. Field trials and evaluation	Interventionist	Grounded theory. Participant observation. Illuminative evaluation.

The agricultural model	*The anthropological model*
Experiments to improve your products by manipulating treatments	Go and live there and see what it is like

because a spectrum has no sharp boundaries, and also (if it is not straining the metaphor) because you get white light by mixing all the different frequencies!

Categories 1 and 2 represent the empirical tradition, which has a strong Scottish-American flavour. The Scots—Thomson, Rusk, Drever, Boyd—who set up the first educational research council in Europe in 1928 believed in it, and the idea can be traced back to Herbert Spencer and to Alexander Bain, who as a professor in Aberdeen University was responsible for the teaching of philosophy, logic, rhetoric, English literature and language and psychology, and also wrote a book called *Education as a Science* in 1879. In fact, in 1946, in Aberdeen Training College (as it was then called), the Departments of Education and Psychology were combined into a Department of Educational Science—an innovation which was subsequently abandoned. The concept of a science of education is based on the belief that educational problems should—and can—be solved by objective empirical evidence, that precise and accurate research can build up a structure of knowledge which will generate new hypotheses and new experiments, until the whole field is uncovered. This was a common aspiration in the 1920s and 1930s, and it has an initial appeal to each new generation of researchers. It is based on the faith that, if only one could design a good enough experiment, with effective controls, precise evaluative measurement and appropriate sensitive statistical analysis, it should be possible to establish objectively the one best method, the ideal curriculum, the optimum period of instruction, the correct use of aids to learning. Once these points have been established by experiment, and adopted in the educational system, any change must be for the worse. So the Scottish researchers tried to decide whether it was better to teach children to add up a column or down a column; whether in subtraction, the method of 'equal addition' was superior to the method of 'decomposition'; whether 'phonics' was better than 'look and say'; and today, the educational technologists try to determine whether programmed learning is better than traditional methods, whether television is better than a live teacher, whether colour is better than black-and-white; and in higher education, we are asked, 'Which is better, lecture or tutorial?' or 'Is there any evidence to show what is the optimum length of a lecture?' The educational science idea keeps recurring: in 1964, Sanford, in *The American College*, wrote: 'Practice in higher education, as in politics, remains largely untouched by the facts and principles of science. What our colleges do, tends either to be governed by tradition, or to be improvised in the face of diverse—and usually unanticipated—pressures.' So Sanford envisages 'a science of higher education . . . the notion that the field (of research) may ultimately be constituted as a body of fact and theory, a discipline of sorts, in which individuals become specialists.'

But most educational researchers today no longer hold this faith in their power. Perhaps we have lost what was a guiding star to the pioneers, and a great source of strength, but it was always a myth. There is no one best method. Most empirical research studies are, to use Ashby's (1958) phrase, 'miniscule analyses'. This is hardly surprising: all science proceeds by 'miniscule analyses', and the building of a coherent theory is a very slow process on which we have only just begun. For the present, the problems which can be resolved empirically are relatively minor, compared with the major issues which require a judgment of values. Nevertheless, in these major issues, research has an important contribution to make, in defining objectives, in evaluation, in assembling relevant and adequate evidence on which to base our judgments.

And this takes me to the second category in my 'spectrum'. One of the distinctive developments of educational research in the past twenty years has been the recognition that too often educational decisions are made without an adequate knowledge base. A major area of achievement is the fact-finding survey type of research, such as the national reading surveys every four years (approximately) since 1948, or the National Child Development study, or the Isle of Wight study, from which we can tell how many children are deaf, stutter, have behaviour problems, are left-handed, wet the bed (and at what ages) and so on. All the major educational reports—Crowther, Newsom, Robbins, Plowden—have been accompanied by extensive surveys, and are much the better for it.

But there is also a potential weakness in this kind of research, for much of it is news rather than science:

> Children in the North of England watch television more than children in the South of England;
> Eighteen per cent of junior school teachers do not know how to begin teaching reading;
> Thirty per cent of medical students live at home.

In the absence of theory or hypotheses, these are useless pieces of information. To quote one reviewer (Holmes, 1972):

> At first sight . . . research might appear to be thriving. But this impression results from the use of the term 'research' to cover work which might better be designated as . . . development, survey or information. This umbrella usage tends to obscure the fact that controlled evaluative research . . . is rare.

My third category is curriculum development, which is the largest single growth area since 1960. It occupies a middle position between my two extremes, drawing on theory and survey, using experimental work and field trials, prepared to venture into open-ended inquiries—as is appropriate for practical-oriented development work which attempts to bridge the gap between theory and practice. If there is a danger of weakness here, it is that curriculum development is inclined to isolate itself as a special new kind of discipline, with its own specialists, its own techniques, its own jargon and even its own funding organisation, instead of recognising how much it has to gain from well designed experiment and evaluation on the one hand, and interventionist and exploratory-type studies on the other hand.

And so we come to the last two categories, which offer a promise of transforming the whole field of educational research, if only we can prevent them from being used by people as a short-cut to 'instant research', to avoid the trouble of thought and planning, or to cover up a lack of knowledge or a willingness to submit one's ideas to the test of hard evidence. It was Michael Young (1965) who pointed out the calamity of the gap between research and innovation; there is innovation without research—new ideas based on hunches, never tested objectively; and there is research without innovation—academic studies which make no impact and are unintelligible except to other researchers. Bringing research and innovation together in 'interventionist-type studies' gives 'action research', in which research monitors change, research is a guide to action, and the results of action are a guide to research.

Halsey's (1972) review of action research in Chapter 13 of *Educational Priority*, Volume 1, is as lucid an analysis as is to be found; and I doubt if there is much I can add to what is said there. As I see it, the problem is to keep research alive beside its dominant and vigorous partner; but the action men in the Educational Priority Area (EPA) studies saw the problem as winning freedom for action from the cold restrictions imposed by the researchers. The tension exists between the two concepts, action and research: action has all the popular qualities—commitment, involvement, belief, enthusiasm; the qualities needed in research have a more limited appeal—detachment, suspension of belief, scepticism. Or to use the vocabulary of Elizabeth Richardson (1975): for action, there must be loyalty, and loyalty is 'a collusion to maintain the pretence of infallibility'; but research requires a tolerance of heresy, 'a willingness to submit the most sacred ideas to the test of reality'.

Action research developed as a protest against the scientific detachment of traditional psychological and psychometric studies. This protest has now been carried to its logical extreme in the last of my five categories of research. On the anthropological model, to understand the educational process, to do any effective research in education, one must see it from the viewpoint of the learner. Traditional empirical research, especially when it involves testing, experiment and statistical analysis, starts from *our* assumptions, *our* framework of thought, and it imposes that framework on what we innocently call the 'subjects' in our experiments. Not surprisingly, the framework usually does not fit; and so we adjust our control mechanisms until we have a situation where we can use our preconceived models—and, not surprisingly, this kind of research produces results of limited value and limited application.

So we have a new style of research, and it is one which we must come to terms with. Just as psychology dominated the 'educational science' style, so sociology dominates this opposite extreme. Here it is important to build constructs on the basis of open-ended inquiry. The case study reveals the unique features of a situation. Participant observation enables the observer to get inside the skin of a situation, instead of studying it in a detached way. Grounded theory is built up from observation, not imposed *a priori*. The descriptions used by different participants to explain their experience provide an exploratory tool; and thus theory is grounded in the everyday life of the people who are being studied. Illuminative evaluation uncovers the nature of what has happened; it does not prove that *x* is better or worse than *y* (How could it be? They are different, and comparison is irrelevant.).

This style of research, like the others, has its potential weaknesses. It can be an excuse for indiscriminate data collection, for tiresome transcripts of trite interview exchanges—research without ideas, which is research without interest, the anecdotal model, rather than the anthropological model. But at its best, this is a highly sophisticated and perceptive style of research (and I wish we knew how to teach the skills on which it depends). It can be even more demanding than the relatively straightforward laboratory experiment, and it may require the use of complex statistical analysis or elaborate procedures like the repertory grid.

We are often presented with this style of research as a challenge to the traditional model. To some extent it is; but my position is that no one of these styles is 'right', and none is altogether 'wrong'. The most effective research employs a variety of strategies, across the spectrum.

Structure in educational research

Structure includes both the organisational structure of research funding and the infrastructure of research support, and here there is clearly a need for a meeting place like the British Educational Research Association, to bring interested parties into effective communication with each other. But many people would want to go further. For example, the Universities Council on the Education of Teachers, in a 1971 research policy document, stated:

> There should be consideration at national level of the possibility of establishing better machinery than at present for the identification and discussion of research priorities and the co-ordination of research policies and initiatives.

Can we envisage the creation of an organised and integrated structure for educational research, for planning, funding, monitoring, for developing research support services, overseeing the provision of research training and financing postgraduate students? I confess that the creation of such a structure is a grand ambition—or, perhaps, a pipe-dream—which I have had myself from time to time. I suspect it was in the minds of some when the Schools Council was set up in 1964, and again when the Educational Research Board was established, in 1965. In both cases, if people had such expectations, they have been disappointed. But from time to time there is talk of creating an Educational Research Council, a supreme body, which would oversee the work of the wide range of institutions concerned with research and development in education, integrating their activities and determining their priorities.

None of the bodies involved in research funding is enthusiastic about this kind of monolithic structure. Perhaps they are merely defending their vested interests, but the argument against it is well made in W. C. Radford's report, *Research into Education in Australia, 1972*:

> Co-ordination is useful, provided it does not throttle intellectual independence and initiative. In the complexities of the social sciences, complete co-ordination

> of research would require omniscience and should never be attempted. (Quoted from Conrad, 1960)

> The development of a subject is to a large extent a gradual uneven growth ... and the most that can be done is to ensure that the system ... discourages the growth from being too uneven or too gradual. (Quoted from Cunningham, 1972)

> Let me make clear immediately that I do not believe in the laying down of priorities in research by a central body ... My reason is simple. Such a laying down of priorities to me implies an impossible omniscience, and lays up trouble for itself ... Provided that those engaged in research develop adequate channels of communication between themselves ... I believe there will not be any greater gap between the nature of problems and the information from research available to solve them, than there would be were there to be a central determination of a limited number of priority areas in which alone study would be supported. It is as well to remember that, not very many years ago, 'education as investment' and 'manpower studies' loomed very much larger as matters of research than now seems warranted by later experience ... Had the major part of the research apparatus swung over to such studies in 1965 or 1966, a good deal of work now known to be more valuable would not have been done.

I am reminded of Berlyne's story (see Yates, 1971) of the response of an imaginary advisory council in 1810, asked to forecast the development of the transport system. 'One thing', they concluded, 'has stood the test of time over several thousand years: the horse has come to stay. Authorities as diverse as Genghis Khan, Dick Turpin, Julius Caesar and Buffalo Bill, all agree on one thing, from long experience, that there is no better way of getting from one place to another than on a horse.'

So the attitude of the Educational Research Board has been mainly responsive. 'Responsive' does not mean waiting for others to make suggestions: it means being ready to respond to imaginative ideas, and resisting the temptation to impose one's own ideas. Few other bodies are prepared to do this; few are able to do it with public money. Mrs Thatcher (then Secretary of State for Education), in 1970, expressed the directly opposite view for DES-sponsored research:

> There was clearly only one direction that the Department's research policy could sensibly take. It had to move from a basis of patronage—the rather passive support of ideas which were essentially other people's, related to problems which were often of other people's choosing—to a basis of commission. This meant the active initiation of work by the Department on problems of its own choosing, within a procedure and timetable which were relevant to its needs. Above all, it meant focusing much more on issues which offered a real possibility of yielding useable conclusions.

This is an appropriate view for a government department, but it is also appropriate for a body like ERB to be prepared to operate outside the limits of established policy. The 1973 report of ERB said:

> When the Board reviewed the problem early in 1973, its decision was to reaffirm the 1971 policy statement, that whereas 'the other major bodies are chiefly concerned with policy-oriented research, SSRC should have a more basic and intellectually innovating role'. The distinction between policy-oriented and basic research is open to question, and there is no implication in the statement quoted that SSRC is interested only in 'pure' social science inquiries: the intention is to bring out an emphasis on the theoretical contribution which each approved project should make as at least part of its results. This is an aspect of educational research which does not seem to be adequately dealt with by the other funding agencies.

There is a place for both approaches and a need for partnership between them. There is a place also for each, occasionally, to do something of the other's role; thus, the ERB has recently embarked on the task of instituting a programme of research in pre-school education, and this will be developed in conjunction with the national programme of the DES, DHSS and the Scottish Education Department.

There is, however, one aspect of the organisation of educational research where there is an obligation—an urgent need—to undertake positive initiatives. This is to build up an extensive *infrastructure* for research and development. William Taylor (1972) has argued this point persuasively in writing and in speeches: the most effective way to improve the quality of educational research, he says, is to build an adequate 'research floor'—funds, equipment, personnel, procedures, training programmes, communication, information retrieval, and so on. To take only one example, information retrieval, the Educational Research Board brought together the representatives of fifteen different organisations to agree on a common format for abstracts of research; and with feasibility studies begun by the National Foundation for Educational Research in England and Wales and the Scottish Council for Research in Education, working in collaboration with the Council of Europe EUDISED thesaurus of educational terms, we have the basis for a possible information retrieval service covering the whole European scene, to match the ERIC system on the other side of the Atlantic.

To summarise, I think that recent years have seen a move away from the naive idea that problems are solved by educational research; that is the old 'educational science' idea, and it is a myth. Educational research can strengthen the information base of decision-making; its procedures of inquiry and evaluation can inject rigour into the flabby educational thinking which has satisfied us for too long in the past. The most important contribution of research is, I suggest, indirect. This is important: in one sense, educational researchers are the unacknowledged legislators of the next generation. As Taylor says in his book *Research Perspectives in Education* (1973) a primary function of research in education is to sensitise—to make people aware of problems. Also, in assessing the achievements of educational research, we have to consider its effect on the attitude of those who teach. Vigorous research activity or, to use a less pretentious title, investigation into teaching and learning, sharpens thinking, directs attention to important issues, clarifies problems, encourages debate and the exchange of views, and thus deepens understanding, prevents ossification of thinking, promotes flexibility and adaptation to changing demands. Research of this kind aims to increase the problem-solving capacity of the educational system, rather than to provide final answers to questions, or objective evidence to settle controversies. On this view, educational research is a mode of thinking rather than a shortcut to answers. In the long run, the real influence of educational research is through its effect on the attitudes of those who teach.

Note: This paper was originally given as an address to the inaugural meeting of the British Educational Research Association in Birmingham on 5 April 1974 by John Nisbet.

W. B. Dockrell

2. The Contribution of Research to Knowledge and Practice Truth—What is that?

That there is a considerable malaise in educational research is perhaps more obvious to those who read research proposals or review articles for inclusion in journals than to those who only read published reports. More striking to the journal reader might be the continued existence of 'normal science' in educational research. In the nearly fifty years of its existence, the editors of the *British Journal of Educational Psychology* seem to have shared the same assumptions about the nature of research. It is not merely that the questions for investigation are remarkably similar but that the pragmatic approach, the kind of questions asked and the methods used, are essentially the same.

If R. B. Cattell were to submit 'The assessment of teaching ability' (1931) to the current editor of the *British Journal of Educational Psychology*, it might not be accepted for publication in volume 50 as it was in volume 1. We have developed more refined statistical techniques and accumulated a great deal more information in the intervening years. Yet the techniques which Cattell used to develop 'a rating scale for the assessment of teachers about to leave college' and 'an abbreviated and simplified scale . . . suggested for use in the selection of teachers from among pupils leaving school' are essentially those we would use today and the pragmatic approach of the study would, I suspect, be still generally acceptable.

Indeed, the article by Austin 'An analysis of the motives of adolescents for the choice of the teaching profession' (1931) might be accepted by the editor of a contemporary journal for publication today. Amos's study 'Examination and intelligence-test forecasts of school achievement' (1931) has, in fact, been replicated recently but this time with reference to admission to university and not to secondary school. As with the contemporary study, he looks at the correlations between his predictors and first and subsequent years. He examines sub-groups. He uses partial correlations and combines predictors as do contemporary researchers. In his discussion of his findings and their implication, he explicitly takes account of sociological investigations of the social distribution of intelligence.

To go even further back, in the first volume of the *Journal of Educational Psychology* published in 1910 not only are the concerns and the techniques the same, but a discussion of a publication of Cyril Burt which had as one of its concerns the contribution of environmental influence and inheritance to general intelligence has a decidedly contemporary ring. The educational research journals are of more recent foundation so perhaps it is not surprising that the current issues of the British and American journals are very similar to the earlier volumes.

There have, of course, been many developments in educational research over the last fifty years, but the appropriate puzzles to be solved are apparently those defined in the early years of this century. The basic concepts have remained essentially the same as has the definition of legitimate techniques of investigation.

If the surface has an appearance of calm, it is misleading. For over the last fifty years, there has been a great expansion of educational research, a tremendous expenditure of public funds and a fashion among administrators and politicians for referring to research findings as a justification for their actions. What was a fairly small pool has become, if not an ocean, at least a fair size loch. Research journals and monographs of all kinds have proliferated and the number of research reports has increased to the point where only a computerised retrieval system can hope to provide a reasonably comprehensive list of references on any topic. All this should perhaps be a cause for euphoria not dismay.

Educational research, like Janus, has two faces. A research report can be read in two ways, as a guide to action or as a contribution to understanding. This is not to say that some research is of itself applied and some theoretical. It is not a difference that inheres in the study itself. Rather it is a distinction that lies in the mind of the reader, in the use that the reader puts the study to. The reader's interpretation does not necessarily coincide with the writer's intention. Indeed, the reader may see implications that are completely outside the researcher's frame of reference. The distinction drawn between decision oriented and conclusion oriented research is unhelpful precisely because it focusses on the writer's intention. What the reader needs are criteria that will help him to see the relevance of a report to his own concerns, practical or theoretical.

The evidence of disarray is of two kinds relating to these two aspects of research as a guide to action and as a body of knowledge.

My major concern is with the evidence of breakdown which is internal to educational research itself and how some of the difficulties might be overcome. It is, though, worth noting first some of the external difficulties since it is the external funders who in the long run will determine the amount of effort that can be devoted to research and are more and more trying to determine the kind of research that will be carried on.

Administrators and politicians seem no longer to be convinced that educational research adequately funded and left to run its own house will tell them what they want to know. The attempt by the 'consumers' to determine what research will be carried on is a major piece of evidence of this disillusion. In Britain, this change is associated with the Rothschild Report and is, therefore, easily dismissed as part of a general attitude to government financed research. It is part of this general climate but it is more than that. The difficulties which have beset the American National Institute of Education are more obviously a response to the disenchantment of the politicians and officials not with research in general but specifically with research in education. Less dramatic changes but equally important both in policy and expectations in Sweden, the country where educational research has been most closely related to decision making, illustrate the same growing caution on the part of the decision makers.

Berlyne (1966) argued that the best way of getting research done is 'to pick out capable researchers and give them their freedom to proceed' (page 117). He went on to argue that 'if somebody had been asked to do research about the year 1800 on how transportation could be improved, what would he have done? He might have looked for some improvement in diet which would give horses greater stamina. He might have sought some way of breeding faster horses. He might have wondered whether coaching inns could be better spaced along the highways or more pliable springs could be installed in stage coaches . . . Any one concerned to improve transportation should have sought ways of improving equitation' (pages 118–19). He goes on to point out 'this was not the kind of research that leads to such advances as the steam locomotive, the internal combustion engine and the aeroplane'. Watt and Galvani were at work but the significance of their work for transportation was not clear to themselves nor to anybody else. Without support their work would not have developed and we would not have transport as we know it today.

Berlyne's paper was read at the Ontario Institute for Studies in Education and its basic premise was accepted. The Institute was generously funded and allowed to devise its own research programme. However, it is an argument which the 'customers' are now less likely to accept. They might fairly argue that for a good many years better horses and coaches would have been more valuable than Galvani's research, that it was practical businessmen who exploited on a gradual and pragmatic basis the possibilities of the steam engine for transportation, that no-one would want to interfere with Galvani's experiments on frogs' legs except possibly the Royal Society for the Prevention of Cruelty to Animals but that it was impossible to tell which of the many schemes proposed to them were going to lead to the type of breakthrough which is exemplified by the discovery and exploitation of electricity.

If the administrators and politicians were merely trying to keep in their own hands the designation of areas for research because assigning substantial amounts of public money is essentially a political decision, they would have a strong case. They would, of course, need informed advice on which were likely to be the most productive lines to pursue. It could be argued too that in the past much British educational research has been in areas of public concern anyhow and that it has covered the very areas which should have been designated by the customers. Hence there should be no cause for anxiety.

It is true too that over the last fifty years, the educational researchers who have been most deeply immersed in practical issues have made the most important theoretical developments. Burt and Thomson, Vernon and Wiseman are examples of men whose work has been intimately involved in practical concerns and which has been of general theoretical significance. It can be argued too that their theoretical studies were in a sense commissioned either directly as in the case of Burt's surveys for the London County Council or indirectly in the case of Thomson and his colleagues by the purchase of Moray House tests.

Why then is the Rothschild principle being applied to education and does it matter? It is not obvious that the research of the last twenty-five years even in areas of general concern has contributed to the formation of policy or when it has apparently been taken into account that it has been properly understood. Educational practice has changed, new official policies have been adopted in areas where there has been research but the findings of the research have been Delphic, even when the opinions of the researchers have been emphatically expressed.

The attempt by administrators to make more use of research involves not only the designation by them of the problem areas but also the formulation of the questions and the definition of the role of researchers. Here lies the real danger. There is a risk that unsophisticated administrators wanting to obtain information which is directly relevant to immediate issues will try to restrict research to the provision of data for they do not realise that the mere gathering of figures will not tell them what they want to know. Information is important but figures are not facts. Truth is elusive.

Even apparently straightforward sets of data need care in interpretation. The difficulties of the unsophisticated interpretation of research are well illustrated by the reaction to Wells and Start's research on reading which was published just before the Bullock Committee on reading was set up. This study provided no basis for concern about reading standards. The figures in the report showed no evidence of declining standards in literacy. Yet they have been cited as evidence of a general decline.

Politicians and public alike who have learned to view opinion polls as predictors of election results with considerable caution seem not to be aware that many similar limitations apply to educational research. The significance of the wording of the question, the willingness of those questioned to answer accurately, the importance of sample size and representativeness are all considered at length in the press and on television when a poll is being discussed. Results of polls are now frequently accompanied by comments on the probable range of error. Yet reports of educational research are rarely considered in the same sophisticated way.

As phrasing the questions is the first problem for opinion pollsters so arriving at an acceptable definition of the criteria of what is meant by, for example, reading and preparing or selecting appropriate tests is the first task of the educational researcher. In the case of reading, all the usual measures from word recognition to use of library are fairly highly correlated so that the same general conclusion is likely to be drawn no matter which measure is used. Changes in usage which make words or expressions more or less familiar are gradual and should not make large differences to scores on reading tests. In the broader context of the achievement of schools with different objectives, however, there are important problems. Unless the measures used are chosen carefully, results can be misleading. The modern primary school, for example, has objectives which the traditional school does not have. The measurement of the modern school by the criteria which were established for traditional education is at best to miss the essential features of the new approach and at worst to create a false impression of the effectiveness of these schools.

There are problems with the response in education as there are in opinion polls. Children's performance on the researchers' tests are influenced by many factors. Haggard (1954) demonstrated many years ago that different groups of children seemed to respond differently to routine testing, a point that has been recently repeated by Jencks. This has been dramatically illustrated by Labov (1970) in the case of language usage. It has important implications for the meaning of group differences in scores on achievement tests. If children from one social group get consistently lower scores on reading tests than children from another group, lower level of reading skill is only one possible explanation of this difference. Attitude to testing in general, to the particular test or to the tester might be equally plausible alternative explanations. Any conclusions about the real level of attainment of radically different social groups drawn on the basis of test scores is open to doubt.

Even the more obvious difficulties that arise from sampling are often missed by officials and politicians. In the reading survey, the authors drew attention to some of the limitations of their sample. As with opinion polling, educational research is dependent upon the willing cooperation of teachers and pupils. Any bias in the sampling may result in false conclusions being drawn. The big difference between educational research and opinion polling is that in research there is no equivalent to the election. There is no ultimate test of the conclusions. In reading, for example, we do not know whether the scores obtained from the sample used in a particular research are representative of the country as a whole or not. All we can do is draw another sample and conduct another study which may have parallel or countervailing weaknesses.

Even in apparently straightforward situations, the figures that educational research can provide are tentative and need to be interpreted if reasonable conclusions are to be drawn. Where the researcher's statistical techniques are more complex, as for example in path analysis or multiple regression analysis, assumptions which have been built in to the statistical procedures determine the answers which can emerge. Misunderstandings of complex statistical tables of this kind give rise to obviously nonsensical statements like the assertion that schools do not make any difference to academic achievement because all is determined beforehand by home circumstances.

Not all of the misapprehensions of the politicians and administrators can be attributed to reading the research with insufficient care. The researchers themselves must accept some of the responsibility. Major sources of misunderstandings, confusion between speculation and evidence, between precise findings and vague impressions, and between generally valid conclusions and results applicable to a small and possibly unrepresentative group, which are examined in detail later, can be found in the reports of the researchers. Bloom's speculations about the importance of the first five years for the growth of intelligence in *Stability and Change in Human Characteristics* (1964) which greatly influenced the American Head Start Program were wrongly read by some researchers as firm conclusions. Similarly, general assertions about comprehensive education or progressive primary education have been based on a case study of a single secondary school or a survey of a few teachers in one district.

Another set of difficulties has arisen from the researchers' use of statistics. It is obviously misleading to use statistical tests to give weight to impressions when the assumptions necessary for the use of these statistics have not been met. It is equally misleading to produce tables and talk about differences between percentages without the usual indications of statistical significance. Floud, Halsey and Martin's *Social Class and Educational Opportunity* (1956) made an important contribution to the debate on the relative merits of comprehensive and selective schooling. On its last page is a note on the statistical reliability of tables. Is it reasonable to expect politicians or administrators even to notice a warning about the absence of statistical significance or if they do to understand that these data 'are subject to considerable error from chance fluctuation so that the conclusions based on them must be regarded as to that extent tentative' and to revise the impressions they had gained from reading the book?

The design and limitations of particular studies are often not spelled out. Svennson's *Ability Grouping and Scholastic Achievement* (1962) was influential in providing support for the Swedish school reform. His conclusion that children did not benefit from streaming seemed to provide justification for the adoption of the comprehensive system. Yet as his critics have pointed out, his conclusion that high ability groups made the same score no matter what type of school they were in may well have been an artefact of the data. These high ability pupils were obtaining marks so close to the maximum of the test that no differences among them could show up. It is surely the responsibility of the researchers to underline these limitations in their data.

It should not be surprising that most administrators lack sophistication in interpreting research findings and in turning questions about significant educational issues into researchable form. Yet the disenchantment of politicians and officials may put responsibility for educational research into just such unsophisticated hands. To overcome this danger, some national systems of education are appointing intermediaries who are themselves skilled researchers. Their major duty is to communicate the findings of research to the administrators and the concerns of the administrators to the researchers. These interpreters of research are unlikely to make the crass errors of the unsophisticated since they are aware of the limitations to the contribution which research can make to the formulation of policy. They realise that research cannot be expected to provide definitive answers to policy questions. While there is not yet general agreement about the contribution of research to forming policy there are suggestions emerging from practice in Sweden and speculation elsewhere (Cohen and Garet, 1975) of the more subtle reciprocal relationship which allows the researchers' studies to inform the decisions of politicians and administrators but does not try to preempt them.

Three roles have been suggested for research. One is the traditional provision of research findings where they are available but with considerably more emphasis than in the past on the tentative nature of the conclusions and the limitations to their general application. Research would thus provide suggestions for policy rather than authoritative guidance. A second role is the stimulation of thought by raising new issues, by questioning assumptions and by pointing to the weaknesses of current practice. The third is the contribution of form and structure to the evaluation of new curricula and techniques.

In an approach of this kind, there is a danger of the researcher becoming a court jester, a licensed fool who is allowed to make outrageous comments from time to time but is not to be taken seriously by practical men. Only a relationship of mutual understanding and mutual respect can prevent this. The alternative risk is that the researchers will be coopted into the educational mainstream which they have helped to establish and direct. Something of the kind may have happened with the researchers who participated in selection for secondary education by preparing tests or in the design of programmes for Educational Priority Area. There may be a risk that individual researchers would become committed to particular activities. It is unlikely, however, that the whole research community would become uncritical where there are a number of research centres and alternative sources of funding.

There is then evidence of considerable disillusion among officials and politicians about the traditional claim of educational research to make an authoritative contribution to policy decisions. This is most obvious in the United States where the National Institute of Education is having difficulty in obtaining adequate funding and in Canada where the basis of funding for the Ontario Institute for Studies in Education has been changed. There is too evidence in Europe of changing attitudes which may make for restriction in the resources available for research and for the extension of greater control by officials. However, different and more realistic expectations of the contribution of research to practice are emerging. This more limited concept of the 'truth' that research can contribute to policy-making may provide the basis for a renewed commitment to educational research and ultimately to fewer constraints on the researchers.

The more important source of difficulty in knowing what truth emerges from educational research lies in the confusion among educational researchers about the status of their conclusions. It is not merely that educational researchers include advocates of the big sweep approach to the acquisition of knowledge, as for example, the study on which the Coleman Report was based in the US or the National Child Development Study in the UK, and the brick by brick approach exemplified in the United States by the work of Bloom and his colleagues on mastery learning and in the UK by the investigations of Bernstein and his associates into the relationship between language and learning; or that educational theory includes those who seek the grand design like the followers of Piaget and those who accept the jigsaw puzzle approach, content to develop concepts which facilitate understanding of one small aspect of human learning. These differences exist in most fields. Among educational researchers there is the more important confusion about the contribution to knowledge made by particular studies. Whitehead in his paper 'The Rhythm of Education' (1932) adapts Hegel's thesis, antithesis and synthesis: 'In relation to educational progress I would term them the stage of romance, the stage of precision and the stage of generalisation'. There is widespread confusion among the researchers about the contribution to educational thinking of any particular study.

A case study which provides an interesting basis for speculation (the stage of romance) is all too often interpreted as providing definitive findings of general validity (the stage of generalisation). This confusion is well illustrated in the studies of compensatory education which made up a major part of the research effort in the US in the last decade and provided the basis for the largest single research activity mounted in the UK. The confusion is not limited to this work. Research in other areas, for example, secondary organisation or primary methods, shows the same difficulties. However, for the rest of this article the illustrations will be drawn primarily from the work on educational deprivation.

According to Whitehead, the first stage, 'the stage of romance', is where knowledge is not dominated by systematic procedures. It is when we experience 'the excitement consequent on the transition from the bare facts to the first realisations of their import, of their unexplored relationships'. In the area of compensatory education, the work of researchers like Hebb and Kretch played an early and important role. They had demonstrated that the performance of adult animals can be markedly depressed by environmental deprivation when young, and conversely could be boosted by environmental richness. McV. Hunt's book *Intelligence and Experience* (1961) revolutionised thinking in psychology and education about intelligence. Before this, relatively little stress had been placed on experience in the development of human intelligence and the research which had emphasised it had often been discounted. Hunt brought these researches together and began the exploration of their relationship. Perhaps more important in its impact on education was Bloom's *Stability and Change in Human Characteristics* (1964). This too is an exploratory speculative book which on the basis of existing evidence questioned established beliefs and suggested the possible importance of experience in the early years for both school learning and adult intelligence. Hunt and Bloom's work was at the first of Whitehead's stages. They were speculations about previously unexplored relationships. They were concerned with plausible argument rather than with empirical verification.

This exploratory stage is, according to Whitehead, an essential part of human thinking and is now generally accepted by researchers. The problem is not to agree that research of this kind is important but to recognise it when it is carried out. There is an easy but mistaken tendency to equate the case study with this approach and indeed Smith and Geoffrey in *Complexities of an Urban Classroom* (1968) do just this. They assert that the kind of study that they are reporting is more appropriately a means of generating hypotheses than of testing them. Yet other researchers seem surprised when they find that the conclusions drawn from one case study are different from those arising from another. As Fisher pointed out in *The Design of Experiments* (1937) statistically significant relationships which emerge in the course of a study but which have not previously been hypothesised cannot be treated as findings. They are instead the basis of hypotheses for future studies. This is because the conclusions are properly hypotheses not generalisations. The observation of regularities which lead to fruitful speculation is not, however, restricted to the case study. At the other end of the spectrum psychometric studies can be used to generate hypotheses. They can suggest relationships which had not previously been noted. Statistical tables, casual observation of children, theoretical writings in other fields, all can lead to the crystallisation of ideas.

The researcher is right to publish his exploratory studies and to put forward his hypotheses derived from them provided that they are clearly presented as tentative hypotheses and not as definitive conclusions.

The second of Whitehead's stages, the stage of precision, is where 'width of relationship is subordinated to exactness of formulation. It is the stage of grammar, the grammar of language and the grammar of science. It proceeds by forcing on the students' acceptance, a given way of analysing the facts bit by bit. New facts are added but they are the facts which fit into the analysis'.

It is true of educational research as of education itself that 'we tend to confine it to the second stage of the cycle; namely to our stage of precision' and as Whitehead goes on to assert 'a stage of precision is barren without the previous stage of romance: unless there are facts which have already been vaguely apprehended in their broad generality, the previous analysis is an analysis of nothing. It is simply a series of meaningless statements about bare facts, produced artificially and without any further relevance'. In educational research, those experiments which test trivial or inadequately formulated hypotheses with well designed experiments contribute no more to our understanding than studies of 'ideas with possibilities of wide significance' without 'the systematic order' imposed by carefully controlled investigations.

The task at this stage for those involved in the study of deprivation was three-fold. The first task was to formulate exactly the nature of the handicap suffered by deprived children. Were the deficiencies linguistic (Bernstein)? Were they motivational (Zigler)? Was it a matter of attentiveness (Kagan)?

The second step was to define the differences between the early environment of deprived children and those not deprived. Here the studies of Hess and Shipman (1965) were crucial. The third step was to devise and test compensatory procedures to see which were most effective. At each step the facts had to be analysed systematically and new facts fitted into the analysis. An equally important part of this stage of precision is the experimental verification of the exact formulations developed.

The studies of deprivation, like so many others in social science, suffered from deficiencies both at the stage of romance and the stage of precision. Some investigated what, with hindsight, are far too simplistic notions of deprivation. Others faced with the choice between 'egalitarian policies or obscurities of unnecessary research' (Halsey, 1972) embraced enthusiastically policies which they failed to evaluate. Thus both groups contributed to frustrating the expressed objective of the Educational Priorities Area Studies which was to define the approaches which were most effective.

In educational research precision is of no value without romance; romance unhelpful without precision.

Just as at the stage of romance, the contribution of experiments or psychometric manipulation of data may be undervalued as a basis for speculation about previously unexplored relations, so at the stage of precision the contribution of case studies of individuals or institutions may be undervalued. The anthropologist can enter the classroom with precise questions to ask, precise hypotheses to test, and he may not need an interaction schedule to help him. The fundamental confusion is between techniques and the significance of the results. Statistical significance does not indicate a definitive finding. It may simply suggest an interesting area to explore. Field notes, projective tests may not only provide a rich basis for speculation but a precise test of exactly formulated hypotheses.

It is tempting to assume at this point that the process is complete, that the answer has been found. However, even if the hypotheses derived from the stage of romance are 'of wide significance' and the experiments derived to test them were well defined, we cannot make generalisations. Given the complexity of education and the great variety of factors which can contribute to a particular outcome, we cannot be sure that even well based findings apply generally without proceeding to Whitehead's third stage—the stage of generalisation. Strangely, for an article entitled 'The Rhythm of Education' Whitehead has little to say about generalisation. 'It is the return to romanticism with the added advantage of classified ideas and relevant techniques.' Perhaps he thought it too obvious to warrant emphasis that it is necessary to ensure that relationships examined at the stage of precision are generally valid.

The most disappointing outcome of the great research effort put into compensatory education is that so few of the benefits from any of the multifarious approaches turned out to be generally valid. The analysis of Head Start in the United States carried out under the sponsorship of the Westinghouse Learning Corporation (1969) could find no evidence for general conclusions which could be of value to teachers. Even in a determinedly optimistic point of view, Bronfenbrenner (1974) could find only a very few plausible general conclusions.

Findings which have seemed well substantiated in carefully carried out investigations, particularly laboratory studies, have not produced conclusions which have been found to be generally valid. It is essential to test conclusions for general validity. A small number of children may not be typical of all five year olds. Yorkshire mining villages may have traditions different from those of the Welsh valleys. Five or six other West Indian children speaking the same dialect may provide a safe retreat from the pressures of the classroom, a retreat not so easily available when there are only two or three West Indians in the class.

Many of the techniques of educational measurement have been devised with just this purpose in mind, to test 'the wide significance' of conclusions derived from precise studies. It is surprising and disturbing how often researchers assume that because their investigations have been carefully carried out, their conclusions are of general significance and require no further validation. But it is only when conclusions derived from the studies of specific groups have been submitted to testing on a broader sample that conclusions about general validity can be drawn.

In education, as indeed most of the social sciences, these generalisations are of a probablistic nature. The generalisations refer to general tendencies. These generalisations are true of most children but not all of them and conspicuously false of some. The Educational Priorities Area Report (1972) focuses in part on the language handicaps of children from mining villages. The generalisation may be valid though it is relevant to note that D. H. Lawrence was the son of a miner and grew up in such a village. The generalisation, if indeed it proves to be valid, would be 'that children growing up in an isolated mining village are likely to be linguistically retarded when compared with other similar children'.

Survey research is not to be equated with generalisability, partly because as noted earlier surveys can generate hypotheses as well as test their general validity and partly because the survey technique cannot be applied economically to many important educational questions, for example, studies which require detailed observations of classroom behaviour or clinical interviews. A series of individual investigations each testing the same hypotheses in widely different circumstances and all producing similar results would be as convincing as a survey of a large random sample. The generalised conclusion though is only as good as the original speculation and the exact formulation.

It would be wrong to draw too sharp a distinction between the various stages for as Whitehead points out it is easy to 'exaggerate into sharpness the distinction between the three stages . . . romance, precision, generalisation are all present throughout'. This is certainly true in the researcher's mind. An experiment which is designed to help in precise formulation may give rise to half disclosed glimpses which set him off on further speculation. Data which are designed to test the general validity of a statement may in turn give rise to generalisations or provide an opportunity for making more precise earlier general notions. The researcher may be working at different levels but his statements are at one level or the other: they are either speculations based on casual observation or theory or they are precise formulations based on structured observation or experiment or they are generalisations based on carefully drawn samples or repeated experiments in different circumstances. The contribution to truth must be distinguished from the many levels of thought in the author's mind.

The malaise within educational research arises from two sources. The officials approach bearing gifts in the form of research contracts but with simplistic notions of what educational research can contribute to practice, its truth value. Within research the broadening of the disciplinary basis of educational research and the rediscovery or more general use of techniques outside the psychometric traditions have led to confusion about the contribution of a particular study to knowledge, truth value in a different sense.

The first difficulty may be resolved by the appointment of senior scientists, as intermediaries, who can appreciate the limitations of research findings and the complexities of research which is to make a useful contribution to practice. The second difficulty can be resolved by the researchers specifying carefully to themselves and to their readers the level (in Whitehead's terms the stage) of a specific study's contribution to understanding. More ambitious taxonomies will have to wait on more precise specification by researchers and more careful teaching of graduate students.

Jerome Bruner

3. The Role of the Researcher as an Adviser to the Educational Policy Maker

At first glance, this topic appears to be principally technical, indeed rather politically and socially innocent. But this impression is based, I think, on an incorrect interpretation of the role of expertise, one that traces its origin to that patron saint of technocrats, Saint Simon. For him, as for his contemporary followers, the role of the expert was that of a neutral party who, in the light of reason, advised as to the best course to be followed in achieving the implicit objectives of the state. The political process, by this dispensation, was regarded as something of a nuisance. The important thing was to get on with the rational organisation of the enterprise. 'Imagine', said Saint Simon, 'that the nation loses monsieur, princes, cardinals, bishops, judges, and in addition, ten thousand of the richest property owners among those who live off their incomes without producing. What would the result be? This accident would certainly afflict all the French . . . but no political harm to the state would result.' But if France lost those who produced knowledge or devised managerial organisation, it 'would become a body without soul' and would need 'at least a generation to repair the damage'.

But the world has changed, not only politically, but even with respect to our understanding of the physical universe in which we live. One rightly wonders whether the Saint Simonian expert provides a proper model. As Robert Oppenheimer put it:

> In an important sense this world of ours is a new world, in which the unit of knowledge, the nature of human communities, the order of society, the order of ideas, the very notions of society and culture have changed and will not return to what they have been in the past. What is new is new not because it has never been there before, but because it has changed in quality. One thing that is new is the prevalence of newness, the changing scale and scope of change itself, so that the world alters as we walk in it, so that the years of man's life measure not some small growth or rearrangement or moderation of what he learned in childhood, but a great upheaval. What is new is that in one generation our knowledge of the natural world engulfs, upsets, and complements all knowledge of the natural world before.

One is reminded of Lord Keynes' dictum. He noted that once an economy can be brought back into equilibrium, the laws of classical economics will generally apply. But the deep question is whether economies can ever be brought back into equilibrium. So George Kelly distinguishes two types of expertise, reflecting Keynes' distinction. One of them is *microexpertise* in which one derives the advice one gives from a body of theory about known situations, about 'classical conditions'. But the contrast is *macroexpertise*. 'Macroexpertise', he noted, 'is a constellation of particular types of advice given to the secular authority to meet situations of crisis without any implication that its application shall become universal. It will perhaps not endure into calmer times nor be relevant to the next crisis.' Under crisis conditions, then, the expert is less a neutral adviser than an historical actor involved in guiding the ship of state much as a pilot might guide a real ship in a storm through dangerous and uncharted waters, decidedly non-classic conditions. The expert's hold on power slackens only as the crisis recedes, though that power is in principle at all times politically revocable, however much the expert may covet power for himself and devise ways for increasing his hold on it. Yet, it always remains a moot question, given the expert's role in such crisis management, whether he is or will remain an historical actor or, rather, whether he is there merely to help arrange the props on the stage of history, perhaps to help the actors through their lines from the prompt box.

You will be quite correct if you infer from my introduction that I believe the field of education to be in a state of crisis, crisis in the deepest sense, reflecting changes much as those expressed in the dark words of Robert Oppenheimer. Under these patently non-classic conditions, it is quite plain that educational innovation will not and cannot come from the efforts of the educational researcher operating solely within the constraints of classically defined educational objectives. The researcher's advice, where educational innovation is concerned, must take into account that the nature of the crisis, the new demands and pressures that shape our educational system, forces us far beyond those that are classically considered to influence the 'effectiveness' of schools. The new forces reflect at least four unpredictable areas of change.

Skill requirements in the maintenance of a labour force for the future.
Changing conceptions of class structure and mobility.
Changing presuppositions about the perfectibility of men, our implicit theory of human growth and development.
Transformations in our implicit notions about the ways in which rare resources should be allocated.

Efforts to reform the educational system, to introduce innovation, most often fail or become diluted because they fail to take full account of these radically changed conditions and how they affect educational decisions. I believe that these changes have produced a highly unstable state, one that requires the educational researcher to become an historical actor rather than merely a neutral adviser. Before developing this point, let me first run briefly over the four destabilising factors mentioned, better to assess them.

With respect to the requirements of the labour force of the future there are several obvious if 'non-classic' conditions to be noted. The first, of course, is acceleration in the technological revolution that places major emphasis on control and information in a highly automated production network. It is not simply that new modes of production and distribution require a more highly skilled and technically fluent work force. Such a work force could easily be produced by slight modifications in our systems of education. Rather, the result of the shift to capital intensive economies is that wealth is produced in a new way without a corresponding redefinition of human work. The confusion is deep. A high official in the Nigerian Federal Government in Lagos told me that the effect on his country of the new highly automated petrochemical industry in Nigeria would be nil since it would require so few workers that Nigerian education would have no problem. But what happens to conceptions of work in Nigeria when capital intensification transforms a few of its industries while the rest of the economy staggers along in its traditional labour intensive way?

In Europe, increases in capital intensification have already produced the image of the bimodal work force, with increasing technical skill at one end for a few and dull, almost unskilled work at the other, often carried out by acquiescent 'guest workers', with all that implies in social problems. It is an image, and because it fails to comprise the 'service' enterprises, a very faulty one. But it is an image that is having a powerful effect, particularly on the young, who see work as either a rat race or as deadly dull. Because of this view of work, there is increasing resistance to participating in a system that is seen as humanly destroying. The capital intensive economics we are constructing, rather than being seen as filling man's energies for new enterprises, are seen as a source of degradation. And perhaps that is what they are—until such a time as we can face the consequences more directly. We cannot expect the young to go about the process of education with anything less than rebelliousness and dissatisfaction if they cannot have a fuller sense of what it is they are preparing for. No surprise that students at Glasgow elect Jimmy Reid their Chancellor for voicing the sentiment that 'The rat race is for rats, not for men'!

Our failure to reflect the changing requirements of work in our schooling is a result neither of callousness nor of stupidity. It comes rather, from the fragmented pattern of planning that too sharply separates educational planning from social and economic planning and, most importantly, from social and economic debate.

With respect to issues of social class, I think again there have been some major changes that have shaken our conception in the school as a major instrument of mobility and opportunity. I think it is now plain that schools *by themselves* cannot be a major instrument of egalitarianism. They are effective only when opportunities for mobility are present in the social and economic fabric of the country in which they exist. Critics like Bernstein and Illich and Coleman have documented the fact that schools and their dominant teaching methods, strongly middle-class orientated, often end up by creating or deepening the felt powerlessness of the working-class child, the immigrant, the underprivileged. Schools, as the saying goes, are part of the problem of social class, not the solution. When social class is combined with ethnic prejudices the problem is compounded. It is a problem that cannot be solved at the educational level; if it can be solved at all, it will have to be at a more embracing social, political, economic level.

A third point relates to a culture's presuppositions about perfectibility, its implicit theory of growth and development. We have all noted with dismay the emergence of a new and covert hereditarianism, based on presumed genetic differences in intelligence and educability between races and between social classes, most often supported by highly controversial interpretations of statistical correlations presented by Jensen, Herrnstein, Eysenck, and others. This is not the occasion for re-examining the evidence, nor do I wish to urge that there are no genetic components in intelligence. It suffices to note that only a few years ago, two distinguished geneticists, W. F. Bodmer and L. L. Cavalli-Sforza, in assessing the evidence of genetic and environmental influences on race–IQ differences, came to the not very startling conclusion that current techniques and data could not resolve the question.

But the issue goes deeper than that. Whatever the sources are that produce IQ differences, what educational action flows from the knowledge of their existence? This has yet to be debated openly, either in educational circles or in the general community. After all, Jencks has recently reported that there are many factors involved in the determination of economic and social success in our society and measured IQ is only a small part of the story. In the crowded conditions of the contemporary world, the persistence of hereditarianism has a powerful and explosive potential as never before. Until we bring these issues into the open they will constrain and distort efforts to change and refresh educational policy. One need only take the example of Head Start in America, killed before ever it had a chance to become stabilised, with a hereditarian bias shaping the denunciation of the critics.

Finally there is the allocation of rare resources in our societies. Education is costly. There are other demands on our national treasuries by way of social services, national security, etc. So goes the classical argument. But are we now operating under classic conditions? I believe again that there is a profound change stirring, one that questions the very idea of education as exclusively a 'launching' exercise. There are many voices questioning whether education of the young should be separated from the task of aiding human beings through all the critical periods of the life cycle, before and after school. Is education a launching or might it be a support system from cradle to rocking-chair? What are we to make of the emergence of 'further education' and educational television?

The questions we have examined are beyond the competence of conventional educational research, whose principal task is to evaluate practices as they exist. It has little or no hand in the planning function, and even if it did, it would be too narrowly conceived to deal with the crisis that faces us. What I would propose, rather, is the creation of a new type of educational research, *research that seeks not evaluation of present practice, but rather the formulation of alternative plans for dealing with our deeper problems.* Such an effort must involve the collaboration of the educational researcher with the psychologist, the anthropologist, the sociologist, the economist, and the politician. This is the range of experts I see being joined together in a *task force involved in the planning of alternatives.* Such an effort is required if we are to put our educational problems into the perspective they require for manageable solution. But even at that, I would urge that the task force not be viewed in Saint Simonian terms—for its function goes beyond that, a matter to which we will turn later.

Let it be clear that what faces our task force is a series of structured contradictions. These are contradictions inherent in the aims of education. For there are at least *three objectives in any democratic educational system that, in the nature of things, are inherently at odds with each other.* They are the following:

Education as a means of providing skills and knowledge useful for servicing the society and its economy.
Education as a means of assuring equal opportunity to its citizens.
Education as a means of assuring self-realisation and fullness in life.
Consider these in ensemble.

A corollary of our increasing technological mode of production is that skill to be useful must be general. The same rule holds for the acquisition of skill in a world where change is rapid and where the only guarantee that skill will not be obsolete is to assure that it will be general. That is to say, it must consist of a set of component skills or sub-routines that can be recombined in a fashion to be appropriate to a wide variety of tasks, many unforeseeable. This is as true in the distribution industries or in social service pursuits as it is in the technical fields of production. Neither the social worker nor the engineer can be adequately trained during a period of change either by reference to old routines or standardised requirements. We have moved toward an era which places greater emphasis upon the generalist, whatever his occupational affiliation, and less upon the craftsman. This is a truism, but its implications for education and its planning are enormous.

What characterises the training of general skills? First, they depend upon linkage of the human operator with powerful techniques for amplifying his powers. Typical is the use of mathematics, a means whereby thinking about order is made much more powerful by the use of culturally transmitted languages for describing and analysing order. But the same holds for disciplines dealing with the social world. One trains a more effective manager by assuring mastery of powerful ideas in economics and the management sciences. Secondly, general skills depend upon an attitude, a point of view, a willingness to try out abstractions. The cultivation of the 'abstract attitude' begins early in life and is furthered enormously by the typical regimen of middle-class homes. Work by Hess and Shipman, and by Schoggen and Schoggen indicates that right from the start, in the form of questions asked at home, in the form of how tasks are set, the middle-class child has much more opportunity for and encouragement in abstract thinking than his working-class brother. Early on, the gap begins to open between the middle-class child and the child not favoured by a supporting environment at home.

Make no mistake about it. What this implies inexorably is that *early* opportunity will constrain later opportunity. The hidden curriculum of the middle-class home, with its covert training in and rewards for abstraction and decontextualised problem solving, almost assures that the potentially able child with the 'wrong' background will not find equal opportunity in our present school systems.

It will be a formidable task for our task force to find ways of broadening the base of early ability in a manner to assure recruitment of skilful leaders from all social backgrounds through schooling. If they cannot, then we shall have to learn to live with an explosive contradiction in our midst. So too in reconciling the narrow aims of 'getting ahead' with the broader ones of 'finding' oneself, cultivating one's self and so on. These are the contradictions to which I alluded. How best to proceed? How shall our task force work?

Decisions about educational objectives (as other objectives of the society) have usually been made by separate organs of the society, usually without reference to overall social aims or overall impact. As Jacques Ellul has noted, each profession has its own aims and seeks to emerge with a technical solution to its problems that is *the* best solution for *that* kind of problem. I believe this approach only deepens the contradictions within our educational enterprise and makes the manageable solutions more difficult to achieve. Can our task force overcome this danger? Can such task forces succeed as 'professionals' advising the state in the sense of Saint Simon? I do not believe so. I think, rather, that the task force, whether at the level of the local community, at the level of the nation state, or even at the Council of Europe, must 'go public', must do something akin to 'consciousness raising'. By 'consciousness raising', a term I borrow from Women's Lib, I mean enlivening the public sense of alternatives, stirring the debate, bringing issues into the open. It is in this sense that the educational researcher via the educational research task force, acts not as 'expert' in the narrow sense, but as an actor on the historical stage. It is only *after* such debate that we can move toward the compromises and the reformulation that are required.

The failure of educational research to innovate, has been precisely by virtue of the *absence of such public debate*. For educational research operates poorly 'from the inside', has no leverage in the way that development by medical researchers of penicillin, say, could alter the practice of medicine from the inside.

A few examples of recent failures make the case clearer. Take the curriculum reform movement in America. Its success was marginal despite the unprecedented work of distinguished scholars and teachers in preparing new and often brilliant teaching materials, as well as new approaches to teacher education. Its modest impact stems principally, I think, from the fact that its underlying assumptions were never aired publicly. The assumptions were too narrow. They related only to such matters as the capacity of the young to understand theoretical issues in far more depth than was supposed, that human beings could be given a far better grasp of their world than was previously believed, etc. But many of these curriculum efforts soon became trivialised, their broader implications were never publicly developed, never related to the debates by which a culture comes to decisions about the deployment of its resources. If at all, the issue was presented as if it were a matter of catching up with the Russians in scientific know-how in order to close a knowledge gap. There is nothing so dead as a closed gap.

I am sure, to take another contemporary example, that the importance of early childhood as a forming ground for basic skills and attitudes will not be discussed until they tap concerns within the culture beyond those ordinarily reached by discussions of education. Nursery education is not the issue. What is at stake is the idea of the family, the extent to which child rearing is a private option exclusively, etc.

It is for these reasons that much of the impact on education in the last decades has come *from outside*, from social critics like Basil Bernstein who accuse formal education and the schools of creating an exploitable working class, or, writers like Ivan Illich, who have proposed the radical alternatives of deschooling, A. S. Neill, whose writings strike at the crisis of authority in conventional school practice.

It will be a *tragedy if educational enquiry continues to be divided between those who operate from within with well designed research dictated by our present educational presuppositions and those, on the other hand, who are critics on the outside working intuitively on central issues beyond the school, but crucial to it*. Perhaps the educational research task force can bring them together, can bring before the community for scrutiny the powerful factors that shape our decisions about schooling; economic, social, political, cultural, as well as the technical requirements of education itself.

One last note. Some will say that to open such debate, such controversy over basic issues will only serve to divide the community and make education a political football. I would wish to argue the contrary. Our constituency as educators is each new generation. It is each new generation, each time, that would most take heart from such debate. I am *not* proposing that the debate be handed over to the young, for that would surely defeat the purpose. It would surely serve the public interest if, to take a grim analogy, we refreshed our educational practices to meet new conditions at least as intelligently as we changed our concepts of national defence to meet the new realities of our changing world.

Note: This paper originally appeared in the *Oxford Review of Education*, Vol. 1, No. 3, 1975.

Rob Walker

4. The Conduct of Educational Case Studies: Ethics, Theory and Procedures

This paper was originally written as a pre-fieldwork guide early in the life of a research project. The project is Ford SAFARI *(an acronym for 'Success and Failure and Recent Innovation'), a study of the effects of a number of recently completed curriculum development projects in British Secondary Schools. Given its audience and origin it is inevitable that the paper lacks the authority of research accomplished. Instead it aims to draw on past experiences, to relate these to research traditions and then to push out into new areas and to signal new approaches.*

As I write this introduction the fieldwork phase of the research is under way and gathering momentum (available materials include MacDonald and Walker, 1976; Brugelmann, 1976; Walker and MacDonald, 1976; Pick and Walker, 1976). Already there are things I could add, things I might change, emphases that have shifted; but since it is too soon to re-write the paper completely I have chosen to retain its speculative character and rather loose structure. In research we often talk about the value of revealing our errors, mistakes, miscalculations and misjudgements so that others may learn from them. In publishing this version of our case study methodology I am describing an approach before I know of its outcome. Some of the mistakes I shall probably know by the time the book is in print.

Introduction

A glance at the literature reveals that it is usual for the case study researcher to encounter severe problems over such issues as conduct in the field, confidentiality, publication, and control over the use of data (McCall and Simmons, 1969; Becker, 1964). A key element of such studies is that they usually involve the immersion of the researcher in the field for relatively long periods of time. Long-term study is justified in terms of the need to determine areas of significance and to check the reliability and consistency of data. Long-term studies also have the incidental effect that personal relationships are established with those being studied, and to some extent these relationships protect the case study worker during the period of research and after its publication.

In the field of education there are now a number of such long-term field studies, for example Smith and Geoffrey (1968), Becker (1961, 1968), Lacey (1970), Hargreaves (1967), Wolcott (1967), and we take these along with related studies in criminology, industrial sociology and community studies, to constitute something of a research tradition. This is a tradition that finds some roots in the Chicago Sociology of the 1920s, that finds inspiration in the methods and techniques of social anthropology and, in the case of Education, has established a niche for itself in the Child Development field and in the sociology of education.

Recently this research tradition, with its stress on naturalistic observation, and on the study of individual instances in some depth, has received considerable attention in other areas of educational research, and particularly in the evaluation of educational development programmes (Parlett and Hamilton, 1972; Hamilton *et al.* 1977). It is an approach highly suited to the problems being pursued by SAFARI, which, as we have framed them, demand the close study of individual events, institutions and people. Yet the long time-scale of appropriate research methods imposes restrictions that we find difficult to handle. If we set out to provide the information people need to know in order to make particular policy decisions we often find ourselves committed to timetables that preclude use of 'anthropological' methods in the collection of data.

It is this double-bind resulting from simultaneous commitments to study in depth *and* to rapid reporting, that creates the starting point for this paper. It is also this double commitment that leads us to attempt to formulate a position for the case study worker that is midway between the worlds of academic research and educational practice.*

The central dilemma†

Our conception of the case study starts from a double-bind. We find ourselves advocating two things that often seem to be in conflict with one another.

1. First is a commitment to studies of the individual instance. We feel that the study of curriculum innovation in its post-development phase has been weighed down by generalities and theories and that there is a need to confront and portray what is actually happening in schools, classrooms and LEA offices at a level of some detail. At the surface level the problem is less one of theory and more one of access to knowledge.

* Throughout this paper we use a distinction between 'researchers' on the one hand, and 'practitioners' on the other. This is a convention adopted to sharpen what, in fact, is an indistinct separation of roles. By 'practitioners' we mean teachers, head teachers, advisers, education officers, DES staff—all those who work in education. In other contexts researchers too may well be practitioners.

† This theme has since been explored more fully in Norris (1977), especially by Helen Simons.

2. Second is a commitment to forms of research that start from, and remain close to, educational practice. This involves us in a form of action research that attempts to inform decision-taking and policy-making by, for example, the fast turn-round of data to those being studied. This has action implications if we accept that knowledge is often the spring for action and that access to knowledge is frequently used as a mechanism of control.

These aspirations conflict in that the first tends to push us towards methods of research that seem to require long term immersion both in the field and subsequently in the data. On the other hand the second tends to push us towards short-term, almost journalistic styles of reporting in which the researcher has little time to check his interpretations against either the data or continuing events.

What we propose is a way out of the dilemma which involves a shift away from reliance on the personal integrity and authority of the researcher. That is to say a shift away from the notion of the researcher as the prime interpreter. We propose instead the establishment of sets of rules and procedures which to some extent free the researcher from responsibility for what is reported, and which allow rapid access to, and publication of, information. At the same time such procedures are designed to protect those being studied from the consequences of the research.

Are the problems really technical?

We have already noted that case study research is a field commonly thought to be fraught with problems of method and technique:

Should the observer become involved in the situation being studied?
Is it possible to offer informants confidentiality?
Is it right to do so?
How should requests for access to data during the course of the study be handled?
What procedures should be adopted in obtaining release for final publication?

Usually these problems are considered to be technical problems. That is to say, given accepted notions about the nature of research and the role of the researcher, then the problem is essentially one of evolving procedures which mobilise the normal ethics of research in fieldwork situations.

In this paper we take a different view. We believe that the difficulties of doing case study research do not stem primarily from technical issues, that is, issues about means, but from deeper value concerns. In order to create a way out of the case study research dilemma with which we opened this paper we feel it is necessary to raise questions about what research and researchers in the field of education should be doing. We intend to challenge the frame.

Case Study—a definition

Case study is the examination of an instance in action. The study of particular incidents and events, and the selective collection of information on biography, personality, intentions and values, allows the case study worker to capture and portray those elements of a situation that give it meaning. In educational evaluation or research the case study worker may attempt to study and portray the impact in a school of a particular innovation, the experience of a curriculum development project team, the development of an idea through a number of social organisations, the influence of a social and professional network, or a day in the life of a teacher, administrator or pupil. These very different studies have in common some commitment to the study and portrayal of the idiosyncratic and the particular as legitimate in themselves.

Case Study—background to the definition

In the past, case study methods have generally been utilised and developed where there has been a clear need to confront the idiosyncrasy of individual instances, (for example, in attempting historical reconstruction, or in biography, journalism and documentary film making). Or where there has been no clear vision of an appropriate theoretical base from which to operate (for example, in applied social science research). Of academic disciplines (as opposed to practitioner-disciplines like clinical medicine, town planning and social work), only anthropology and ethology appear to have developed procedures for using case study research cumulatively. As a result case study research has a generally low status as a research method. The Open University Course E341 on Educational Research dismissed case study in a section of three brief paragraphs whose opening sentence was: 'The simplest approach to educational research is the case study.' (Entwistle, 1973, p. 19)*

Case Study—pros and cons

The justification usually given for case study research is that it gives insight into specific instances, events or situations. The case study reveals, 'what institutions *mean* to individuals (and) helps us get beyond form and structure to the realities of human life, or to use Malinowski's term, "it puts flesh and blood on the skeleton"' (see Lewis, 1959, p. 3). Part of the appeal of case study is that it offers some escape from the language of theory, but the case study

* The section continues by raising the generalisation problems and only briefly mentions method: '. . . very often case studies are not representative and hence the results apply only to that group and to the specific situation involved. Nevertheless, a case study can be a useful starting point for a piece of research; it can also be used by students to gain the flavour of research without being involved in unnecessary complications.' (p. 20)

may contribute *to* theory, for it promises to reveal how theoretical abstractions relate to common sense perceptions of everyday life.

The objection most often raised to case study is the 'generalisation problem'. This is seen in terms of the limited reliability and validity of the case study and is often framed in terms of two questions:

> How can you justify studying only one instance?
> Even if it is justifiable theoretically, what use can be made of the study by those who have to take action?

The first question touches on the problem of studying representative situations and events. The case study worker seems to reject ideas of sampling and control, both key aspects of experimental design.

In one sense the criticism is inappropriate. The vast readership of books like Bel Kaufman's *Up the Down Staircase* (1964) testify to the fact that large numbers of people find truth even in the fictionalised instance. The problem for the case study worker is not whether it is *worth* studying individual events, but whether he can do so in a way that captures the attention of his audience. Yet in research terms a fundamental problem of design is raised by single-sample studies (though to phrase the problem in this way is itself misleading; to define case study research as 'research on samples where *N* equals 1' is to allude to a set of research values that are not necessarily appropriate). When only one instance is studied it does not really matter *which* instance is studied. The sampling problem is not really a problem at all; one instance is likely to be as typical and as atypical as another. The problem of generalising ceases to become a problem for the author. It is the reader who has to ask, what is there in this study that I can apply to my own situation, and what clearly does not apply?

The question 'What use is the case study?' raises more clearly the issue of the relationship of research to the making and taking of decisions. In some ways this is a more serious issue and it is a continuous concern in this paper. At this juncture we simply make the point that many educational practitioners are in fact 'natural' case study workers. Teachers, advisers, heads, administrators, curriculum developers—they all tend to make judgements on the basis of knowledge of the particular instance, rather than by reference to research findings. Some researchers may disapprove of practitioner-lore as a basis for action, but if that is how the system works we would do well to know more about it.* Perhaps we might even try to improve such 'research' rather than merely condemn it.

* This idea provides the central theme for a research project funded by the SSRC and based at the Centre for Applied Research in Education, University of East Anglia (1977–79) 'Classroom Observation, the Practice of Advisers, Head Teachers and Teachers'.

To restate the argument

Users of case study methods have encountered a number of difficulties in conducting their research. As we have seen, a list of these difficulties would include:

problems of the researcher becoming involved in the issues, events or situations under study;
problems over confidentiality of data;
problems stemming from competition from different interest groups for access to, and control over, the data;
problems concerning publication, such as the need to preserve anonymity of subjects;
problems arising from the audience being unable to distinguish data from the researcher's interpretation of the data

Problems of this kind are usually considered as 'methodological' problems, that is to say they are seen as isolated technical problems that can be overcome within existing frames of research. Whenever they dominate particular studies there is a suspicion that the research has been poorly executed; that unspoken professional norms have been violated. The risks that case study workers run are frequently reflected in the hesitancy with which sponsors approach proposals for such research. Any proposals we make that attempt to resolve the dilemma posed between depth study and rapid reporting will have to cope with these issues and this may mean recasting accepted notions about the nature of research and the role of the researcher.

Evaluation and research

The tradition of case study research that has emerged in the social sciences has evolved under conditions rather different from those which constrain the work of the evaluator. The social scientist normally reports to his peers rather than to his subjects, and usually he is relatively free from pressures either to complete his fieldwork fast or to report quickly. Field studies typically involve periods of several months in the field and final reports are often delayed by several years.

The evaluator, however, usually works in situations which are more politically intense. The people he studies may well be part of the audience he reports to; he may have the opportunity to spend only a few days in the field and have to produce his report in weeks or months rather than years.

The evaluator often finds himself in situations where he has to account for his research in terms outside the normal constraints and values of the researcher; his need to reconcile research and practical affairs is consequently more urgent and compulsive than it would be in pure research. Not only in relation to case study, but more generally, evaluators have tended to find accepted notions of educational research wanting when they have been applied to evaluation problems.

This difference between research and evaluation is essentially one of degree, for the researcher too in choosing to respond to the interests and needs of one group rather than another, enters a web of political relationships, perhaps less pressing but just as real as those enclosing the evaluator. Whether we are working as researchers or evaluators we are primarily concerned with the creation, production and communication of knowledge. We enter the political arena because that knowledge is often the basis on which power is legitimated. As researchers and evaluators we are frequently hired by those with power to study those who are powerless; and in the particular case of education, knowledge is not only the basis of power but the medium through which power is exerted.

In a related paper, Barry MacDonald (1974, pp. 11–12) has looked more closely at the inherently political nature of evaluation and sketched out three models by which evaluators can secure their enterprise. He outlines his three types of evaluation as follows:

> *Bureaucratic evaluation*
> Bureaucratic evaluation is an unconditional service to those government agencies which have major control over the allocation of education resources. The evaluator accepts the values of those who hold office, and offers information which will help them to accomplish their policy objectives. He acts as a management consultant, and his criterion of success is client satisfaction. His technique of study must be credible to the policy makers and not lay them open to public criticism. He has no independence, no control over the use that is made of his information, and no court of appeal. The report is owned by the bureaucracy and lodged in its files. The key concepts of bureaucratic evaluation are 'service', 'utility', and 'efficiency'. Its key justificatory concept is 'the reality of power'.
>
> *Autocratic evaluation*
> Autocratic evaluation is a conditional service to those government agencies which have major control over the allocational resources. It offers external validation of policy in exchange for compliance with its recommendations. Its values are derived from the evaluator's perception of the constitutional and moral obligations of the bureaucracy. He focusses upon issues of educational merit, and acts as expert adviser. His technique of study must yield scientific proof, because his power base is the academic research community. His contractual arrangements guarantee non-interference by the client, and he retains ownership of the study. His report is lodged in the files of the bureaucracy, but is also published in academic journals. If his recommendations are rejected, policy is not validated. His court of appeal is the research community, and higher levels in the bureaucracy. The key concepts of the autocratic evaluator are 'principle' and 'objectivity'. Its key justificatory concept is 'the responsibility of office'.
>
> *Democratic evaluation*
> Democratic evaluation is an information service to the community about the characteristics of an educational programme. Sponsorship of the evaluation does

not in itself confer a special claim upon this service. The democratic evaluator recognises value pluralism and seeks to represent a range of interests in his issue formulation. The basic value is an informed citizenry, and the evaluator acts as broker in exchange of information between groups who want knowledge of each other. His techniques of data gathering and presentation must be accessible to non-specialist audiences. His main activity is the collection of definitions of, and reactions to, the programme. He offers confidentiality to informants and gives them control over the use of the information they provide. The report is non-recommendatory, and the evaluator has no concept of information misuse. The evaluator engages in periodic negotiation of his relationships with sponsors and programme participants. The criterion of success is the range of audience served. The report aspires to 'best-sellers' status. The key concepts of democratic evaluation are 'confidentiality', 'negotiation' and 'accessibility'. The key justificatory concept is 'the right to know'.

Recasting notions of research

We see the democratic mode as particularly appropriate in case study research, or in evaluation activities using case study techniques. This places the case study worker in the position of having to *negotiate* his interpretations with those involved in the study rather than being free to impose them on the data. The shift involved is a shift in power, a move away from *researchers'* concerns, descriptions and problems towards *practitioners'* concerns, descriptions and problems. This is essentially what we mean when we talk about recasting our notions of the nature of research and the role of the researcher. Put this way we may seem to be back in the mainstream of contemporary sociology, but we are not simply arguing for the validity of 'members' categories', we are arguing for the rights of informants over the control of what is published. In relation to our central dilemma we see the democratic mode of evaluation as a possible source of resolution but in terms of MacDonald's typology this shift towards acknowledging practitioners' perceptions could also be accommodated within the bureaucratic mode. The difference is a fundamental difference in the answers each mode gives to the questions 'Who is the research for?' and 'Who owns the data?'.

The possibility of a move towards the bureaucratic mode as a means of moving from researchers' to practitioners' problems is clear in Mrs Thatcher's statement about DES sponsored research:

> There was clearly only one direction that the Department's research policy could sensibly take. It had to move from a basis of patronage—the rather passive support of ideas which were essentially other people's, related to problems which were often of other people's choosing, to a basis of commission. This meant the active initiation of work by the Department on problems of its own choosing, within a procedure and timetable which were relevant to its needs. Above all, it meant focussing much more on issues which offered a real possibility of yielding useable conclusions. (Quoted in Nisbet, 1974)

Perhaps the difference between the views of Mrs Thatcher and the 'democratic' mode evaluator is a fine one, but one which almost certainly will work out to be significant in practice. On a DES commission the democratic mode researcher would include the DES in the field he was studying, and the DES would be involved in the negotiations that could constitute a significant element of the research. Ideally the researcher would act as a communication point between the commissioners of the research and those being studied.

The general issue is not which of MacDonald's modes of research is 'best' but which is most appropriate to certain problems and conditions. Our feeling is that the democratic mode is best suited to exploratory studies or to the study of situations of some political sensitivity, for it is a mode of research in which all those engaged have the means continuously to direct and to influence the research from the proposal stage through to publication. Democratic evaluation studies can only work when there is involvement by all the significant people and groups implicated in the problem area.

The major limitation of the democratic mode is likely to be its inherent inertia. Any proposal that requires the support of multiple audiences before decisions are taken is likely to lead to complication if not to confrontation. As Oettinger points out, 'The observation that decisions were made by relatively few people is true of most of the major military-industrial developments of recent decades, including not only the Manhattan Project but the development of the national air defence system . . . . the design of the Polaris submarine, and the race of the moon'. He quotes Alvin Weinberg, Director of the Oak Ridge Laboratory, on the same point: 'Many fewer people were involved in our decision to go ahead with the Manhattan Project than were involved in our decision to adopt pay-as-you-go income tax. In consequence it was easier to start on the atomic bomb than to modify the income tax laws' (1969, p. 59).

The democratic mode of evaluation is conservative in that it presupposes values in the existing situation that need protection. Its negative aspect is inertia, which is inherently conservative precisely because it offers support, perhaps even unthinking support to the *status quo*. It seems clear therefore that democratic evaluation ought logically to attract support when a threatened system appears capable of being shored up by a restatement of consensus values. But it should also attract conservative support where the activity under review is commonly perceived as likely to get *dramatically* worse. Here the necessary changes would be arguably better controlled by establishing as wide a basis as possible for fully-discussed cautious progress. It is potentially a way of screening out the possibility of really radical review. Whether this logic ever gets turned into practice is another matter.

Case studies in education

Case study research has previously been used in education but mostly in an autocratic mode. That is to say it has been carried out primarily as a piece of 'pure' research directed to an audience of research professionals. The interpretations made have been essentially the interpretations of the researcher. The responsibility for the final account has been his alone.

In evaluation this approach has been complicated by the fact that the evaluator has often had a dual role, that of case study worker *and* that of change-agent, and the assumption has been that these two roles are not incompatible. We hold strongly to the view that the two roles are incompatible and that the evaluator should strive for neutrality. A problem that highlights this issue, and which frequently emerges at the design stage of a study, is how to set up procedures that ensure the credibility of the evaluation. In other words how to insulate the roles of evaluator and change-agent from each other even when the same people are operating in both roles.

To return to the dilemma with which we opened this paper, what is distinctive about the use of case study in evaluation as opposed to research is that the case study worker hopes to work in such a way that he is not overtaken by events. He has to design the research so that he can report before the normal passage of events irretrievably changes the situation under study. In contrast to an evaluation report most educational case studies read to the practitioner like history. Howard Becker writes in the introduction to *Making the Grade* (1968):

> We started our fieldwork in 1955 and completed it in 1961. The university has changed greatly in the interim, and it should be clear that the figures we present and other organisational features we describe represent the university at that time. Some of the things we describe are characteristic of most American universities. Others are to be found only in certain kinds of universities, particularly the large state schools. Still others may be unique to Kansas. The generalisability of our analysis is problematic (p. 16).

Educational case studies, within a democratic mode, will have a commitment to feeding back information quickly to participants in the situation under study. For the evaluator it is less important to generalise than it is to report accurately. If case studies are to be used in evaluation this will involve some reappraisal not only of the time scales involved, but also of the social context within which the 'meanings' will be generated. The 'generalisability' problem can be to some extent ameliorated if the initial audience is confined to *those involved in the study*. The final report then becomes a report on the process of research and publication becomes part of that process.

Characteristics of the case study

Application of the democratic mode to case study research reveals a number of questions which all relate to accepted notions of the nature of research and the role of the researcher:

to whose needs and interest does the research respond?
who owns the data (the researcher, the subject, the sponsor . . .)?

who has access to the data? (Who is excluded or denied?)
what is the status of the researcher's interpretation of events vis à vis the interpretations made by others? (Who decides who tells the truth?)
what obligations does the researcher owe to: his subjects, his sponsors, his fellow professionals, others?
who is the research for?

The implications of such questions is to reaffirm that research is inherently a social process leading to a social product. Case studies are public documents about individuals and events with consequences for the lives of those portrayed as well as for the reader. In order to maintain the integrity of both the record and those under study the fine line between what is public and what is private needs to be carefully negotiated.

Equally, case studies are identifiable, at least to those involved and usually to wider audiences. By this we do not mean that people and institutions can always be recognised, but that the kinds of issues, problems, paradoxes, conflicts, situations and events portrayed ring true. In this way case studies may create images of reality that become part of the reality itself. Thus Elizabeth Richardson's study of Nailsea School (Richardson, 1973), and Roger Graef's film 'Space Between Words' (Graef, n.d.), have become part of the vocabulary of thinking of many teachers, headteachers and administrators.

The best case studies transcend the boundaries between art and science, retaining both coherence and complexity. Inevitably, the case study worker finds himself part historian, part psychologist, part sociologist and part anthropologist. Often he is also part scientist and part artist, sometimes to his own surprise. (Freud wrote: 'It still strikes me . . . as strange that the case studies I write should read like short stories' (1953, p. 160).)

The difficulty that case study workers within the democratic mode are likely to encounter in retaining their identity as specialists in particular disciplines raises major problems for the status of the case study itself as a form of knowledge. In related papers, Hans Brugelmann and John Elliott (1974) have pointed out that a triangulation approach such as we suggest in this paper tends to lead to a relative view of truth in terms of the reports and perceptions of differently located observers. There is little attempt in this paper to locate those reports relative either to objective truth or to theoretical propositions at the level of subject disciplines. The case study worker may produce a study which is internally consistent and acceptable to all those involved, but which in fact relates only marginally to the 'truth'. This is not to claim that all reality is necessarily relative, but simply to suggest a methodological stance in relation to fieldwork situations. The stress on 'definitions of the situation' and the application of increasingly rigorous procedures in order to validate subjective data, constitutes a method and related sets of techniques which I feel are applicable in the particular case of educational case studies. It is not intended to prescribe a world view or to exclude the validity of alternative approaches. I am not claiming that all truth is relative, and all reality necessarily multiple, but that in some situations it is a useful strategy to treat them as if they were.

Research and policy

Recognition of the issues raised has consequences for the conduct of research. Yet questions of this kind have only recently been considered by educational researchers, perhaps because the social sciences have themselves rarely been taken seriously by decision-makers, but also because those areas of study that *have* influenced decision-making (economics, demography, psychometrics) have held a strong allegiance to a positive, rational, scientific model which has effectively precluded research from asking reflexive questions. For the most part the questions we have outlined here have not been asked because the answers have not been required.

Within policy making bodies, despite an apparent increasing sophistication of research, there has been a growing sense of unease at the lack of fit between research and practice; a feeling that research defines its own problems irrespective of the problems faced by practitioners and that its audience is primarily an audience of fellow researchers rather than its sponsors, subjects or fellow citizens. Mrs Thatcher's statement echoes this feeling clearly.

Perhaps the main appeal of measurement data is that it is relatively easy to condense, and so amenable to rapid handling. On the other hand case study data does offer some things to the practitioner that conventional educational research does not. Louis Smith has summarised some of these aspects of the case study in relation to the educational administrator as follows:

> . . . case studies . . . have a quality of *undeniability*. That is someone is actually doing something; it is not hypothetical. As such cases accumulate, in varying settings and with varying support, personnel and rationale, it becomes difficult to excuse one's own inaction. It forces one to back off from his 'rationalisations' and to confront the basic choices and dilemmas in values underlying his decisions in his district.
>
> Second, the case studies are totalities, that is they have a 'holistic' or 'systematic' quality. By their very nature, they constrain or attend to all the elements.
>
> Third, a cluster of elements seem summarisable as a particularistic quality. There is a concreteness, vividness . . . and detail. The nooks and crannies of a phenomenon, an event, an experience, are explored.
>
> Fourth . . . the case study can be individualised. Each person can clarify the similarities and the differences in his own setting, his own organisation, his own personality. With even minimal discussion he can ask the questions which 'bug him', work through the immediate perceptions of possible difficulty 'at home', test his experience against the elements of the case.

> Fifth, the case studies accent process, change over time. This has a particular utility for 'men of action', persons who want to do something—administer, supervise, teach. Data are revealed on where and how one begins, implements and terminates. The critical decisions at each point in time are highlighted, along with such elements as alternatives, prediction systems, subjective probabilities, value systems, utilities, costs and benefits (Smith, 1974, p. 7).

What is interesting here is that case study is seen as close to the real world of the administrator, in a way that research produced by orthodox experimental design or survey research is not.

Louis Smith writes about the relationship between the *completed* case study and its audience. The problems we are looking at concern the *production* of case studies—and here there are often tremendous difficulties. For example, since educational case studies are usually financed by people who have, directly or indirectly, power over those studied and portrayed, the case study worker may be operating, or perceived as operating, under a series of constraints from sponsors. This effect may be amplified by the fact that case study methods rely heavily on human instruments (researchers and subjects) about which only limited knowledge can be obtained and whose private expectations, desires and interests may bias the study in unanticipated and unacknowledged ways. Lack of rules for case study leaves research opportunities open to abuse. Not only will people and institutions studied give their own accounts as to why they are being studied, they might well have their own reasons for *wanting* to be studied and these may not always be made explicit to the researcher. This again may influence and constrain the research in unacknowledged ways especially when, as we are suggesting, their own perceptions and responses may be built-in to research procedures.

Recently some Local Education Authorities have established their own research units, or attempted to move their advisers into research roles. Research has been established in colleges of education, polytechnics and even schools. If research roles become diffused through the system then as research gets closer to practice it may face the need for new forms of theory and new methods which allow audiences to generalise directly *to* other situations and not simply generalise *from* situations into areas of abstraction. If this happens on a large scale it is likely that the specialist research role will once again turn to problems which will sophisticate methodology rather than pursue raw data. This in turn will involve small scale, situationally specific research pursued through limited funding and access.

Beginning to resolve the dilemma—Condensed Fieldwork

Characteristic of traditional case study research in the social sciences is the long time spans involved—both in the field and in analysis and presentation. If case study methods are to be used within a democratic mode it is inevitable that one of the key features of the method will have to be revised—the use of *long term* participant observation or fieldwork.

In developing ways of using case study methods within a democratic mode of research we have to think in terms of *condensed fieldwork*; we have to find ways of collecting and presenting our data with some speed.* Inevitably this takes us even closer to the endemic problems of case study research, especially the problems of reliability and validity, confidentiality, consultation, publication and control over data. It is one thing to publish a study five years after the period of fieldwork, but quite another to spend a week in a school and to produce the case study a week later.

The notion of condensed fieldwork in part cuts us off from the traditions of case study research in the social sciences and draws us closer to other traditions in journalism, documentary film making and the writing of biography. What we retain most strongly from social science is the attempt to be objective, impartial and well-informed.

In part condensed fieldwork is an inevitable consequence of the demands of a democratic mode of research. If the researcher is to engage in continuous negotiation with his sponsors and subjects he is unable to make a long term study his main preoccupation. He cannot insulate himself from his sponsors or his subjects. People will not only want to know what he is doing, they will want results. Another facet of the democratic mode, however, is that the method of research should, through the process of the research, become available to those being studied, so that when the project terminates they will have, not just a copy of the report, but access to skills which allow them to continue to research unaided. 'Anthropological' style research which is usually held up as the distinguishing mark of case study research is rarely feasible in democratic mode evaluation or research, there is simply not time for such methods as they are normally practised and they are rarely accessible to practitioners.

Reliability and validity

Perhaps the heart of the problem is that case studies are inevitably always partial accounts involving selection at every stage, from choosing cases for study, to sampling events and instances, and to editing and presenting material. Since educational case studies are almost always conducted under severe constraints of time and resources, reliability and validity pose considerable problems.

Superficially case study is often set against quantitative research as belonging to a different 'paradigm', but in some ways this distinction is misleading, the case study worker is often more 'quantitative' in orientation than is realized. Howard Becker writes:

* Examples of such work are becoming available. See for example the Understanding Computer Assisted Learning Evaluation (CARE, Norwich 1974–7) and *The Case Studies in Science Education Project* (University of Illinois 1976–8).

> The observer, possessing many provisional problems, concepts and indicators . . . wishes to know which of these are worth pursuing as major foci of his study. He does this, in part, by discovering if the events that prompted their development are typical and widespread, and by seeing how these events are distributed among categories of people and organizational sub-units. *He reaches conclusions that are essentially quantitative*, using them to describe the organization he is studying. (1958, p. 656)

Although Becker works primarily within a descriptive frame, his concern is often with what is recurring, typical or widespread. Even when he looks at single instances the focus is often on the single instance as running counter to the main trend. For example, in the study *Boys in White* a major theme concerns the development and functioning of the 'perspectives' of medical students. The data used to construct perspectives was generated by studying the frequency with which items appeared in field notes but 'the final step in the analysis . . . . was a consideration of those cases found in the field notes which run counter to the preposition that students shared a particular perspective' (Becker, 1961, p. 43).

The analysis of these 'negative cases' was used to explore the boundaries within which the perspective in fact operated.

The approach we are exploring moves further away from quantitative methods than that developed by Becker and his colleagues. As a result it is not easy to apply accepted notions of reliability and validity to the kinds of data we collect and the forms of presentation we adopt. We find, instead, that we need to start by questioning the meanings of these concepts and then to see if we can rework them into our methods and procedures.

Reliability

We see reliability as concerned with the degree of fit between construct and data. Given high reliability it should be routine for other researchers to reach the same representations from the same events, and further to gather their own data and be able to handle that in a manner that is free from ambiguity or confusion. This seems to us essentially the same definition as that used in testing. For instance, Guilford defines reliability as 'the accuracy with which a score represents the status of an individual in whatever aspect the test measures him' (1954, p. 398). The critical point is that reliability is concerned with the relation between events and representations.

In the case study, however, the emphasis is towards '*collecting* definitions of situations' (multiple representations) and the presentation of material in forms where it is open to multiple interpretations. If it proves feasible to do this, to some extent we are by-passing the usual problems of reliability by passing responsibility for them on to the audience. In other words, the relationship between our representations of events and the events themselves is not critical because no claim is made for our representations as against those made by anyone else. What we have done is to put the audience in a situation where *their* representations are as significant as ours; the fit between events and their representations of it presenting a more subtle set of problems than is usual in testing or survey research.

It is common in research to use the term reliability to refer to a further difficulty and one which often dominates discussion of case study research: the problem of replicability. Would another researcher entering the same situation produce similar results? We suggest that in our emphasis on procedures rather than personal intuition we are moving to a kind of case study research that has high reliability in this sense. Educational situations are rarely replicable and this proposition would be difficult to test, but in theory it would seem that where procedures are clear and explicit then reliability in this sense would be higher than it would given a free hand to the researcher in the design and conduct of the case study.

Validity

Consideration of validity takes us to the interface between the findings of the study and the reality from which they were extracted, with what Guilford describes as 'the concern with *what* a test measures and with what it will predict' (p. 400). Validity is essentially about truth conditions.

The news the educational researcher brings is generally of one of two kinds. He may enter the system in order to seek truth through explanation, or alternatively he may enter it to seek truth through the portrayal of reality. Case study belongs to the second tradition. The news it brings is news which gives the reader a feeling of vicarious experience (Stake, forthcoming). Case study research relies heavily on face validity—the judgement that the results *seem* to fit the reality. This is a form of validity strongly distrusted by psychometricians:

> Looking valid by itself is no guarantee of any form of genuine validity, even to experienced psychologists, one can have little confidence in such information. This is why some psychologists facetiously refer to the acceptance of some tests as a matter of 'faith validity'. Apart from any confidence in superficial appearance, or lack thereof, it is sometimes said that for the sake of good public relations it often pays to make a test relevant to the layman who takes it, or who has any administrative decisions to make concerning it. (Guilford, 1954, p. 400)

In the case study, face validity is of much greater significance, for the case study worker is critically concerned to capture just those 'commonsense' meanings which constitute mere interference to the test designer. The case study worker constantly attempts to capture and portray the world as it appears to the people in it. In a sense for the case study worker what *seems* true is more important than what *is* true. For the case study worker as opposed to the psychometrician the internal judgements made by those he studies, or who are close to the situation, are often more significant than the judgements of outsiders.

This brings us to a further problem of validity which arises when the audience is not a research audience but an audience of practitioners. Descriptive accounts of individual instances may be accepted as true by practitioners but they are not likely to create appropriate and convincing bases for policy or decision making. The problem seems to be that such descriptive accounts are highly persuasive to a primary audience, but not to secondary audiences. Case studies do not readily lend themselves to 'data collapse', and where it may be easy to extract key statistics from a set of tables in order to pursue a course of action it seems less credible to extract an incident from a descriptive account. This might seem at first sight a convincing argument against case study research. However, our point is that when descriptive or personal data is missing from a research report, then those taking decisions will 'fill-in' from their own experience. Our conception of the case study is basically concerned with how to systematise this informal data. The question the decision-taker has to ask him, or herself, is how well do they really want to be informed?

What we are suggesting is that in educational research we need to go beyond the effective portrayal of individual instances and to find ways to be on guard against using case study to smuggle our own, or single values into the system.

Some will see this emphasis on practitioner lore as a dismaying denial of a basic value distinction between high order and lower order conceptual frameworks of understanding. (Rather as some educational reforms are seen as conceeding high standards in order to gain popularity with the pupils.) Perhaps a warning analogy can be drawn here with what has happened to the theory of film, with the implications that has for education. Since the war, film theory has received considerable interest, encouraged by the formation of the British Film Institute's Education Department. But despite its concern with popular film and the mass media (as opposed to what were disparagingly referred to as 'Art House Movies'), the kind of theory it developed was mainly derived from academic literary criticism and from sociology. As such it was often largely inaccessible to the audience who watched the films. What set out as an attempt to produce an accessible theory of the mass media often became a purely esoteric intellectual pursuit.

We feel it is important that Educational Research should attempt to avoid a similar fate. It is rare for educational researchers not to claim teachers as a primary audience, but in practice few researchers can claim the audience of teachers captured by John Holt or Bel Kaufmann. Most educational research simply does not directly connect with the world it purports to study.

New models of procedure

In the case study worker's search for models of procedure, conduct and technique he/she often turns to the ethnographer working in an exotic culture. Recently the terms 'anthropology', 'ethnography' and 'participant observational' have begun to appear in education research studies (e.g. Parlett and Hamilton, 1972; Cronbach, 1974), but we believe that although the ethnographic analogy is in some ways helpful, in other ways it is misleading.

Perhaps the attraction of the ethnographic model stems from the recognition that the research itself is *social*; it proceeds through a set of social processes that influence and shape it from its inception through the fieldwork phase and into its final presentation, reception and usage. Social and cultural anthropologists seem particularly sensitive to the social processes involved in the fieldwork phase of research and echo many of the feelings felt by educational researchers who work within the educational process.

At the heart of this is a problem of identifying for the researcher how he relates his own sense of self to the person he feels himself becoming in the field situation. One anthropologist, Alan Beals, writes:

> Except under extraordinary circumstances, there will always be a kind of clear plastic film separating the fieldworker from the rest of the community. The fieldworker does not fully understand the motives of others, he may in fact come to display a kind of paranoia arising in the fact that he knows that he is a centre of attention, but is not sure why. The fieldworker who behaves like a mechanical man, who treats others as subjects, or who coldly calculates the degree of friendship to be extended in each case, is going to appear less than human. People will be puzzled and dismayed by his behaviour. Certain kinds of information are available to the dispassionate observer. He is not likely to make enemies or become involved in disputes. On the other hand, he may have a considerable impact simply because his behaviour is impossible to understand or predict. Perhaps the ideal fieldworker would be a person who learned to behave in a natural and predictable manner, involved but not strongly involved. For our part, we came to feel at home in Gopalpur. Even today we can remember each friend and each enemy as we remember our friends and enemies at home. We were a part of the community and we shall not forget it. (Quoted in Spindler, 1970, p. 40)

The fieldworker engaged in long-term participant observation in an exotic culture, has this curious and periodic identity crisis about being part in, and part outside the culture; of being, as Hortense Powdermaker (1967) puts it, both 'stranger and friend', or what the linguist Labov (1973) describes (adopting the vernacular of the Harlem youth groups he studied) as 'being a lame'. The short-term case study worker rarely meets these problems, yet there is something in the way an anthropologist like Alan Beals writes that seems familiar. He seems to be describing what it is like to 'make a strange journey in a familiar land' (Blythe, 1969).

Ethnographers often talk about 'culture shock' resulting from sudden immersion in an alien culture. The effect is to put the fieldworker in the position of constantly asking: what kind of person am I in this situation? For the fieldworker can never fully take himself for granted. Lacking the knowledge to become a real member of the culture the ethnographic fieldworker is frequently seen by those he is studying as incompetent, in the way that a child is seen as incompetent. Perceiving this view of himself only compounds the psychological disorder accompanying 'culture shock':

> At first we had a hard time just getting along from day to day among people in whose terms we were weird and barely comprehensible outsiders with the social and technical skills of a Semai four-year old. This initial social situation produced in us a psychological condition anthropologists call 'culture shock'. We felt depressed, incompetent, unattractive, and very lonely. I can easily understand the response of the great anthropologist, Malinowski when he writes in his field diary that one trivial frustrating incident, 'drives me to a state of white rage and hatred of bronze-coloured skin, combined with depression', a desire to 'sit down and cry' and a further longing to 'get out of this'. For all that I decide to resist and work today—'business as usual', despite everything. (Dentan, in Spindler, 1970, p. 88)

For the educational case study worker the world being studied is mostly mundane, part of our commonsense experience. Yet you do not have to travel far to encounter the paradoxes, ambiguities and curiosities which constitute the exotic.

Charting multiple realities

In the educational case study we are dealing with more familiar worlds, yet when we begin to collect data we soon realise that the perceptions of our informants often differ. Somehow we have to produce 'research' which fits in to a grammar created by multiple rules; we have to find ways of working where what we do fits to some extent the language, norms and expectations of diverse groups. We cannot do this by immersing ourselves in the field for a period of time and then extracting ourselves with no obligations to return, and besides, we are part of the culture we portray.

The study of multiple realities belongs to a considerable academic tradition stemming particularly from the work of William James (1890) in psychology, from Alfred Schultz in social psychology and from W. I. Thomas in sociology. Nevertheless, the scientifically trained fieldworker often finds it hard to suspend his belief in his own reality, and to find a way of capturing the complexities of multiple interpretation. This may create for him a sense of inner confusion. An anthropologist working in Chicago writes:

> When you are an infant in age, it is one thing to be helpless, but when you are 29 years old, it is quite something else. This feeling of helplessness was very difficult for me to handle. In the early part of my research it often made me feel so nervous and anxious that the events occurring around me seemed to merge in a blur of meaningless action. I despaired of ever making any sense out of anything. Vice Lords sensed my feelings and I could see it made some people uncomfortable. This increased the difficulty of gaining the rapport necessary to carry out successful research. (Keisar, in Spindler, 1970, pp. 234–5)

The educational researcher may share some of these feelings on entering a school, classroom or an LEA office, but is unlikely to be perceived as quite so helpless, and indeed may often be seen as an authority or expert. Yet the extent of his or her own sense of confusion constitutes some sort of test for the researcher, for it would seem that the degree of 'culture shock' experienced in the initial stages of fieldwork is in part a function of the degree to which the taken-for-granted assumptions of the world under study have become problematic. It is unlikely that an educational researcher will experience the kind of cultural shock met by anthropologists working in exotic cultures—to do so within one's own culture would perhaps be classified as insanity.

Conduct in the field

As you read accounts by anthropologists about the experience of fieldwork (e.g. Spindler, 1970; Malinowski, 1967; Powdermaker, 1967; Mead, 1975), it is clear that the research is highly personal—that the knowledge gained is often personal knowledge gained by the researcher. Little comes out of the final monograph for the reader that is not carefully worked and understood by the writer. This marks the process off from the kind of case study role we have been suggesting—for we have talked about the possibility of case study sustaining multiple interpretations, of portraying reality rather than explaining it. To this end we have suggested relying on carefully considered procedures rather than on personal intuition.

This is not to say that some of the initial problems met by the field anthropologist are not very similar to those met by the educational case study worker. Consider for instance this point raised by an experienced ethnographic fieldworker:

> I became aware of another factor which happens everywhere I think, and which should be carefully watched by every fieldworker. In another society, the anthropologist, (stranger or outsider) is taken in and made welcome by one group or faction, who henceforward tend to monopolise him. He, therefore, becomes an object of suspicion or (at best) indifference to rival groups or factions. One has always to find a way to break away from one's original welcomers or sponsors. (Hart, in Spindler, 1970, p. 46)

This is a familiar problem in the case study of schools. How to gain acceptance by the Head, the staff and the pupils without being captured by any one interest, or group. To gain access to the school you need to first approach the Local Education Authority; to gain access to the staff, you need to approach the Head; to gain access to the pupils you need to approach the staff. Each fieldwork contact is thus sponsored by someone in authority over those you wish to study, and relationships between 'sponsors' and researchers cannot be broken if the research is to continue. Somehow the fieldworker has to construct some kind of compromise, relying on the passage of time for him to become as a *person* rather than in his official status. This, in fact, is one of the main reasons that fieldwork takes so long to conduct—it is not so much that the data itself demands long immersion in the field, but that the mutual trust required in research relationships takes time to create.

This is part of what is involved when Alan Beals writes of 'feeling at home in Gopalpur', 'being part of the community', and of 'remembering each friend and enemy as we remember our friends and enemies at home'. The point is not the field anthropologist is in *danger* of becoming part of the situation under study, but that he fails unless he does. This, perhaps more than any other single issue, stands between the view of research held by those with a commitment to 'objectivity' derived from experimental design and personal non-intervention and those who believe in 'objectivity' acquired from *within* the situation under study. John Dollard, who probably more than any other social scientist has attempted to reconcile the difference and conflict between the research methods of the anthropological fieldworker, the methods of psychoanalytic case study and the methods of experimental psychology, finally recognised a significant discontinuity in method when he wrote 'but not every *n*th person can be a friend' (Dollard, 1949).

Those who have been involved in fieldwork recognise truth in this and are aware of the critical and often precarious friendships they have made in the course of their work. But to the untrained observer such statements only serve to mystify even further the methods and procedures of the anthropological fieldworker. Margaret Mead recalls how, having trained in psychology, she attended anthropology classes given by Franz Boas:

> Professor Boas always spoke of the Kwakiutl as 'my dear friends', but this wasn't followed by anything that helped me to know what it was like to live among them . . . there was, in fact, no *how* in our education. What we learned was *what* to look for. Years later Camilla Wedgewood, on her first trip to Manam Island, reflected on this point when she wrote back: 'How anyone knows who is anybody's mother's brother, only God and Malinowski knows'. (Mead, 1975, pp. 148–51)

Later Margaret Mead attempted to teach her own students more explicitly about the methods and procedures involved in fieldwork and evolved a view close to the one we want to promote in the context of educational research:

> For fieldwork is a very difficult thing to do: to do it well, one has to sweep one's mind clear of every pre-supposition. In the field one can take nothing for granted. For as soon as one does, one cannot see what is before one's eyes as fresh and distinctive, and when one treats what is new merely as a variant of something already known, this may lead one far astray . . . the point of going into the field at all is to extend further what is already known, and so there is little value merely in identifying new versions of the familiar when we might, instead, find something wholly new. But to clear one's mind of pre-suppositions is a very hard thing to do and, without years of practice, all but impossible when one is working in one's own culture or in another that is very close to it. (Mead, 1975, pp. 154–5)

Margaret Mead's stress on fieldwork to extend what is already known despite the difficulties she foresees, is critical for the use of case study research in education as we envisage it. Many people in and around education today detect a growing feeling of cultural fragmentation. People at different points of the educational system feel increasingly isolated from people at other points. Classroom teachers becoming divorced from the concerns of teachers whose roles are managerial or pastoral. Schools becoming isolated from the concerns of local authorities; colleges of education from the concerns of schools. The ultimate effect is one of division and suspicion at a number of levels in the system, anarchy at the periphery as seen from the centre; malign conspiracy at the centre as seen from the periphery.

There seems also a distinct move in the administration of research funds towards the adoption of criteria of social usefulness and towards accountability of researchers to their sponsors. For researchers this means justifying their research as a means and not as an end, and so demands either that they commit themselves to non-technical values, or that they take up roles in bureaucratic institutions where value positions relating to their research are taken by others. Other trends could perhaps be added, but these seem to indicate a growing separation between the worlds of controllers and controlled throughout the educational system. Under the conditions brought about by these kinds of change, case study research offers glimpses of the culture of the other groups. It offers to short-circuit the insulation each interest group has accumulated for its protection. More than any other reason, this explains the delicacy with which the case study worker has to proceed.

A democratic ethic

In fieldwork most of the researcher's time and energy is frequently taken up in initiating and sustaining the relationships that make the research possible. Once the relationships are established the business of data collection can often be accomplished quite quickly. One of the main suggestions we make in this paper is for 'condensed fieldwork' to replace long immersion in the field as the legitimate methodological basis for case study in educational research. Rather than waiting for personal relationships between researcher and subjects to create trust we believe it may be possible to substitute sets of rules and procedures which synthesise an ethic that makes feasible a research strategy that is genuinely 'democratic'.

There are, of course, a number of dangers in using a word like 'democratic' in the context of educational research. The word itself has so many associations, subtle shades of meaning, and raises many paradoxes. For example, in the way we have used it here there is some conflict between, on the one hand, the attempt to formulate a set of research practices which give those being studied more control over the study itself, and on the other hand a move on the part of the researcher towards more freedom from the constraints of the academic community. More fundamentally there is a tension between the claim that individuals and interest groups have a right to know about what is happening in areas of the system that are structurally invisible to them, and the claim that such knowledge is personal, that people own the facts of their lives and have the right to deny others access to them.

Normally in case study research the case study worker is heavily dependent on personal trust. Instead of relying entirely on personal trust we feel that in the contexts we work in it may be possible to maintain trust through holding strongly to a carefully formulated ethic. The trust we seek depends on generating a style of educational research in which methods and procedures are explicit and visible. We are interested in attempting to play down the *personal* expertise of the researcher in order to enhance his professionalism. Just as people will put trust in a doctor, or policeman (while knowing some doctors are unprofessional and some policemen corrupt) so we believe it should be possible for the educational case study worker to establish a similar professional identity. In other words for people to trust us because of what we do rather than because 'we are people just like them'. The cost may be the loss of personal freedom now allowed to the researcher, but the gain could be that case study research will gain in credibility and begin to be used more effectively by educational practitioners.

The researcher attempting to produce a case study of a school or curriculum project faces a problem, for in presenting *his* interpretations of persons and events, how does he account for the interpretations made by others? What kinds of responsibility do they have for the finished product? Marie Kurchak (1974) describes the educational researcher's problem as well as the film maker's when she writes:

> What the film maker has presented is her private vision, packaged in celluloid. The family's isolation is reinforced as the film maker impotently withdraws the camera and hopes the message will reach someone 'in a position to do something about it'.

Since the case study is a *selective* mirror of events, accounts and definition of what happens, then whenever selections are made they must be related, as far as possible to named issues and negotiated with participants as to relevance and accuracy. By according confidentiality to informants for the term of the study and thereafter negotiating for release of material when it is needed for publication many initial field problems can be overcome, but the deeper issues remain.

Film as example and analogy

In documentary film making as in educational research the confusion of roles between observer and change agent recurs. The film maker feels impotent because he expects to bring about change, but in the way we have described a democratic mode of research that would be no part of his responsibility. The non-involved stance of the observer being validated by the increased involvement of his subjects in, and their responsibility for, both the process of research and its finished product.

Some of these ideas have already been practised by documentary film makers. Through its 'Challenge for Change' programme the National Film Board of Canada has been experimenting with ways of overcoming the alienating effects of the social documentary film on those portrayed. One of their most influential projects involved making a film on the island of Fogo, off Newfoundland, and the procedures adopted there have become known by film makers as 'The Fogo Process':

> Film maker Low shot 20 hours of footage oriented around several personalities and events. He screened the film, unedited, to the participants, and asked them to approve screenings to other members of the community. They had the option of cutting out film they might later regret.
>
> Low then made a series of short films (which he called 'vertical' films) each about a single personality or event. The films were screened for groups all over the island. In their work as a catalyst to discussion of mutual problems, the films allowed people, who may have been reluctant to speak in public, to allow their films to speak for them. People with opposing views had something external to mediate the hostility that might have occurred in face-to-face confrontation.
>
> One of the members of the film team remarked that in a 'horizontal' documentary intercutting of opinions immediately creates a hierarchy of who is right and who is wrong, thereby putting down some members of the community. The goal of trying to get people to talk to each other is then impeded.
>
> With the permission of the islanders, the films were shown to the decision makers, and their comments were recorded for the islanders.
>
> The technique of using film as a catalyst, mirror and third party mediator has been used since the Fogo experiment from the Mississippi Delta to Alaska. In some cases, half inch video (vtr) has been used in place of, or in conjunction with, film. (Kurchak, 1974)

Educational research, like film making, has traditionally worked with the notion of producing a final, 'finished' product. It too has seen its work left unrecognised, become suddenly popular, misinterpreted or misused, leaving the researcher with uncertain responsibilities.

Vertical studies

The film makers' idea of the 'vertical documentary' coupled with Barry MacDonald's notion of 'democratic evaluation' raise intriguing possibilities for the case study worker. Perhaps rather than engage in lengthy fieldwork and finally producing an account (as both Howard Becker and Louis Smith did), it might be possible to work by producing initial case studies on the basis of limited fieldwork and then using responses to these to redirect later work.

For example, after a week in a school the case study worker could produce limited 'vertical' studies—an account of a single event, a recording of a lesson, an interview with the Head. After working through these with the people involved they could circulate to a limited audience, and on the basis of that audience's response perhaps circulate more widely.

Visual records

In producing 'vertical' studies there are considerable advantages in using visual presentations, even in educational research. We have worked previously mainly with classroom recordings though more recently we have been experimenting with other visual records. For example we have recorded on tape-slide a whole working day in the life of an LEA adviser as he visits schools. We have also considered using an exhibition of photographs of a school and its immediate environment as a stimulus for interviewing pupils. The visual record has advantages for the researcher who has to work fast, what Collier (1967, p. 12) calls its 'can opener' effect. It gives the researcher a clear identity and an immediate visible product, and used skilfully this can provide him with a rapid introduction to the field. Since the early 1960s, video-tape recording has become more easily available, accessible and simpler to use. This increased availability of the technology represents a considerable challenge both to research and teaching. Video-tape makes it possible to capture and to replay some aspects of classroom action, so creating an enormous potential for research in the form of new kinds of data.

Negotiating interpretations

In terms of research design the point is not simply that vertical studies are circulated for approval, but for validation; the responses to the study perhaps being added to the study itself when they reveal significant new interpretations. Like works of art, case studies are never finished, only left.

This is the kind of process we have in mind when we suggest that democratic mode research may demand school case studies that can be completed within a week. Under such circumstances the researcher cannot become an expert in the detailed workings of the institutions under study, and is unable to become the person who knows the full story of the schools. Unable to produce the authoritative study from personal own resources the case study worker needs to proceed in such a way that his or her accounts are viewed as tentative and provisional. In admitting the fragility of their own interpretations case study workers might strengthen their accounts by mobilising the responses of participants as part of the final study.

For example in SAFARI one of the projects we are studying is Nuffield Secondary Science. Quite early on we realised that people in science education were referring to a range of different and often complex issues when they used the phrase 'The Nuffield Approach'. When we asked what the phrase meant we failed to obtain a clear, unambiguous formulation which might constitute a definition. What we did in this instance was simply to collect a range of comments, definitions, anecdotes and accounts which surrounded the phrase and seemed as a collection to retain some of the complexities of meaning the phrase has in use. By circulating this collection to people with an interest in the area we continuously obtained new fragments to add to the collection, it thus became self-validating and as our research continued a source for checking later ideas and hypotheses. The point is that we produced this collection at the *start* of the research and then used it as one way into the field, rather than simply opening a file which we wrote up at the end.

Confidentiality

For the case study worker confidentiality represents a continuous rather than an intermittent concern. It is not simply a question of negotiating access to the field at the start of the research and publication at the end. Given the sort of research we have outlined, and the constraints of the democratic model, confidentiality necessarily assumes the status of a continuous and predominant concern. At every stage of the research and with almost every encounter the case study worker must continually monitor what is said in order not to breach the confidentiality given to other participants.

The nature of case study is such that participants can often only judge the full consequences of release of data in retrospect, when the full study is available. We have adopted the procedure of offering blanket confidentiality in order to gain faster access to relevant data and to protect informants from the need continuously to monitor what they say. Release of data is then progressively negotiated between case study worker and informants according to the context of publication and the audience being informed.

We emphasise that confidentiality is not simply a mechanical procedure but a continuous methodological concern closely related to the values contained and communicated by the research. To return to the analogy with documentary film making:

> The problem with social documentaries is that they can be exploitative. The film maker may be sensitive as he goes about the act of embalming their misery, but when the lights are gone the family is still hungry. This is not the only problem: after *The Things I Cannot Change* was aired on CBC TV, the family was exposed to the teasing and mocking of their neighbours. (Kurchak, 1974)

The researcher attempting to produce a case study of a school or curriculum project faces similar problems. In presenting *his* (or her) interpretation of persons and events, what account is made of the interpretations made by others? The researcher is caught in the tension between meeting the obligations owed to the audience and the obligations owed to the subjects. The democratic model does not dissolve this tension but formalises the need for negotiation.

*Interviews**

One of the implications of using condensed fieldwork methods is a much heavier reliance on the unstructured interview than is usual in participant

* For a more detailed account see Helen Simons's paper on interviewing in Norris (ed.) (1977).

observation. Few of the handbooks available on interviewing, however, describe adequately the kind of interview often adopted in case study of the kind we have described. The reason is perhaps that those we interview not only have greater knowledge than we do about the areas under study, but that they assume that we have some knowledge too. The educational researcher is part of the educational scene in a way that, say, the organisational sociologist is not. Areas of knowledge and expertise over-lap. This also gives the unstructured interview a certain cutting edge. Many of the procedures we are recommending here are necessary because the interview is a penetrating device which requires greater protection for those studied than is necessary for observation of their routine social behaviour.

In the hands of a skilled interviewer most people are inexperienced and will reveal things they do not intend. Only by allowing retrospective control of editing and release of data to informants can the case study worker protect his subjects from the penetrative power of the research as well as checking his own misinterpretations or misunderstandings. Ethically this involves taking the view that people own the facts of their lives and should be able to control the use that is made of them in research.

The sharing of control over data with participants does mean that the researcher often has to face the fact that some of the finest data is lost, diluted or permanently consigned to the files. On the other hand access to knowledge about what are sensitive issues to his (or her) informants may guide the research in significant and unexpected ways.

The critical skills for interviewing are perhaps psychological mobility and emotional intelligence. 'Psychological mobility' is a phrase used by the American anthropologist Hortense Powdermaker (1967) to describe the fieldworker's ability 'to step in and out of the role of people with different value systems'. She ascribes her failures in conducting a study of the Hollywood film industry to her inability to make psychological transitions smoothly. In retrospect she wrote:

> I think of what the book might have been if some of my involvement had not been hidden, if I had possessed the psychological mobility and the sociological opportunity to enter and understand all the contending groups, if my value system had not so aggressively dominated the whole study, if I had known more humility and compassion.

In an interview the interviewee will often react to or against what is perceived to be the interviewer's frame of reference and definition of the situation. He will attempt either to 'tell the interviewer what he wants to know' or to take issue with what he perceives as the interviewer's point of view. Either way the interviewer's values enter the interview, and unless he/she is 'psychologically mobile' the interviewer may not realise the extent to which he or she is dominating or controlling what is said. Hortense Powdermaker warns, 'Conscious involvements are not a handicap for the social scientist. Unconscious ones are always dangerous' (Powdermaker, 1967).

The phrase 'emotional intelligence' extends the psychological mobility of the interviewer in order to emphasise with the interviewee. It is not enough simply to be self-aware and to know how your own values are entering the situation. You need to enter the world of the other. As the novelist Sybille Bedford writes of the interview, 'it takes two to tell the truth':

> It takes two to tell the truth.
> One for one side, one for the other?
> That's not what I mean. I mean one to tell, one to
> hear. A speaker and receiver. To tell the truth
> about any complex situation requires a certain
> attitude in the receiver.
> What is required in the receiver?
> I would say first of all a level of emotional intelligence . . .
> Imagination,
> Disciplined.
> Sympathy, Attention,
> And patience. (Bedford, 1968, p. 18)

For most interviewees the research interview clearly presents a novel and somewhat paradoxical situation. It is quite common to find people who treat the interview as mildly inconveniencing, who initially offer to talk for 'twenty minutes' but then go and talk for two hours. Given an interviewer who is both emotionally intelligent and psychologically mobile interviewees will frequently divulge personal information, and subsequently add, 'I don't know why I'm telling you this but . . .' or, 'I don't know why I told you, I've never told anyone else before'.

A problem with using the interview is that the interviewer can almost always force a response. Having acceded to the interview only very few people are able to resist the rule of the game that required a response to a question. Given a response, even if it is intended as flippant or off-hand, a skilled interviewer can use it to force a subsequent reply:

Teacher Don't expect me to tell you anything about the Headmaster, I won't say anything about the Head . . .
Interviewer You just *have*,

Later,

Teacher The Head is a well-meaning man.
Interviewer You mean misguided?

The skilled interviewer has to be sensitive to the different stages of the interview. Initially the interviewee generally assumes that the interviewer has limited knowledge about him and that he cannot be entrusted with some kinds of information. At critical stages of the interview the interviewer may be able to reveal to the interviewee a knowledge of his situation that was unsuspected. If he or she is able to do this he may be able to move the interviewee into a new phase based on increased trust, recognition and unanticipated shared meanings.

Other social processes at work in the interview may work against the interviewer, for example the interview situation may set up social opportunities for the interviewee to release information not relevant to the research but which attempts to restrict the researcher in other activities related to the research.

Overall perhaps the main problem with the interview is that it releases more of the truth than the case study worker can handle. Consequently the basic value of the interviewer is respect for the privacy of the interviewee and a recognition that people own the facts of their lives.

The report

Case study methods lend themselves to a variety of means of presentation, written reports, audio-visual recordings, displays and exhibitions. Generally these presentations should be devoid of indications of praise or blame from the point of view of the researcher. They should present contingency relationships only, leaving it to the audience to infer cause. They should attempt to be explicit about rationale and procedure, and the principles governing the selection and presentation of content. One consequence of this is to reduce the researcher's control over the content of the case study. The researcher may feel after a period of time that the study needs rewriting, but may be unable to rewrite because the procedures that were adopted prevent a reassertion of control over the data.

Wherever appropriate the case study should contain the expressed reactions (unedited and unglossed) of the principal characters portrayed to the report in its final draft form. It is implicit in the notion of case study that there is no one true definition of the situation. Within the confines of the study we act as though truth in social situations is multiple: the case study worker acts as a collector of definitions, not the conductor of truth.

Postscript

During 1975 we circulated short discussion papers and preliminary versions of the paper reproduced here (see MacDonald and Walker, 1975). The response to these papers indicates a number of areas of concern which give rise to an emerging structure for the rash of ideas, suggestions and speculations we have put forward here. Briefly these areas of concern can be labelled: Evaluation and Research, New Paradigms for Educational Research, and Anthropology as Inspiration. They derive in part from the traditions, expectations and values of slightly different, even if overlapping, audiences. It would be inappropriate here to examine each detail but we can at least give some indication of what lies behind each label.

Evaluation and research

One way of looking at the paper is as a working truce between the different priorities of evaluation and research in the face of a particular research project. A common response to our earlier papers has been (*a*) that we have confused evaluation and research and (*b*) that what we propose is perhaps new and significant for evaluators but that it has been well-rehearsed over a number of years in the social sciences, and particularly in sociology.

On the first point, we hope that what we have arrived at is a synthesis rather than a confusion. From our views of both evaluation and research we have arrived at a consensus on two major points.

One is that understanding of organised attempts at change in education must depend on developing understanding of the processes and milieux of the programme. It is a view which stresses the significance of locale and subculture.

The second point of consensus concerns the professional role of the researcher and stresses his or her social accountability both in the conduct of research and the dissemination of the results.

Our emphasis on these two areas of consensus has made our project feasible in terms of synthesising differing priorities and practices from evaluation and research. The cost perhaps has been a lack of concern on our part with what to many are the critical problems in educational research at the present time. Our stress on the creation of working relationships between research and practice has led us away from *formal* debates about alternative paradigms and the nature of knowledge. This has confused some readers who felt perhaps we should acknowledge the literature more fully, and has led some to claim that while the questions and issues we raise may be new for evaluators they are well rehearsed in the social sciences. This has some truth. Some of the problems of case study as we perceive them have antecedents in sociology, notably the Chicago school and community studies. This is a research tradition that has lost some of its impetus in the last two decades, except in some specialised areas (notably criminology). In education it is best known through the work of Willard Waller (1932).

We have felt for some time that educational research has failed to meet the challenge that Waller's research represents. There are few contemporary works that can claim such strong descriptive data as Waller presents in *The Sociology of Teaching*. One of our starting points in SAFARI was to attempt to match the quality of Waller's data. In asking ourselves how we might do this given modern methods of data collection and contemporary trends within the system we were led to formulate the procedures we have related here.

We also see our conception of the case study as a break with that tradition of research in the social sciences. The case study tradition of research (community studies, participant observations, anthropological studies) in the social sciences is, in Barry MacDonald's use of the term 'autocratic'. Admittedly the research is subject to the security of the academic community, but it is still basically the *researcher's* interpretation that gives coherence to the final report. The methods, procedures, techniques of research are open to question, but the right of the researcher to impose his view on the situation, often without reference to those of his informants (outside the frames of his research instruments), is taken for granted. It is not an issue. For us, it is *the* central issue.

What we have attempted is to design a form of case study research in which the case study worker relinquishes some authority over interpretation in the attempt to gain greater credibility and influence. We feel that what we are suggesting *is* radically different to the debate within sociology about the relation of theory to research. We are not simply trying to devise forms of research which map alternative realities in terms of different sets of taken-for-granted assumptions, but mobilise these differences within sets of negotiated relationships. There are strong action implications underlying our conception of educational research; hence the need for procedures to protect individuals from the consequence of the research.

New paradigms for research

The last few years have seen considerable debate about alternative paradigms for educational research (see, for example, Parlett and Hamilton, 1972; Young, 1971). There is at present some talk about a shift away from the funding of testing and survey programmes and towards 'descriptive', 'illuminative', 'phenomenological' or 'applied' research.

This trend is illustrated by a keynote address given by a leading American educational psychologist, Lee Cronbach. After reviewing ATI studies in education, that is studies which attempt to cross-breed experimental and correlational approaches by looking at Aptitude v. Treatment Interactions, Cronbach (1974) comes to the conclusion that in educational research the number of variables, and their consequent interactions, demand sample sizes that involve large scale research efforts. This causes him to review the closed nature of much contemporary educational psychology and suggest the use of observational approaches rather than an exclusive reliance on hypothesis testing:

> There *are* more things in heaven and earth than are dreamt of in our hypotheses, and our observations should be open to them. From Ockham to Lloyd Morgan, the canon has referred to parsimony in theorising, not in observing. The theorist performs a dramatist's function; if a plot with a few characters will tell the story, it is more satisfying than one with a crowded stage. But the observer should be a

journalist, not a dramatist. To suppress a variation that might not recur is bad observing.

Cronbach suggests a new direction for education psychology which has some parallels with the case study:

> Instead of making generalisation the ruling consideration in our research, I suggest that we reverse our priorities. An observer collecting data in one particular situation is in a position to appraise a practice or proposition in that setting, observing effects in context. In trying to describe and account for what happened, he will give attention to whatever variables were controlled, but he will give equally careful attention to uncontrolled conditions, to personal characteristics, and to events that occurred during treatment and measurement. As he goes from situation to situation, his first task is to describe and interpret the effect anew in each locale, perhaps taking into account factors that were unique to that locale, or series of events. As results accumulate, a person who seeks understanding will do his best to trace how the uncontrolled factors could have caused local departures from the modal effect. This is, generalisation comes late, and the exception is taken as seriously as the rule.

Cronbach remember is writing from within the context of the discipline; he writes as an educational psychologist. Yet he too finds himself looking out to other disciplines for inspiration and reference:

> The two scientific disciplines—experimental control and systematic correlation—answer formal questions stated in advance. Intensive local observation goes beyond discipline to an open-eyed, open-minded appreciation of the surprises Nature deposits in the investigative net. This kind of interpretation is historical more than scientific. I suspect that if the psychologist were to read more widely in history, ethnology, and the centuries of humanistic writings on man and society, he would be better prepared for this part of his work.

Cronbach's paper is significant because, despite his references to description and to history, he is attempting to shift the emphasis away from accounting for the past. The emphasis instead is on helping the practitioner decide how to take the next step:

> The psychologist can describe the conditions under which generalisations *have* held, or the domain of which they provide an actuarial summary. He cannot often state the boundaries defining how far they *will* hold. . . As Meehl has said, when we step outside the range of experience we have to use our heads. Though enduring systematic theories about man in society are not likely to be achieved, systematic inquiry can realistically hope to make two contributions. One reasonable aspiration is to assess local events accurately to improve short-run control. The other reasonable aspiration is to develop explanatory concepts, concepts that will help people use their heads.

Lee Cronbach is not making the same case as the one we propose in this paper, yet there are points of similarity and contact. We quote his paper here to indicate that there are changes currently being debated within the social sciences about the nature and scope of research. Cronbach's final paragraph makes the point strongly:

> Social scientists are rightly proud of the discipline we draw from the natural-science side of our ancestry. Scientific discipline is what we uniquely add to the time-honoured ways of studying man. Too narrow an identification with science, however, has fixed our eyes upon an inappropriate goal. The goal of our work, I have argued here, is not to amass generalisations atop which a theoretical tower can someday be erected. The special task of the social scientist in each generation is to pin down the contemporary facts. Beyond that, he shares with the humanistic scholar and the artist in the effort to gain insight into contemporary relationships, and to realign the culture's view of man with present realities. To know man as he is, is no mean aspiration.

Anthropology as inspiration

It is currently fashionable in educational research to look to anthropology as a reference and inspiration. In this paper we have used anthropological research in a highly selective way; what we have referred to is the *fieldwork* tradition. This explains why some of the anthropologists we have quoted have been those, who though distinguished in anthropological circles might be thought of as fringe members for one reason or another. For example, Hortense Powdermaker's field studies were all unusual at the time she worked—studies of the Hollywood star system, of the American Deep South, of urban Africa. Her techniques too seem unorthodox, particularly her disciplined and sensitive use of the interview. Perhaps her early training as a Union organiser gives her fieldwork an inquiring style and a political edge that many anthropologists lack. She herself hints at some of the isolation she feels from the discipline in some of the stories she tells:

> I did not see how Europeans could be omitted from the study of contemporary African life, but at that time I was apparently the only anthropologist in Northern Rhodesia with that view. Western civilisation was not completely unimportant in rural society either. One anthropologist, working in the latter, boasted about getting into a physical fight in a bar with a European because of the man's remarks about Africans. My answer was, 'But you should have been taking notes'. (Powdermaker, 1967, p. 250)

We have also quoted Margaret Mead, who may not seem a 'fringe figure'. Yet her success has mainly been recognised outside academic anthropological circles. In the discipline her greatest achievements, notably her fieldwork with Gregory Bateson on Bali, remain largely neglected. Their unorthodox use of film

> meant we had to wait 25 years before our work had much impact on anthropological fieldwork. And there are still no records of human interaction that compare with those Gregory made in Bali and then in Iatmul. (Mead, 1975, p. 257)

Margaret Mead has undoubtedly been an influential figure in American anthropology, yet her skill was mainly a fieldwork skill. We have quoted her in this paper for that reason.

There are of course other areas of anthropology that offer inspiration to the educational researcher (ethnosemantics, philosophical anthropology, studies of material culture), but it is the fieldwork tradition we stress here. Some people reading our papers have not appreciated this and have pointed to the failures of anthropology in dealing with complex urban situations. We believe that if there is a failure this is a failure of theory not a failure of method.

Acknowledgements: To Barry MacDonald and David Jenkin for detailed and extensive comments; also to Clem Adelman, David Hamilton, Helen Simons and Bob Stake.

R. A. Becher

5. Research into Practice

The purpose of this paper is to consider the ways in which the educational researcher might be seen as an agent of classroom innovation. There is, of course, a wide spectrum of different types of activity which might be described by the term educational research. At the one end of the spectrum it could be claimed that the neurophysiologist, carrying out fundamental studies on the nature of the human brain, is helping us to understand the mysteries of the learning process and is in that sense engaged in educational research. At the other, it might be said that the intelligent and conscientious teacher, who sets out to improve his or her professional competence by a systematic process of trial-and-error, is also engaged in a form of research into the process of education. But it will not be helpful for my present purpose to adopt such a liberal interpretation. I shall confine myself instead to what seems to have been the dominant post-war tradition of the major educational research institutes in Western Europe and North America. The mainstream of this tradition derives historically from the psychometric testing movement of the pre-war years, and from the influence of statisticians such as Fisher on the social sciences in general. It is with educational research of this specific and specialised type that my remarks will be concerned.

It must be acknowledged at the outset that very little of the educational research that is done appears to have any noticeable impact on the ordinary teacher and his work. It is not easy to get round this difficulty by saying that research consists in the pursuit of knowledge for its own sake. In the long term, if it is not to be seen as an expensive self-indulgence, there must be a pay-off of some kind. So it is, I think, right for all of us—teachers, policy-makers and the tax-paying public, as well as the researchers themselves—to look for ways in which the present situation can be improved.

Many researchers, to their credit, have made serious attempts to make their work more relevant to innovation in the classroom. The major difficulty has usually been seen as one of communication. As a result, researchers have looked for new and more effective ways of passing on to the practitioner the wisdom and the insights generated by their investigations. Simple guides have been written for teachers on how to interpret research findings, and the findings themselves have often been published in a form more readily understandable to the layman. When this approach has been seen to give disappointing results, the researchers have gone further. In the last two decades there has been increasing emphasis on development projects and action research programmes, some of which have themselves been based on the results of research. The expectation behind such programmes has been a reasonable one: namely that once the relevant research findings could be translated into specific practical recommendations, and once the results could be diffused into the educational system, the communication gap could at last be bridged.

But even this imaginative strategy has not so far paid off. Major action programmes—such as Operation Headstart in the USA, or the Educational Priority Areas Project in Britain—have been found, on investigation, to make much less impact than had at first been hoped. Major research-based development schemes—such as the IMU Mathematics Project in Sweden or the Individually Programmed Instruction Project in the USA— have not clearly shown themselves to justify the substantial costs involved. Nobody yet knows the answer to this new, and unexpected dilemma. The optimists may be inclined to blame faulty techniques, and to put increasing efforts into improving the available dissemination procedures. The pessimists may want to blame the inherent conservatism of the teachers, and give up in despair. But there is another alternative which we should perhaps be prepared to consider.

If a particular malady fails to yield to treatment, it may be because the patient refuses to take his medicine. Or it may be because the medicine itself is not sufficiently powerful or effective. But it may also be because the original diagnosis was mistaken. Perhaps we should look again at how the problem has been formulated, rather than at why the attempted solutions have not so far produced the results we hoped for.

Consider the following hypothesis. The difficulty is not that the teacher wilfully refuses to listen to the researcher, but that however carefully he listens the researcher has little of interest to tell him. The fault lies not with the practitioner, not with the communication system, but with our current conceptions of educational research itself. I want to pursue this hypothesis by considering some of the dominant assumptions of the research community, and to conclude by suggesting some ways in which these assumptions may need to be modified if the work of the researcher is to achieve a greater relevance to both professional decisions and public policy.

Let me reiterate, first, that this argument is not concerned with the wider definition of educational research. My remarks are not relevant to the specialised work of the clinical psychologists, or of those philosophers or sociologists or economists who happen to take a broad general interest in educational problems. Rather, I am concerned to focus attention on those specialists in learning theory, aptitude testing, curriculum evaluation, interaction analysis, and the like who form the main body of the educational research profession today.

The main assumption shared by most of them is that different learning situations are sufficiently alike in certain significant respects to justify the search for the general laws which govern them. The study of education is, in this tradition, modelled predominantly on the study of physical science. I want to look at some of the implications of this view, and to contrast them with the implications of the converse assumption. I mean, of course, the assumption that learning situations are sufficiently different in certain significant ways to invalidate the search for the general laws which govern them. In making this contrast, I shall be arguing the case for a different tradition, namely one which regards the study of education as a branch of the human, rather than the physical, sciences.

It may be helpful to draw out the significant contrasts in a number of different ways. First, consider the process of innovation itself—a process which has been studied in a variety of contexts. One helpful set of distinctions is made by Donald Schon, in his book *Beyond the Stable State* (1971). He describes the differences between what he calls centre-periphery models of innovation and periphery-periphery models. The former—the centre-periphery models—represent situations in which innovative ideas are generated at some central controlling point in the system, and are then delivered to practitioners engaged at its periphery. New weapon systems developed under wartime conditions provide one example of this process. The latter—periphery-periphery models—cover situations in which an innovation occurs at some point of practice, and then spreads along the periphery to other practitioners. An example here might be some new surgical technique worked out not in a medical research centre but in a general hospital. There is also a third possibility, which Schon does not discuss as fully as either of these—namely periphery-centre models. These cover the cases in which innovative messages are generated at the periphery of the system but then pass for processing to the centre. Market-oriented industries represent one instance of this process, where the demands of the consumer are carefully studied, and in large part determine the nature of the goods or services supplied.

In terms of these models, the majority of current educational research and development assumes the appropriateness of a centre-periphery pattern of innovation. The researchers and the developers do their work at the centre, where they are relatively remote from everyday concerns of the practitioner. They then try to find ways of disseminating their results to the periphery of the system, much as if they were operating an oil refinery and working out the best means of delivering their products to the expectant customers in their houses and their cars. Their approach seems to suggest that what is really important is to get the logistic structures right. If only they can change the framework of the management system in the appropriate ways, it is assumed that the actual processes of teaching and learning will look after themselves.

Unfortunately, there are now several examples which suggest that this assumption is too tidy-minded to match the complexity of human activities in general and education in particular. It is true that people's attitudes and expectations are to some extent shaped by the structure of the institutions in which they work. It is also however true that human institutions are themselves to some extent shaped by the attitudes and expectations of those who work in them. So a structural innovation—one which is formulated at the centre but has to be implemented at the periphery—can take on a surprising variety of different forms, according to how it is perceived or interpreted by those who are required to carry it out. Consider, for example, the reorganisation of secondary schools along comprehensive lines. The happy political myth is often sadly matched by the practical reality, in which pupils remain segregated by ability within the framework of a school which is itself designated as non-selective (Ford, 1969). Or consider the bewildering variety of different forms which an innovation such as team teaching may take, ranging from schools where teachers in different subjects genuinely plan and work together to those in which they have a formal meeting once a term to exchange information on their respective syllabuses. Or consider, again, how very diversely a given curriculum programme may be applied in practice, depending on the presuppositions of the teacher concerned and the procedures with which he feels comfortably familiar.

These examples suggest that the processes in education—that is, the actual transactions between teachers and students—are more important, because more basic and fundamental, than the structures. Unless careful attention is given to them, before modifying the surrounding framework, what very often results is superficial change without fundamental innovation. This is only another way of saying that the initial focus should be at the periphery, rather than at the centre, of the system. To put it more specifically, the problems on which educational research and development should engage should be those which are defined by a close study of educational practice.

I want now to come at the point another way, by considering what role the educational researcher should see himself as performing in relation to the teacher. The issue is closely related to questions about the sources of recruitment and methods of training for educational research: but I shall not go into such questions here, important though they undoubtedly are. Instead, let me simply note that the majority of research workers, whether or not they have had any experience as practising teachers, tend to see themselves as operating outside the educational system itself and as possessing some external and independent expertise. This expertise, whatever its nature may be, and from whatever specialist discipline it may derive, powerfully conditions the range of interests which the researcher is prepared to pursue. It also, of course, provides a professional context for the knowledge which he generates and helps to preserve his status with his fellow-researchers.

Typically, the educational researcher begins by selecting a particular aspect of education which lends itself to study in terms of the approach dictated by his own specialism. He goes to conduct his study within the limits which that specialism imposes. If questions arise which are not regarded as falling within the legitimate boundaries of his discipline, he ignores them—

for they are not his affair. He bends his subject-matter to his professional requirements, not his requirements to his subject-matter. If his disciplinary loyalties are to experimental psychology, he may set up an artificial laboratory-type investigation. If he is statistically inclined, he may try to create some kind of controlled situation in the field. What he very seldom does is to explore the environment as it occurs in ordinary everyday educational practice. That is much too unsatisfactory a business for anyone who sees himself as a man of science: for human concerns (and education is after all one of them) are too uncomfortably messy to be equated with the tidy certainties of classical physics. So the researcher contents himself with the hope that he can find the right way of abstracting the hard nuggets of truth from the shifting sands of reality, and thus eventually transform the craft of teaching into the engineering of the learning process.

What, though, might be the consequences of abandoning the pursuit of certainties, the search for general laws, the notion that education is a regrettably unsatisfactory kind of physical science in which the universal truth persists in wearing a heavy disguise? Suppose that the researcher were no longer to insist on dividing up the field of educational practice into colonial territories yielding to different types of expertise, and adopted instead a more holistic approach. In that case, I suggest, he would begin to place himself in a very different tradition. He would find himself embarking on a complex exercise in which he would be constrained to look at the learning milieu as a totality, to put the educational process in its wider social environment and to try and make some sense of what was actually taking place in that environment.

This alternative way of identifying research issues—through a study of educational practice, rather than by following the prior dictates of some specialised expertise—would have major implications for the researcher's role. He could no longer see himself as the outside expert coming in to investigate some carefully formulated topic of his own choosing and then trying to find ways of communicating to the teacher the benefits of his wisdom. His function would more closely resemble that of a consultant, working alongside the teacher. His concern would be to help the practitioner first to identify, and eventually to resolve, the actual problems which arise in the course of the educational process.

Such an approach would not deny the researcher the exercise of any expertise. But it would demand in him a readiness to venture beyond the limits of a single disciplinary specialism and to draw wherever necessary on the insights and findings of other research fields. He would often find himself in unfamiliar and uncertain territory where—like the teachers he aimed to help—he was in the position of a seeker after new understanding. His skill would lie in the tasks both of achieving that understanding and of formulating it in terms meaningful to the practitioner—terms which could help unravel the tangled complexities of the classroom world and show its problems in a new and illuminating light.

The alternative research tradition with which this paper is concerned can be approached, not only through considering the process of innovation itself, or through a discussion of possible changes in the researcher's role, but also more directly by looking at methodological issues. As long as educational research is seen as a search for the general laws governing a variety of educational situations, it is likely to put a considerable emphasis on quantitative techniques. For it is of the essence of an exact science that its results must be objective, capable of replication by independent investigators, and expressible in numerical or probabilistic terms.

One typical strategy in current educational research is to take large samples of the population to be investigated; to apply to them some standardised instrument, measure or procedure; to record the results as far as possible in quantitative form; and then to subject these results to elaborate statistical manipulation. Considering how seldom this strategy has paid off, it is surprising how long it has managed to survive as part of the researcher's normal repertoire. Its deficiences are familiar enough. In the first place, the devices available to measure the aptitudes, skills, or other relevant characteristics of the sample population are extremely crude, and likely to remain so. They are in no sense comparable with those of the quantitative scientist, since scientific instruments apply to the phenomena of the material world, which are considerably simpler than those of human behaviour. Moreover, the number of variables which may need to be taken into account in any educational situation are much larger, and less amenable to control, than those which normally obtain in any exact science. However technically impressive the researcher's statistical analysis of his results may be, there is no disguising the inadequacies of his methods of deriving his basic data. It is not surprising that, in consequence, the findings of most studies which adopt this quasi-numerical approach are insignificant, unenlightening and of little interest to anyone but the research community itself.* In this situation, the researchers have at least the consolation of calling for further research to resolve the inconsistencies of their successive investigations: but no one else is left any the better off.

An alternative methodology which seems worth serious attention is one which models itself on the approaches of the historian, the anthropologist and the interpretative critic.† It places its emphasis on the exercise of informed judgement and illuminative understanding, and seeks an objectivity of a less

* One case in point was the seven-year study of the impact of educational innovation on student performance, carried out by the American Institutes for Research under the title Project Longstep, whose massive but totally uninformative report to the US Office of Education was published in April 1976.

† At the time (1973) when the original version of this paper was written, the style of approach referred to here was in its infancy. It has since gained in stature, and now has its own supporting literature. Its main source-book is David Hamilton, David Jenkins, Christine King, Barry MacDonald, Malcolm Parlett (eds) *Beyond the Numbers Game*, Macmillan Education, 1977.

mechanistic kind than that which underlies the clinical trials of a new drug or the field testing of a new brand of wheat. The small but growing number of researchers in this more humane, less scientistic tradition have not necessarily abandoned quantitative techniques. They see these, however, as being of relatively limited usefulness, and do not expect them to remain valid in every situation. Their work is carried out largely through observational case studies rather than through batteries of questionnaires or standardised tests. They attend as carefully to the varied contexts and processes of learning as to its discernible products. An airline pilot's training concentrates more on how to function in a disastrous or unexpected situation than on how to operate when all is going to plan. So too researchers in this tradition have learnt to interest themselves in those aberrations from the norm—those cases where something atypical has happened—which tend to be given little emphasis in any statistically-based approach.

Research in this alternative style, then, looks for the significant differences, as well as the general similarities, between different learning milieux. But in abandoning the search for universal certainties and infallible laws, it does not—any more than does historical or anthropological study—abandon all attempts at generality. It is rather that the generalisations for which it seeks are of the kind expressed in novels, plays or works of art, not of the kind expressed in scientific texts. They are designed to throw into relief, and make more readily understandable, the underlying features of those human interrelationships that typify the educational process. And above all, the researchers who work within this tradition attempt to present their findings in ways which will be both informative and illuminating for practitioners and policy-makers, and not just technically impressive for their fellow-researchers.

To summarise, I have tried to sketch out an approach to educational research which would demand a radical change in the current assumptions held by many of its practitioners. The persistent gulf between the researcher and the teacher in the classroom cannot, I suggest, be bridged by any less radical measures. What is in question is not the abandonment of scholarly standards, but only the abandonment of an inappropriate and unproductive tradition. If the educational researcher ceases to adopt the camouflage of the quantitative scientist and turns from trying to create artificial laboratory models to a study of the natural phenomena of learning, he is more likely to make intelligible the actual transactions which take place in a variety of educational environments. If he adopts a holistic approach to learning situations, he is better placed to unravel their complex reality than he is by distorting what he sees in terms of his own disciplinary preconceptions. If his role becomes that of a consultant and problem-solver rather than that of an expert in some narrow specialism, he is more likely to gain a sympathetic understanding of the human world of the teacher and the taught. If he concentrates his attention on the process rather than the structure of education, he will help to meet the actual needs at the periphery of practice rather than merely to fulfil the inbred requirements at the centre of the research domain.

Finally, I would argue that if the researcher were to change his style of work in these directions, the problem of communication would solve itself. In addressing his attention to educational realities, the researcher would reach common ground with both the practitioner and the policy-maker. In learning to derive his results from a study not only of the similarities but also of the differences between one context and another, he would become a skilled and authoritative interpreter of the language of experience. There can surely be no better formula than this for an agent of innovation in the classroom.

Note: This paper was commissioned as a keynote lecture at a Council of Europe Colloquium of Directors of Educational Research Organisations held in Paris in November 1973, and printed in an earlier version in the Council of Europe Information Bulletin, July 1974.

Robert E. Stake

6. Program Evaluation, particularly Responsive Evaluation

In this paper I shall write about some recent developments in the methodology of program (or project) evaluation, and about what I call 'responsive evaluation'.

My main attention will be on program evaluation. A program may be strictly or loosely defined. It might be as large as all the teacher-training in the United States or it might be as small as a field-trip for the pupils of one classroom. The evaluation circumstances will be these: that someone is commissioned in some way to evaluate a program, probably an on-going program; that he has some clients or audiences to be of assistance to—usually including the educators responsible for the program; and that he has the responsibility for preparing communications with these audiences.

In 1965 Lee Cronbach, then President of the American Educational Research Association (AERA), asked me to chair a committee to prepare a set of standards for evaluation studies, perhaps like the *Standards for Educational and Psychological Tests and Manuals* compiled by John French and Bill Michael and published in 1966 by the American Psychological Association. Lee Cronbach, Bob Heath, Tom Hastings, Hulda Grobman, and other educational researchers had worked with many of the US curriculum reform projects in the 1950s and early 1960s, and had recognized the difficulty of evaluating curricula, and the great need for guidance on the design of evaluation studies.

Our committee reported that it was too early to decide upon a particular method or set of criteria for evaluating educational programs, that what educational researchers needed was a period of field work and discussion to gain more experience in how evaluative studies could be done. Ben Bloom, successor to Lee Cronbach in the Presidency of AERA, got the AERA to sponsor a *Monograph Series on Curriculum Evaluation* for the purpose we recommended. After seven volumes the series gained the sponsorship of the UCLA Center for the Study of Evaluation. I think this Monograph Series can take a good share of the credit, or blame, for the fact that by my count over two hundred sessions at the 1973 AERA annual meeting programs were directly related to the methods and results of program evaluation studies.

There were two primary models for program evaluation in 1965, and there are two today. One is the informal study, perhaps a self-study, usually using information already available, relying on the insights of professional persons and respected authorities. It is the approach of regional accrediting associations for secondary schools and colleges in the United States, and is exemplified by the Flexner report (1916) of medical education in the USA and by the Coleman report (1966) of equality of educational opportunity. This model is usually referred to as the School Accreditation Model. Most educators are partial to this evaluation model, more so if they can specify who the panel members or examiners are. Researchers do not like it because it relies so much on second-hand information. But there is much good about the model.

Most researchers have preferred the other model, the pretest/post-test model, what I often refer to as Ralph Tyler's model (Tyler, 1949). It uses prespecified statements of behavioural objectives—such as are available from Jim Popham's Instructional Objectives Exchange—and is nicely represented by Tyler's *Eight Year Study*, Husén's *International Educational Study*, and the National Assessment of Educational Progress. The focus of attention with this model is primarily on student performance.

Several of us have proposed other models. In a 1963 article Cronbach suggested that evaluation studies be considered as applied research on instruction, designed to discover what could be learned in general about curriculum development, as in Hilda Taba's Social Studies Curriculum Project. Mike Scriven strongly criticized Cronbach's choice in AERA Monograph No. 1, stating that it was time to give consumers (purchasing agents, taxpayers, and parents) information on how good each existing curriculum is. To this end, Kenneth Komoski established in New York City an Educational Product Information Exchange, which has reviewed equipment, books and teaching aids, but has to this day still not caught the buyer's eye.

Dan Stufflebeam was one who recognized that the designs preferred by researchers did not focus on the variables that educational administrators have control over. With support from Egon Guba, Dave Clark, Bill Gephart and others, he proposed a model for evaluation that emphasized the particular decisions that a program manager will face. Data-gathering would include data on Context, Input, Process and Product, analysis would relate those things to the immediate management of the program (see Stufflebeam *et al.*, 1971). Though Mike Scriven criticized this design too, saying that it had too much bias toward the concerns and the values of the education establishment, this Stufflebeam CIPP model was popular in the US Office of Education for several years. Gradually it fell into disfavour because it was not generating the information—or the protection—that program sponsors and directors needed. But that occurred, I think, not because it was a bad model, but partly because managers were unable or unwilling to *examine their own* operations as part of the evaluation. Actually no evaluation model could have succeeded. A major obstacle was a federal directive which said that no federal office could spend its funds to evaluate its own work, that that could only be done by an office higher up. Perhaps the best examples of evaluation reports following this approach are those done in the Pittsburgh schools by Mal Provus and Esther Kresh (see Provus, 1971).

Before I describe the approach that I have been working on—which I hope will someday challenge the two major models—I will mention several relatively recent developments in the evaluation business.

It is recognized, particularly by Mike Scriven and Ernie House, that cooption is a problem, that the rewards to an evaluator for producing a favourable evaluation report often greatly outweigh the rewards for producing an unfavourable report. I do not know of any evaluators who falsify their reports, but I do know many who consciously or unconsciously choose to emphasize the objectives of the program staff and to concentrate on the issues and variables most likely to show where the program is successful. I often do this myself. Thus the matter of 'meta-evaluation', providing a quality-control for the evaluation activities, has become an increasing concern.

Early in his first term of office, President Nixon created a modest Experimental Schools Program, a program of five-year funding for three carefully selected high schools (from all those in the whole country), and the elementary schools that feed students into them. Three more have been chosen each year, according to their proposal to take advantage of a broad array of knowledge and technical developments, and to show how good a good school can be. The evaluation responsibility was designed to be allocated at three separate levels, one *internal* at the local school level, one *external* at the local school level (i.e., in the community, attending to the working of the local school, but not controlled by it) and a third at the national level, synthesizing results from the local projects and evaluating the organization and effects of the Experimental Schools Program as a whole. Many obstacles and hostilities hampered the work of the first two evaluation teams. And work at the third level—according to Egon Guba who did a feasibility study—was seen to be so likely to fail that it probably should be carried no further.

Mike Scriven has made several suggestions for meta-evaluation, one most widely circulated based on abstinence, called 'Goal-free evaluation' (see Scriven, 1973). Sixten Marklund has jokingly called it 'Aimless evaluation'. But it is a serious notion, not to ignore all idea of goals, but to refrain completely from any personal discussion of goals with the program sponsors or staff. The evaluator, perhaps with the help of colleagues and consultants, then is expected to recognize manifest goals and accomplishments of the program as he works it in the field. Again, with the concern for the consumer of education, Scriven has argued that what is intended is not important, that the program is a failure if its results are so subtle that they do not penetrate the awareness of an alert evaluator. Personally I fault Scriven for expecting us evaluators to be as sensitive, rational and alert as his designs for evaluation require. I sometimes think that Mike Scriven designs evaluation studies that perhaps only Mike Scriven is capable of carrying on.

Another interesting development is the use of adversarial procedures in obtaining evidence of program quality and especially in presenting it to decision makers. Tom Owens, Murray Levine, and Marilyn Kourilsky have taken the initiative here (see, for example, Levine, 1973). They have drawn upon the work of legal theorists who claim that truth emerges when opposing forces submit their evidence to cross-examination directly before the eyes of judges and juries. Graig Gjerde, Terry Denny and I tried something like this in our TCITY Report (Stake and Gjerde, 1974). It was important to us to leave the issue unresolved, to let the reader decide which claim to accept, if any. But we would have served the reader better if we had each written a follow-up statement to challenge the others' claims. At any rate, this is an example of using an adversary technique in an evaluation study.

Now I want to concentrate on the approach for evaluating educational programs presently advocated by Malcolm Parlett of the University of Edinburgh, Barry MacDonald of the University of East Anglia (e.g. MacDonald, 1976), Lou Smith of Washington University of St Louis (e.g. Smith and Pohland, 1974), Bob Rippey of the University of Connecticut (e.g. Rippey, 1973), and myself. Many of you will have had an opportunity to read an excellent booklet written by Malcolm Parlett and David Hamilton (1972). Like they did, I want to emphasize the settings where learning occurs, teaching transactions, judgement data, holistic reporting, and giving assistance to educators. I should not suggest that they endorse all I will say today, but their writings for the most part are harmonious with mine.

Let me start with a basic definition, one that I got from Mike Scriven. Evaluation is an *Observed Value* compared to some *Standard*. It is a simple ratio but this numerator is not simple. In program evaluation it pertains to the whole constellation of values held for the program. And the denominator is not simple, for it pertains to the complex of expectations and criteria that different people have for such a program.

The basic task for an evaluator is made barely tolerable by the fact that he does not have to solve this equation in some numerical way nor to obtain a descriptive summary grade, but needs merely to make a comprehensive statement of what the program is observed to be, with useful references to the satisfaction and dissatisfaction that appropriately selected people feel toward it. Any particular client may want more than this, but this satisfies the minimum concept, I think, of an evaluation study.

If you look carefully at the TCITY Report you will find no direct expression of this formula, but it is in fact the initial idea that guided us. The form of presentation we used was chosen to convey a message about the Twin City Institute to our readers in Minneapolis and St Paul, rather than to be a literal manifestation of our theory of evaluation.

Our theory of evaluation emphasizes the distinction between a preordinate approach and a responsive approach. In the recent past the major distinction being made by methodologists is that between what Scriven called *formative* and *summative* evaluation (see Scriven, 1967). He gave attention to the difference between developing and already developed programs, and implicitly to evaluation for a local audience of a program in specific setting as contrasted to evaluation for many audiences of a potentially generalizable program. These are important distinctions, but I find it even more important to distinguish between preordinate evaluation studies and responsive evaluation studies.

I have made the point that there are many different ways to evaluate educational programs. No one way is the right way. Some highly recommended evaluation procedures do not yield a full description, nor a view of the merit and shortcoming of the program being evaluated. Some procedures ignore pervasive questions that should be raised whenever educational programs are evaluated:

Do all students benefit or only a special few?
Does the program adapt to instructors with unusual qualifications?
Are opportunities for aesthetic experience realized?

Some evaluation procedures are insensitive to the uniqueness of the local conditions. Some are insensitive to the quality of the learning climate provided. Each way of evaluating leaves some things de-emphasized.

I prefer to work with evaluation designs that perform a service. I expect the evaluation study to be useful to specific persons. An evaluation probably will not be useful if the evaluator does not know the interests and language of his audiences. During an evaluation study, a substantial amount of time may be spent learning about the information needs of the persons for whom the evaluation is being done. The evaluator should have a good sense of whom he is working for and their concerns.

Responsive evaluation

To be of service and to emphasize evaluation issues that are important for each particular program, I recommend the *responsive evaluation* approach. It is an approach that sacrifices some precision in measurement, hopefully to increase the usefulness of the findings to persons in and around the program. Many evaluation plans are more 'preordinate', emphasizing (1) statement of goals, (2) use of objective tests, (3) standards held by program personnel, and (4) research-type reports. Responsive evaluation is less reliant on formal communication, more reliant on natural communication.

Responsive evaluation is an alternative, an old alternative. It is evaluation based on what people do naturally to evaluate things: they observe and react. The approach is not new. But it has been avoided in planning documents and institutional regulations because, I believe, it is subjective, poorly suited to formal contracts, and a little too likely to raise the more embarrassing questions. I think we can overcome the worst aspects of subjectivity, at least. Subjectivity can be reduced by replication and operational definition of ambiguous terms, even while we are relying heavily on the insights of personal observation.

An educational evaluation is *responsive evaluation* (1) if it orients more directly to program activities than to program intents, (2) if it responds to audience requirements for information, and (3) if the different value-perspectives of the people at hand are referred to in reporting the success and failure of the program. In these three separate ways an evaluation plan can be responsive.

To do a responsive evaluation, the evaluator of course does many things. He makes a plan of observations and negotiations. He arranges for various persons to observe the program. With their help he prepares brief narratives, portrayals, product displays, graphs, etc. He finds out what is of value to his audiences. He gathers expressions of worth from various individuals whose points of view differ. Of course, he checks the quality of his records. He gets program personnel to react to the accuracy of his portrayals. He gets authority figures to react to the importance of various findings. He gets audience members to react to the relevance of his findings. He does much of this informally, iterating, and keeping a record of action and reaction. He chooses media accessible to his audiences to increase the likelihood and fidelity of communication. He might prepare a final written report, he might not—depending on what he and his clients have agreed on.

Purposes and criteria

Many of you will agree that the book edited by E. F. Lindquist, *Educational Measurement* (1951), has been the bible for us who have specialized in educational measurement. Published in 1951, it contained no materials on program evaluation. The second edition, edited by Bob Thorndike (1971), has a chapter on program evaluation. Unfortunately, the authors of this chapter, Alex Astin and Bob Panos, chose to emphasize but one of the many purposes of evaluation studies. They said: 'The principal purpose of evaluation is to produce information that can guide decisions concerning the adoption or modification of an education program' (p. 749).

People expect evaluation to accomplish many different purposes:

to document events
to record student change
to detect institutional vitality
to place the blame for trouble
to aid administrative decision making
to facilitate corrective action
to increase our understanding of teaching and learning

Each of these purposes is related directly or indirectly to the values of a program, and may be a legitimate purpose for a particular evaluation study. It is very important to realize that each purpose needs separate data, all the purposes cannot be served with a single collection of data. Only a few questions can be given prime attention. We should not let Astin and Panos decide what questions to attend to, or Tyler, or Stake. Each evaluator, in each situation, has to decide what to attend to. The evaluator has to decide.

On what basis will he choose the prime questions? Will he rely on his preconceptions? Or on the formal plans and objectives of the program? Or on actual program activities? Or on the reactions of participants? It is at this choosing that an evaluator himself is tested.

Most evaluators can be faulted for over-reliance on preconceived notions of success. I advise the evaluator to give careful attention to the reasons the evaluation was commissioned, then to pay attention to what is happening in the program, then to choose the value questions and criteria. He should not fail to discover the best and worst of program happenings. He should not let a list of objectives or an early choice of data-gathering instruments draw attention away from the things that most concern the people involved.

Many of my fellow evaluators are committed to the idea that good education results in measurable outcomes: student performance, mastery, ability, attitude. But I believe it is not always best to think of the *instrumental* value of education as a basis for evaluating it. The 'payoff' may be diffuse, long delayed: or it may be even beyond the scrutiny of evaluators. In art education for example it is sometimes the purpose of the program staff or parent to provide artistic experiences—and training—for the *intrinsic* value alone. 'We do these things because they are good things to do', says a ballet teacher. Some science professors speak similarly about the experiential value of reconstructing certain classical experiments. The evaluator or his observers should note whether or not those learning experiences were well arranged. They should find out what appropriately selected people think are the 'costs' and 'benefits' of these experiences in the dance studio or biology laboratory. The evaluator should not presume that only measurable outcomes testify to the worth of the program.

Sometimes it will be important for the evaluator to do his best to measure student outcomes, other times not. I believe that there are few 'critical' data in any study, just as there are few 'critical' components in any learning experience. The learner is capable of using many pathways, many tasks, to gain his measure of skill and aesthetic 'benefit'. The evaluator can take different pathways to reveal program benefit. Tests and other data-gathering should not be seen as essential; neither should they be automatically ruled out. The choice of these instruments in responsive evaluation should be made as a result of observing the program in action and of discovering the purposes important to the various groups having an interest in the program.

Responsive evaluations require planning and structure; but they rely little on formal statements and abstract representations, e.g., flow charts, test scores. Statements of objectives, hypotheses, test batteries, teaching syllabi are, of course, given primary attention if they are primary components of the instructional program. Then they are treated not as the basis for the evaluation plan but as components of the instructional plan. These components are to be evaluated just as other components are. The proper amount of structure for responsive evaluation depends on the program and persons involved.

Substantive structure

Instead of objectives, or hypotheses as 'advanced organizers' for an evaluation study, I prefer *issues.* I think the word 'issues' better reflects a sense of complexity, immediacy, and valuing. After getting acquainted with a program, partly by talking with students, parents, taxpayers, program sponsors, and program staff, the evaluator acknowledges certain issues or problems or potential problems. These issues are a structure for continuing discussions with clients, staff, and audiences. These issues are a structure for the data-gathering plan. The systematic observations to be made, the interviews and tests to be given, if any, should be those that contribute to understanding or resolving the issues identified.

In evaluating TCITY, Graig Gjerde and I became aware of such issue-questions as

Is the admissions policy satisfactory?
Are some teachers too 'permissive'?
Why do so few students stay for the afternoon?
Is opportunity for training younger teachers well used?
Is this Institute a 'lighthouse' for regular school curriculum innovation?

The importance of such questions varies during the evaluation period. Issues which are identified early as being important tend to be given too much attention in a preordinate data plan, and issues identified toward the end are likely to be ignored. Responsive-evaluation procedures allow the evaluator to respond to emerging issues as well as to preconceived issues.

The evaluator usually needs more structure than a set of questions to help him decide 'what data to gather'. To help the evaluator conceptualize his 'shopping list', I once wrote a paper entitled 'The Countenance of Educational Evaluation' (Stake, 1967). It contained the matrix, the thirteen information categories, shown in Figure 1. You may notice that my categories are not very different from those called for in the models of Dan Stufflebeam and Mal Provus.

For different evaluation purposes there will be different emphases on one side of the matrix or the other: descriptive data and judgemental data. And, similarly, there will be different emphases on antecedent, transaction, and outcome information. The 'countenance' article also emphasized the use of multiple and even contradicting sources of information.

It also pointed out the often ignored question about the match-up between intended instruction and observed instruction; and the even more

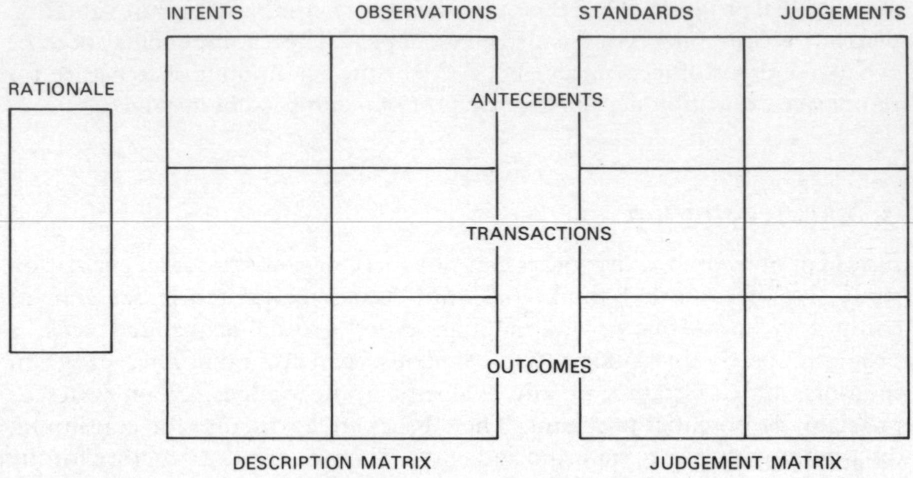

FIGURE 1 *A layout of statements and data to be collected by the evaluator of an educational program*

elusive question about the strength of the contingency of observed outcomes upon observed transactions, under the particular conditions observed. I think these 'countenance' ideas continue to be good ones for planning the content of the evaluation study.

I like to think of all of these data as observations: intents, standards, judgments, and statements of rationale are observed data too. Maybe it was a mistake to label just the second column 'Observations'. Thoreau said: 'Could a greater miracle take place than for us to look through each other's eyes for an instant'.

Human observers are the best instruments we have for many evaluation issues. Performance data and preference data can be psychometrically scaled when objectively quantified data are called for. The important matter for the evaluator is to get his information in sufficient amount from numerous independent and credible sources so that it effectively represents the perceived status of the program, however complex.

Functional structure

'Which data' is one thing but 'how to do the evaluation' is another. My responsive-evaluation plan allocates a large expenditure of evaluation resources to observing the program. The plan is not divided into phases because observation and feedback continue to be the important functions from the first week through the last. I have identified twelve recurring events. I show them as if on the face of a clock. I know some of you would remind me

Talk with clients, program staff, audiences

Identify program scope

Overview program activities

Discover purposes, concerns

Conceptualize issues, problems

Identify data needs, re issues

Select observers, judges; instruments if any

Observe designated antecedents, transactions and outcomes

Thematize; prepare portrayals, case studies

Validate; confirm; attempt to disconfirm

Winnow, match issues to audiences

Format for audience use

FIGURE 2 *Prominent events in a responsive evaluation*

that a clock moves clockwise, so I hurry to say that this clock moves clockwise and counter-clockwise *and* cross-clockwise. In other words, any event can follow any event. Furthermore, many events occur simultaneously, and the evaluator returns to each event many times before the evaluation ends.

For example, take twelve o'clock. The evaluator will discuss many things on many occasions with the program staff and with people who are representative of his audiences. He will want to check his ideas of program scope, activities, purposes, and issues against theirs. He will want to show them his representations (e.g., sketches, displays, portrayals, photographs, tapes) of value questions, activities, curricular content, and student products. Reactions to these representations will help him learn how to communicate in this setting. He should provide useful information. He should not pander to desires for only favourable (or only unfavourable) information, nor should he suppose that only the concerns of evaluators and external authorities are worthy of discussion. (Of course, these admonitions are appropriate for responsive evaluation and preordinate evaluation alike.)

This behaviour of the responsive evaluator is very different from the behaviour of the preordinate evaluator. Here is my estimate as to how the two evaluators would typically spend their time:

	Preordinate %	*Responsive* %
Identifying issues, goals	10	10
Preparing instruments	30	15
Observing the program	5	30
Administering tests, etc.	10	—
Gathering judgements	—	15
Learning client needs, etc.	—	5
Processing formal data	25	5
Preparing informal reports	—	10
Preparing formal reports	20	10

I believe the preordinate evaluator conceptualizes himself as a stimulus, seldom as a response. He does his best to generate standardized stimuli, such as behavioural objective statements, test items, or questionnaire items. The responses that he evokes are what he collects as the substance of his evaluation report.

The responsive evaluator considers the principal stimuli to be those naturally occurring in the program, including responses of students and the subsequent dialogues. At first his job is to record these, learning both of happenings and values. For additional information he assumes a more interventionist role. And with his clients and audience he assumes a still more active role, stimulating their thought (we hope) and adding to their experience with his reports.

Philosopher David Hawkins responded to the idea of reversing S–R roles in this way:

> ...I like the observation that one is reversing the S and R of it. In an experiment one puts the system in a prepared state, and then observes the behaviour of it. Preparation is what psychologists call 'stimulus',... In naturalistic investigation one does not prepare the system, but looks for patterns, structures, significant events, as they appear under conditions not controlled or modified by the investigator, who is himself now a system of interest. He is a resonator, a respondent. He must be in such an initial state that *a* his responses contain important information about the complex of stimuli he is responding to, and *b* they must be maximally decodable by his intended audience. (pers. comm., 1973)

In the next section of this paper I will talk about maximally decodable reports. Let me conclude these two sections on structure by saying that the evaluator should not rely only on his own powers of observation, judgement and responding. He should enlist a platoon of students, teachers, community leaders, curriculum specialists, etc.—his choice depending on the issues to be studied and the audiences to be served. The importance of their information, and the reliability of it, will increase as the number and variety of observers increase.

Portrayal and holistic communication

Maximally decodable reports require a technology of reporting. We educational measurements people have tried to be impersonal, theoretical, generalizable. We have sought the parsimonious explanation. We have not accepted the responsibility for writing in a way that is maximally comprehensible to practicing educators and others concerned about education. According to R. F. Rhyne:

> There is a great and growing need for the kind of powers of communication that help a person gain, vicariously, a feeling for the natures of fields too extensive and diverse to be directly experienced.
>
> Prose and its archetype, the mathematical equation, do not suffice. They offer more specificity within a sharply limited region of discourse than is safe, since the clearly explicit can be so easily mistaken for truth, and the difference can be large when context is slighted. (Rhyne, 1972, pp. 93–104)

We need this power of communication, this opportunity for vicarious experience, in our attempts to solve educational problems.

One of the principal reasons for backing away from the preordinate approach to evaluation is to improve communication with audiences. The conventional style of research-reporting is a 'clearly explicit' way of communicating. In a typical research project the report is limited by the project design. A small number of variables are identified and relationships among them are sought. Individuals are observed, found to differ, and distributions of scores are displayed. Covariations of various kinds are analyzed and interpreted. From a report of such analytic inquiry it is very hard, often impossible, for a reader to know 'what the program was like'. If he is supposed to learn 'what the program was like', the evaluation report should be different from the conventional research report.

As a part of my advocacy of the responsive approach I have urged my fellow evaluators to respond to what I believe are the natural ways in which people assimilate information and arrive at understanding. *Direct* personal experience is an efficient, comprehensive, and satisfying way of creating understanding, but a way not usually available to our evaluation-report audiences. The best substitute for direct experience probably is *vicarious experience*—increasingly better when the evaluator uses 'attending' and 'conceptualizing' styles similar to those which members of the audience use. Such styles are not likely to be those of the specialist in measurement or theoretically minded social scientist. Vicarious experience often will be conceptualized in terms of persons, places, and events.

We need a reporting procedure for facilitating vicarious experience. And it is available. Among the better evangelists, anthropologists, and dramatists are those who have developed the art of story-telling. We need to portray complexity. We need to convey holistic impression, the mood, even the mystery of the experience. The program staff or people in the community may be 'uncertain'. The audiences should feel that uncertainty. More ambiguity rather than less may be needed in our reports. Oversimplification obfuscates. Ionesco said:

> As our knowledge becomes separated from life, our culture no longer contains ourselves (or only an insignificant part of ourselves), for it forms a 'social' context into which we are not integrated.
>
> So the problem becomes that of bringing our life back into contact with our culture, making it a living culture once again. To achieve this, we shall first have to kill 'the respect for what is written down in black and white...' to break up our language so that it can be put together again in order to re-establish contact with 'the absolute', or as I should prefer to say, with 'multiple reality'; it is imperative to 'push human beings again towards seeing themselves as they really are'. (Ionesco, in Esslin, 1966, p. 298)

Some evaluation reports should reveal the 'multiple reality' of an educational experience.

The responsive evaluator will often use portrayals. Some will be short, featuring perhaps a five-minute 'script', a log, or scrapbook. A longer portrayal may require several media: narratives, maps and graphs, exhibits, taped conversations, photographs, even audience role-playing. Which ingredients best convey the sense of the program to a particular audience? The ingredients are determined by the structure chosen by the evaluator:

> Suppose that a junior-high-school art program is to be evaluated. For portrayal of at least one issue, 'how the program affects *every* student', the students might be thought of as being in two groups: those taking at least one fine-arts course and those taking none. (The purpose here is description, not comparison.)
>
> A random sample of ten students from each group might be selected and twenty small case studies developed. The prose description of what each does in classes of various kinds (including any involvement with the arts in school) might be supplemented with such things as (1) excerpts from taped interviews with the youngster, his friend, his teachers, and his parents; (2) art products (or photographs, news clippings, etc, of same) made by him in or out of class; (3) charts of his use of leisure time; and (4) test scores of his attitudes toward the arts. A display (for each student) might be set up in the gymnasium which could be examined reasonably thoroughly in 10–20 minutes.
>
> Other materials, including the plan, program, and staffing for the school, could be provided. Careful attention would be directed toward finding out how the description of these individual youngsters reveals what the school and other sources of art experiences are providing in the way of art education.

It will sometimes be the case that reporting on the quality of education will require a 'two-stage' communication. Some audiences will not be able to take part in such a vicarious experience as that arranged in the example above. A surrogate audience may be selected. The evaluator will present his portrayals to them; then he will question them about the apparent activity, accomplishments, issues, strengths and shortcomings of the program. He will report their reactions, along with a more conventional description of the program, to the true audiences:

> These twenty displays could be examined by people specially invited to review and respond to them. The reviewers might be students, teachers, art curriculum specialists, and patrons of the arts. They might also visit regular school activities, but most attention would be to the displays. These reviewers should be asked to answer such questions as 'Based on these case studies, is the school doing its share of providing good quality art experience for all the young people?' and 'Is there too much emphasis on disciplined creative performance and not enough on sharing the arts in ways that suit each student's own tastes?' Their response to these portrayals and questions would be a major part of the evaluation report.

The portrayal will usually feature descriptions of persons. The evaluator will find that case studies of several students may more interestingly and faithfully represent the educational program than a few measurements on all of the students. The promise of gain is twofold: the readers will comprehend the total program, and some of the important complexity of the program will be preserved. The several students usually cannot be considered a satisfactory representation of the many—a sampling error is present. The protests about the sampling error will be loud; but the size of the error may be small, and it will often be a satisfactory price to pay for the improvement in communication.

There will continue to be many research inquiries needing social survey technology and exact specification of objectives. The work of John Tukey, Torsten Husen, Ralph Tyler, Ben Bloom, and James Popham will continue to serve as a model for such studies.

Often the best strategy will be to select achievement tests, performance tests, or observation checklists to provide evidence that prespecified goals were or were not achieved. The investigator should remember that such a preordinate approach depends on a capability to state the important purposes of education and a capability to discern the accomplishment of those purposes, and those capabilities sometimes are not at our command. The preordinate approach usually is not sensitive to ongoing changes in program purpose, nor to unique ways in which students benefit from contact with teachers and other learners, nor to dissimilar viewpoints that people have as to what is good and bad.

Elliot Eisner nicely summarized these insensitivities in AERA Monograph 3. He advocated consideration of *expressive objectives*—toward outcomes that are idiosyncratic for each learner and that are conceptualized and evaluated *after* the instructional experience; after a product, an awareness, or a feeling has become manifest, at a time when the teacher and learner can reflect upon what has occurred. Eisner implied that sometimes it would be preferable to evaluate the quality of the *opportunity* to learn—the 'intrinsic' merit of the experience rather than the more elusive 'payoff' to use Scriven's terms.

In my own writing on evaluation I have been influenced by Eisner and

Scriven and others who have been dissatisfied with contemporary testing. We see too little good measurement of complex achievements, development of personal styles and sensitivities. I have argued that few, if any, specific learning steps are truly essential for subsequent success in any of life's endeavours. I have argued that students, teachers, and other purposively selected observers exercise the most relevant critical judgements, whether or not their criteria are in any way explicit. I have argued also that the alleviation of instructional problems is most likely to be accomplished by the people most directly experiencing the problem, with aid and comfort perhaps (but not with specific solutions or replacement programs) from consultants or external authorities. I use these arguments as assumptions for what I call the *responsive evaluation* approach.

Utility and legitimacy

The task of evaluating an educational program might be said to be impossible if it were necessary to express verbally its purposes or accomplishments. Fortunately, it is not necessary to be explicit about aim, scope, or probable cause in order to indicate worth. Explication will usually make the evaluation more useful; but it also increases the danger of misstatement of aim, scope, and probable cause.

To layman and professional alike, evaluation means that someone will report on the program's merits and shortcomings. The evaluator reports that a program is 'coherent', 'stimulating', 'parochial', and 'costly'. These descriptive terms are also value-judgement terms. An evaluation has occurred. The validity of these judgements may be strong or weak; their utility may be great or little. But the evaluation was not at all dependent on a careful specification of the program's goals, activities or accomplishments. In planning and carrying out an evaluation study, the evaluator must decide how far to go beyond the bare bones ingredients: values and standards. Many times he will want to examine goals. Many times he will want to provide a portrayal from which audiences may form their own value judgements.

The purposes of the audiences are all important. What would they like to be able to do with the evaluation of the program? Chances are they do not have any plans for using it. They may doubt that the evaluation study will be of use to them. But charts and products and narratives and portrayals do affect people. With these devices persons become better aware of the program, develop a feeling for its vital forces, a sense of its disappointments and potential troubles. They may be better prepared to act on issues such as a change of enrolment or a reallocation of resources. They may be better able to protect the program.

Different styles of evaluation will serve different purposes. A highly subjective evaluation may be useful but not be seen as legitimate. Highly specific language, behavioural tasks, and performance scores are considered by some to be more legitimate. In America, however, there is seldom a greater legitimacy, than the endorsement of large numbers of audience-significant people. The evaluator may need to discover what legitimacies his audiences (and their audiences) honour. Responsive evaluation includes such inquiry.

Responsive evaluation will be particularly useful during formative evaluation when the staff needs help in monitoring the program, when no one is sure what problems will arise. It will be particularly useful in summative evaluation when audiences want an understanding of a program's activities, its strengths and shortcomings and when the evaluator feels that it is his responsibility to provide a vicarious experience.

Preordinate evaluation should be preferred to responsive evaluation when it is important to know if certain goals have been reached, if certain promises have been kept, and when predetermined hypotheses or issues are to be investigated. With greater focus and opportunity for preparation, preordinate measurements made can be expected to be more objective and reliable.

It is wrong to suppose that either a strict preordinate design or responsive design can be fixed upon an educational program to evaluate it. As the program moves in unique and unexpected ways, the evaluation efforts should be adapted to them, drawing from stability and prior experience where possible, stretching to new issues and challenges as needed.

Note: This paper was presented at a conference organized by the Scottish Council for Research in Education in Edinburgh, May 1974.

Ian Westbury

7. Schooling as an Agency of Education: Some Implications for Curriculum Theory

In the year 1949–50 American schools enrolled 28·6 million students; twenty years later, in the Fall of 1970, America's schools enrolled 51·6 million students. In 1949–50, 77 per cent of the population of the United States aged fourteen to seventeen were in school; in 1971, 94 per cent of this age-group were there. Statistics of this kind, and they are repeated again and again in all western societies, reflect the factors which have determined the whole course of the development of schools, and of educational thought, in recent years. In the years since the end of the Second World War the aspiration of the pioneers of public education to school the whole population was achieved to a degree that would have been regarded as scarcely conceivable only twenty-five years ago. The bare statistics cited above can serve to remind us of what was required to achieve this unprecedented expansion of the educational system: buildings had to be provided, teachers trained, and curricula developed for a burgeoning enterprize. There were many vexations to be borne as we struggled with our tasks, but at the same time, there were many satisfactions to be secured inasmuch as something that was fundamental to the ideals of education was being seemingly achieved. We believed in our mission, its implicit conception of education, and our work.

However, now that the frantic years of the 1950s and 1960s have passed public education is seemingly being faced by a pervasive feeling that the achievement of the recent past may have been problematic. There are, it seems, many critics of what was done and their fundamental claim is disconcerting: all that education wrought in what seemed to be its finest hour was the ill-considered, and often shoddy, deployment of an institution whose forms derived more from conventional wisdom, and often expedience, than from planful reflection; expansion has meant little more than the increasing consumption of the services that a particular kind of institution was prepared to offer; the momentum of this whole development derived not from the needs of its putative clients but rather from forces inhering in the institution itself and its interactions with its policies and societies.*

* These paragraphs represent, of course, a bald summary of a complex set of themes. Dreeben (1971) provocatively discusses the meaning of the kind of statistics cited here. These general themes are discussed most comprehensively in the report on youth of the President's Science Advisory Committee, in the literature on accountability (Wise, 1976), and in tracts like

Bold assertions put in this form do no more than sketch a caricature of a mood, albeit one that presses increasingly upon the schools. I believe, however, that there is more than enough reason to take the claims of the critics we face on both the left and the right as suggestive of a possible problem and see if educational theory and research can offer a tentative formulation of what the mood, and the debate we face, might be directing attention to. I see the issues being addressed as centering on the *form* of the institution of the school we know and believe that a formulation of our seeming problem requires us to search for an understanding of what these forms are and why they might be problematic. This is the task I will undertake in this essay.

I should note that it may be that my sense that education faces a problematic situation that has its origins in the agency represented by the school and the school system will not be sustained by the arguments that I offer here. I am not sure, however, that this is as important as the possibility that the exploration of a possibility serves to give educational research reasons for examining holistically and comprehensively what schools are and why they might be as they are. Educational thought is at its core always a search for an understanding of the ways by which the goal of education can be advanced. And, clearly, advancement entails a consideration of both ends *and* means, of instrumentality and goals. Unfortunately educational thought has all too rarely achieved an effective reconciliation between practical and normative thinking—with the consequence that too much educational planning has proceeded in a rudderless way while speculation about what schools might or should be has proceeded without a clear sense of what aspirations might mean for the real world of the schools. It might be that what is important about the mood that I see facing us is simply its invitation that we should examine what schools are doing; that search for understanding should, I would hope, call our attention to the need to find a way of building bridges between practical and speculative thought and, at the same time, nurture a critical perspective on where the schools are and might be. Thus, it is less important that I succeed here in showing how the schools are troubled in any specific way than it is to communicate my sense of some of the ways in which a judgement that the schools *might* be troubled leads us to the view that schooling is intellectually and managerially problematic in some important respects. It is this sense that schooling is an institution that is worthy of reflection and disciplined inquiry which educational research lacked when deployment was the central preoccupation of the agency that provides its *raison d'être*.

Bereiter's *Must We Educate?* (1973). I have attempted a more comprehensive exploration of these ideas in 'Educational policy-making in new contexts: The contribution of curriculum studies' (1977).

Schooling as a planned world

The view of classrooms, the curriculum, and the school system that I will be offering here presumes that we should see them as components of an *agency* that has been designed to perform certain tasks. The primary overt task of the school system is to induct the young into valued aspects of the human experience; the forms and the patterns that we see when we look at schools reflect interpretations of this core task and represent attempts by both planners who develop policies and teachers who implement these policies to systematically offer students worthwhile experiences. Given this viewpoint, we can ask what kinds of structures underlie the surface order of the school; the questions that we should want to investigate in these terms are those that have been fundamental to curriculum research: How is the knowledge and values-transmission task of the school organized and executed? How and why is the knowledge that the school judges worth teaching chosen?

But words like activity, structures, knowledge and the like are abstractions. In the day-to-day world of the schools they stand for things like subjects, periods, classrooms, and lessons. We can readily concede that these order, in Bridgham's (1971) elegant terms, a set of 'envelopes containing a set of "allowed" solutions to the problems envisaged by curriculum designers', but that recognition does not go as far as we need to go to bridge the gap between the world of the organizational analyst and designer and that of the head and the teacher; some more formal language is required to do the job. Dreeben (1973) has offered one way of approaching this problem. He suggests that the concrete reality of schooling can be thought of as a form of *work* on the part of both teachers and students and so become amenable to the kind of analysis offered by Woodward (1965), Perrow (1970) and Stinchcombe (1968) in which organizational and activity forms are seen as functions of *goals, technologies* (or ways and means), and *structures*. Let us follow Dreeben (1970, 1973) and attempt to use these concepts to offer a view of the activity structure of the classroom from the teachers' vantage point before turning to the exploration of the curriculum, and of the school in its systemic aspects.

When we look at schools we see, in traditional settings at least, row upon row of classrooms; and when we look inside these classrooms we see desks, a teacher's table up front and a chalkboard on the front wall of the room. Each such room has seating for thirty or so students and only a limited amount of floor space. When school is in session we usually see a teacher standing or sitting in his place up front and students sitting in their desks, listening to the teacher talk, interacting with him during question-answer exchanges and occasional discussions, or else 'working', answering questions in workbooks or work sheets or writing laboriously. We know that the forward movement of this activity is controlled by explicit and implicit decisions by the teacher about pacing, target groups and the like and that these minute-by-minute, week-by-week decisions are, in their turn, controlled by a curriculum (whether formal or informal) that outlines, and often specifies, what should be covered in the course of a year and years. And, despite many attempts by reformers to change this pattern of school activity, it appears that, with the exception of such innovations as the 'open' school, class teaching of this kind is the dominant method of instruction in at least American schools (see, for example, Adams and Biddle, 1970; Bellack *et al.*, 1966; Cusick, 1973; Cusick *et al.*, 1976; Smith and Geoffrey, 1968; see also Wankowski, 1974).

Let us assume that this view of the classroom is accurate enough for our purposes and further assume that we can characterize the predominant lesson-giving pattern in these rooms as the *recitation* or question-and-answer. When we do this we find that contemporary lessons become merely further instances of a pattern of teaching that has persisted for at least seventy-five years, and it is a pattern of teaching which has been criticized for almost all of these seventy-five years. As Hoekter and Ahlbrand (1969) noted at the conclusion of their extensive review of the literature of classroom observations in this century:

> The studies which have been reviewed in this paper show a remarkable stability of classroom verbal behavior patterns over the past half century, despite the fact that each successive generation of educational thinkers, no matter how else they differ, has condemned the rapid-fire, question-answer pattern of instruction. This opens a number of interesting avenues of inquiry. What is there about the recitation, for instance, that makes it so singularly successful in the evolutionary struggle with other, more highly recommended methods? That is, what survival skills of teachers are met uniquely by the recitation . . . If the recitation is a poor pedagogical method as most teacher educators have long believed, why have they not been able to deter teachers from using it?

For the educational planner Hoekter and Ahlbrand's questions must be fundamental. Barnes (1976) quotes Freire to claim that recitation teaching 'dehumanizes by devaluing and subverting the learner's purposes and sense of reality', a charge that has been made, albeit in different words, again and again by philosophically-oriented critics. Cusick *et al.* (1976) see in this method the source of omnipresent passivity of students in American secondary schools; in their words, the teachers they observed

> did most or almost all of what there was to do [in the classroom], the talking, inquiring, and gesticulating, and this reduced the amount of activity available for students. Indeed, student involvement was discouraged except where students were reacting to the teachers. Furthermore, student involvement was usually singular, one student interacting with the teacher while the others observed the interaction. The teachers seemed to spend more energy supervising the twenty-four or so observers than in interacting with the single respondent. The whole process demanded a large amount of teacher attention to maintenance and supervisory matters which detracted from the instructional process and exaggerated the importance of compliance with maintenance demands for the students.

In an earlier paper (1973), I attempted to answer Hoekter and Ahlbrand's questions and argued that we can exploit the topics of goals, technology and structures to account for the persistence of the recitation. Assume that the classroom makes four goal-like demands on the teacher, no one of which can be achieved without compromising success at achieving another: These goals are the *coverage* of a body of content, the engendering of *mastery* by students of that content, the creation of *affect* on the part of students towards both content and the learning setting and effective management of the class as a unit in the interests of task *attention* and order. Assume further that the teacher has four resources at hand to achieve his goals, himself and his personal resources, a text or two, such group climate as is created by the school and the milieu of the school, and the predispositions to learning that students bring to the classroom. In addition, he has a room with its walls and its desks, structures which maximize the number of students that can be crowded into expensive space, a place and an organizational pattern which he played no part in creating and has no power to change. In this context the recitation in conjunction with the text becomes a usefully adaptive and robust *coping strategy* within the repertoire of the teacher, a technology of ways and means which permits the teacher to meet the conflicting demands of the classroom situation. It gives the teacher a way of securing task attention, gives him control over the activity of students, facilitates coverage of content and offers a drill and practice situation that leads students to a gradual mastery of the facts that schools recognize as the symbols of learning.

In a parallel study Abrahamson (1974) undertook an analysis of the teaching

	Affect	*Coverage*	*Mastery*	*Attention*
Basic Approach				
Homework				
'Do Problems'	(− − −)	+	+	(− − −)
Main In-Class Activity				
'Teacher Explanation'	(−)	(+)	(− − −)	(− − −)
'Student Call-Outs'	(+)	(− − −)	(− − −)	+
Supplementary Maneuvers				
'Make Sure Everyone Is Following Along'	− − −	(−)	(+)	(− − −)
'Go Over It One More Time For Good Measure'	− − −	(−)	(+)	(− − −)
'Sense of Humor'	+	(− − −)	(− − −)	(+)
'Pedagogical Side-Trips And Side-Comments'	+	(−)	(− − −)	(− − −)
'Illustrations On The Board'	(− − −)	(− − −)	(+)	(+)
Supplementary Tactics				
'Selective Choice of Illustrations'	(− − −)	(+)	(− − −)	(− − −)

FIGURE 1 *A rating of the presumed effect of Mrs Moore's basic approach, supplementary manoeuvres and tactics on the four classroom demands, from J. H. Abrahamson (1974) 'Classroom constraints and teacher coping strategies' Ph.D. dissertation, University of Chicago*

behaviours of a sample of six high school teachers to explore if this kind of approach to the analysis of teaching methods as coping technologies had utility for the analysis, not of an ideal-typification of the classroom, but of real teaching. The primary data source for the study was a daily record of class techniques gathered in a non-participant mode. The final result of Abrahamson's study was a grid intersecting the four core elements he identified as making up the essential components of the classroom technology of each of the teachers he observed with the four classroom goals-demands of affect, coverage, mastery and attention (management). Using this grid he attempted to delineate the presumed effects of significant teacher behaviour in the classrooms he observed (see Figure 1). A plus rating on the grid implies an inference that the behaviour could affect the demand; a minus rating implies that the behaviour would impede the accomplishment of the demand; a dash implies that the behaviour has no obvious effect. Parentheses imply that he secured some direct evidence for the presumed effect while a rating without parentheses indicates no direct evidence for the effect. Figure 2 summarizes the results of the study.

Two distinctive teaching styles or teacher coping behaviours seemed to emerge. One group of teachers—the three described in the upper half of Figure 2—seemed to accept responsibility for deferring evenhandedly to all four classroom demands and chose a basic approach to their conventional interpretations of the teaching task that was simple in character and seemed to acquire its coping capability by its match between individual demands and elements of the teacher's method. They coped by virtue of their method. The second group of teachers—those described in the lower half of Figure 2—seemed, on the other hand, less concerned with coping with the pressures of each of our demands and emphasized instead one or another of them. They coped in the setting primarily because of the impact of their personalities on classes, not because of the efficacy of their method.

Abrahamson's study seems to offer some initial empirical support for the plausibility and utility of the way of looking at classrooms I outlined above. It would appear the concepts, goals, technology and structure are topics which, when interpreted in ways that bring them to the classroom, do have analytic power and do permit an analysis of the methods of classroom as a structured technology. However, at this point the best that can be claimed for my functionalism is a face plausibility. To strengthen the case for the form of analysis of the classroom that I have been attempting two further and different arguments must be made; one of these arguments can be developed fairly simply, the other is more complex.

The simpler of these two arguments can be quickly sketched and is amply sustained, at least in its basic outline, by such descriptive-analytic studies as Smith and Geoffrey (1968) and Stebbins (1974) and by process-product studies which are increasingly seeing what Rosenshine (1976) has termed 'direct instruction' as *the* method which is most closely associated with student achievement of a conventional kind (see Figure 3). Direct instruction

Name	Complexity	Adequacy of Main In-Class Activity: Af	C	M	At	Teacher Interpretation	Personal Qualities Needed
Moore	very consistent modal lesson	– +	+ – – –	– – – – – –	– – – +	equal emphasis among four demands	good, fundamental knowledge of math
Jones	very consistent modal lesson	+ + +	+ – –	+ + +	– – – – +	equal emphasis among four demands	disposition that will allow students to do most of the talking
Smith	very consistent modal lesson	– – – + – – –	+ - +	– – – + +	+ – – – – – –	equal emphasis among four demands	be generally supportive of student efforts
Fox	two modal lessons that alternate	modal I – – – modal II –	– +	– – – –	– – – –	strong emphasis on coverage rather than other demands	ability to project a sincere interest in student concerns and possession of a wide and varied range of personal experiences
Schmidt	small segment within most modal lessons that varied	– +	+ – – –	– – – – – –	– – – +	strong emphasis on affect rather than on other demands which is reflected in his supplementary manoeuvres	overwhelming personality, extensive vocabulary, ability to banter, thorough knowledge of student sub-culture, Ivy League athlete
Brown	one modal lesson and one secondary lesson that alternate	modal lesson –	–	+	–	strong emphasis on mastery – ignores coverage to large extent	conviction in the rightness of your approach so that you can purposely create student anxiety and frustration

FIGURE 2 *from J. H. Abrahamson (1974)*

Elements	Suggested Positive Correlates	Suggested Negative Correlates
Time and Activities	Time structured by the teacher	Time spent on arts, crafts, dramatic play, active play, stories
	Time spent on number and reading activities using textbooks and academic workbooks, or in verbal interactions on reading and mathematics	Gamelike activities Number of interest centres Large number of different concurrent activities
	Time spent in seatwork with academic workbooks through which the pupils proceeded at their own pace	Hours of unstructured time Frequent socialization
Work Groupings	Students worked in groups supervised by the teacher	Free work groups Children working independently without supervision of teacher
Teacher's Directions and Questions	Teacher directs activities without giving pupils choice of activities or reasons for the selection of activities	Teacher joins or participates in pupil's activities Teacher organizes learning around pupil's own problem
	Learning is organized around questions posed by the teacher	Teacher approaches subject matter in an indirect, informal way
	Teacher asks narrow question	Teacher encourages pupil to express himself freely
	Teacher asks direct questions that have only a single answer	Teacher permits pupil to suggest additional or alternative answers
	Adult commands, requests, or direct questions that had an academic focus	Pupil initiates activities Pupil has freedom to select activities Teachers commands and requests, nonacademic Teacher open-ended questions, nonacademic
Student Responses	Students give a high percentage of correct answers both in verbal interaction and in workbooks	Child open-ended questions and nonacademic commands Adult nonacademic commands or requests, or open-ended questions Child nonacademic responses Child general comments to adults or among children
Adult Feedback	Teacher immediately reinforces pupil as to right or wrong Adult feedback had an academic focus Teacher asks new question after correct answer Teacher gives answer after incorrect answer	Adult feedback on nonacademic activities (e.g., play, music)

FIGURE 3 *A summary of elements in direct instruction, from B. Rosenshine 'Direct instruction' in N. L. Gage (ed.) (1976)* The psychology of teaching methods, *The 75th Yearbook of the National Society for the Study of Education. Chicago: the Society*

and the recitation achieve the ends of mastery and group control, because they are methods well adapted to the structural and goal parameters of the classroom and the technical and material resources provided for teachers. They achieve maximal group attention under the conditions in which teachers must work; their vitality is not surprising for change away from these methods would require a change in the goal and structural parameters of the classroom setting and the widespread provision of new resources for teaching.

However, this argument begs the question it ostensibly answers by assuming tacitly that recitation-like procedures must have been legitimate technologies, or at least more legitimate educational technologies than they would now seem to be, at some point in the history of the classroom. Otherwise, why would the classrooms we now have been built to support such methods. In other words, the argument I have been making to this point fails to establish the validity of its structural functional premise. To meet this problem we must link the recitation as a technology with both the goals and the structures of the conventional classroom and so break the closed circle of inference and assumption we have been drawing to this point.

In earlier papers (1973, 1978) I suggested, following Stinchcombe (1965), that the link between goals and structures of the classroom and technologies will be found if we examine the milieu in which the classroom as we know it came into being. I hypothesized that, if we can infer that the recitation is an instructional method that is well adapted to the transmission of largely inert information from books to the minds of groups of students we would find that, 1., a purposeful attempt was made at the time of the beginnings of public education as we know it to design a setting in which, 2., inert information could be optimally transmitted from books into the largely empty heads of students. I suggested, in other words, that the reformers who wish to abolish recitation-teaching and the like in the interests of learning by doing, for example, are running headlong against institutions which were deliberately designed to very different things. Some recent research suggests that some inferences of this kind might be warranted.

Cheverst (1972) reports a study which offers considerable support for the expectation that an analysis of conceptions of educational goals through time will find that goals have shifted markedly in character. The direction of this shift appears to be from goals to which the technologies associated with the conventional classroom *might* be adaptive to goals that make these technologies increasingly maladaptive. Table 1 summarizes the results of the analysis of the incidence of 'teacher-centred,' 'subject-centred' and 'child-centred' metaphors in four English official publications about elementary schooling, the 1905 edition of the *Handbook of Suggestions for Teachers in Public or Elementary Schools*, the 1931 Hadow Report on the Primary School, the 1944 edition of the *Handbook of Suggestions for Teachers*, and the 1967 Plowden Report, *Children and Their Primary Schools*. An inspection of the trends indicated in Table 1 reveals clear changes across these publications in the dominant images associated with the goals of schooling. More importantly,

		1905[1]	1931[2]	1944[3]	1968[4]
Child-Centred	Fav.	5·0	32.0	51·0	54·0
	Unf.	10·0	3·5	0·0	0·0
Knowledge-Centred	Fav.	30·0	39·0	3·5	3·5
	Unf.	0·0	14·0	28·0	17·5
Teacher-Centred	Fav.	55·0	11·5	17·5	7·0
	Unf.	0·0	0·0	0·0	17·5
		100·0	100·0	100·0	100·0

[1] The Handbook of Suggestions for Teachers in Public or Elementary Schools, 1905 edition.
[2] The Hadow Report on the Primary School, 1931.
[3] The Handbook of Suggestions for Teachers, 1944 edition.
[4] Children and their Primary Schools, the Plowden Report, 1968.

TABLE I *Trends in types of metaphor (%), from P. H. Taylor (1973) 'New Frontiers in Educational Research'* Paedagogica Europaea, *VIII, p. 28. (Braunschweig: Georg Westermann Verlag)*

the analysis of the 1905 *Handbook* suggests that the teacher- or subject-centred images of the kinds we would infer would be associated with the recitation, had official approval.

It also appears from historical research that we can sustain the notion that the invention of the structural form of the classroom was purposively linked to information-transmission goals and recitation-like technologies. Seaborne's (1971) fascinating study of English school architecture strongly suggests that the form of the elementary classroom that emerged in England in the 1850s was closely associated with a decision on the part of the Committee of the Council for Education to favour simultaneous instruction of groups of students by adult and pupil teachers by means of 'oral lessons' over the older monitorial (peer teaching) and, by implication, the tutorial methods then dominant in the grammar schools. The plan for school design shown in Figure 4, the result of ten or so years of systematic investigation by the Council, foreshadows the modern school very clearly and stands in marked contrast to the structures being built only a decade earlier to suit monitorial methods, structures which would be more adaptive to present-day 'open' methods than most present-day traditional classrooms.

The research that I have been describing, work that has its origins in a search for understanding of the contexts and conditions within which teaching which many theorists regard as basically unsatisfactory seems to take place leads to a recognition that when we consider the classroom and its methods, we are exploring a particular kind of social invention, one that Hamilton (1977) has termed the *classroom system*. This system of schooling was an invention of the nineteenth century and was responsive to a conception on the part of educational policy-makers of that time of what should happen in schools, both technologically and organizationally. Such a conception of a

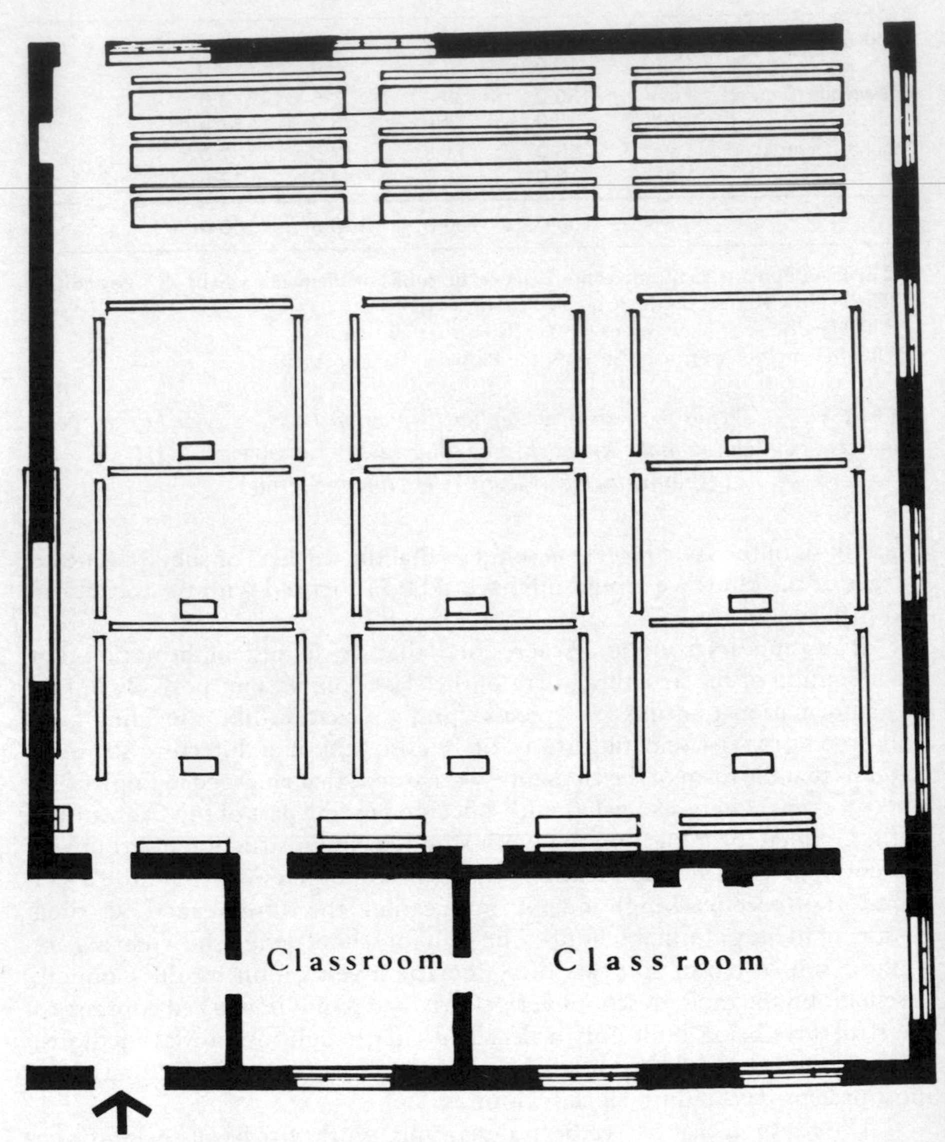

FIGURE 4 *Some nineteenth-century school plans*
A. National Society's Central Boys' School plan, c. 1843

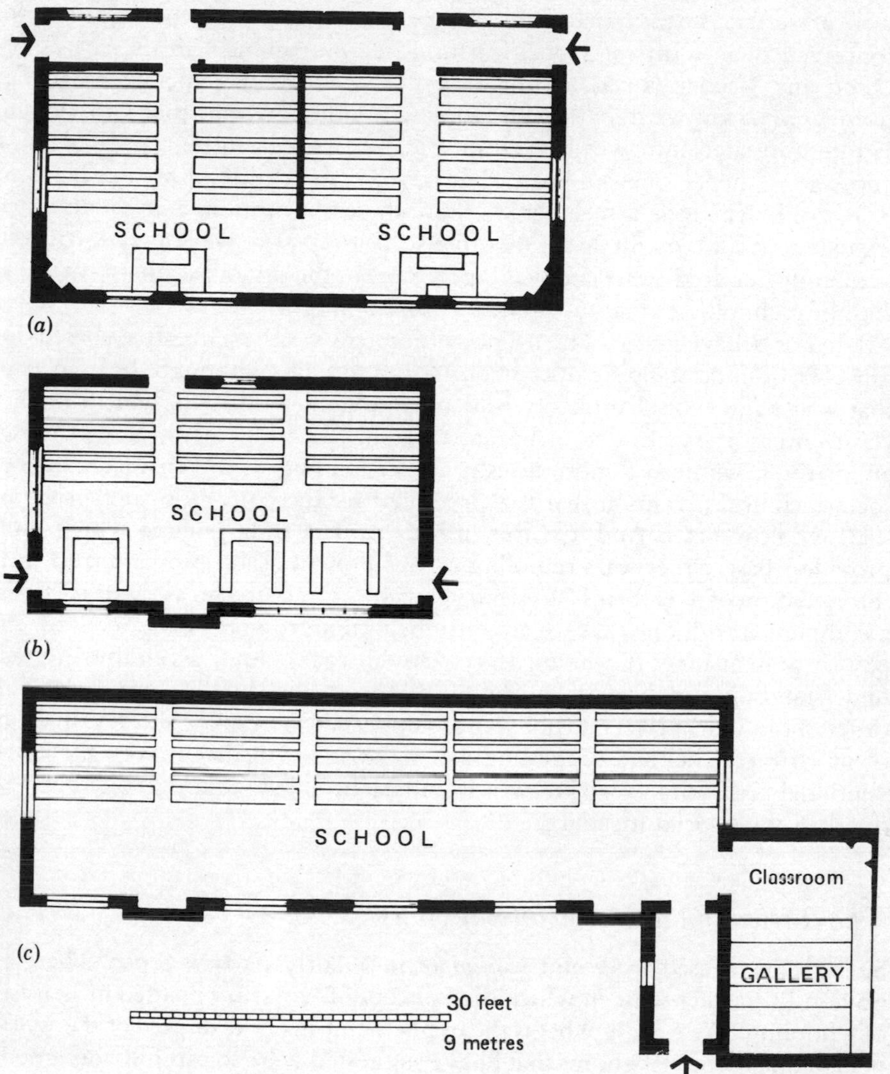

B. *Plans issued by the Committee of Council on Education;* (a) *Plan for 112 children, 1840 (Series B, No. 3);* (b) *Plan for 116 children, 1845 (No. 1);* (c) *Plan for 120 children, 1851 (No. 5) from M. Seaborne (1971)* The English School: Its Architecture and Organization, *Vol. 1, reproduced by permission of Routledge & Kegan Paul Ltd and The University of Toronto Press*

technology and organization was, in its turn, embedded in a conception of the goals of schooling. It is clear from the kinds of texts and examinations that were prescribed by the nineteenth-century inspectorate* that these goals were conceived of in terms of verbal learning, learning which, in the words of Olson and Bruner (1974), assumed that 'the effects of experience can be considered as knowledge, that knowledge is conscious and that knowledge can be translated into words. Symmetrically, words can be translated into knowledge: hence one can learn, that is, one can acquire knowledge, from being told.' The issue is whether we share these assumptions and whether, to the extent that we might do so, we can assume they were well operationalized (from our hundred-years later vantage point) in the organizational structures and the technologies that the pioneers of schooling left us.

I do not believe that we are in a position to answer these questions based on our present understanding of classrooms and teaching although the evidence that is at hand would probably lead to a judgement that the world of the classroom is awry. But to elaborate this kind of judgement, and propose alternatives, we need a more holistic understanding of the character of the socio-technical invention that is represented by the conventional classroom than we now have. And it is this holistic understanding alone which will provide a basis either for a retooling of our present classroom pattern or for the invention of new forms (Westbury, 1978). The classroom as a workplace is a complex world, one that we are only beginning to understand in either its past or present form (Calhoun, 1973; Doyle, 1978). And, given this limited understanding, and the many meanings that are carried by the contrived social order of this workplace, I do not want to undertake here an explicit evaluation of its character beyond suggesting as I have and will that maybe the conventional classroom as we know it is an anachronism, although one heavily overlain with social meaning.

The curriculum as a structure of goals

So far I have used *work* and *workplace* in a fairly narrow sense. There is obviously another sense in which the concept of work can be used in analysis of schooling. We can ask what is the explicit end-in-view or goal of the work being done in the classrooms that I have suggested were so carefully designed. And, if the genetic approach to understanding the classroom has merit, the obvious question is 'What was the nature of the tasks that the nineteenth-century classroom was designed to facilitate?' Clearly, the answer to this question has two aspects: the teaching of reading, writing, arithmetic, grammar, and a smattering of useful and improving knowledge (Calhoun, 1973; Layton, 1973; Sturt, 1967) as well as mental discipline, skill in manipulating abstractions, whether the terminology of grammar or science,

* For examples of nineteenth-century examinations see the appendix to this paper. For a review of nineteenth-century approaches to 'instructional design' see Landon's *School Management* (1887).

the facts of history and geography, the written language, or the computational algorithms of arithmetic, algebra and geometry.

This assessment of the goals of the nineteenth-century school and the twentieth-century successors of those schools is commonplace, so commonplace that it hardly achieves significance. Most of us know that the traditional school sees its goals too narrowly and we know the evils of mental discipline and bottle-filling—but knowing this does not give us the leverage that we need to rehearse possible alternative curricula and explore what the traditional canon of reading, writing, arithmetic and mental discipline might *mean*. To secure this leverage we need to ponder the traditional curriculum from such vantage points as Furth's (1970) 'School for Thinking', an elementary school curriculum deriving from Piaget's insights into the nature of human cognitive development; or, jumping to the secondary school, we need to contrast the 'modern' curriculum that emerged during the last decades of the nineteenth century (English, mathematics, history, French, science and the like) with one that *might* emerge if we were to recreate the schools *de novo* in this second half of the twentieth century. In such a recreated school disciplines like computer science, engineering, agriculture, economics, film, perhaps different foreign languages and so forth would have a more important place than they do in the conventional school (Ausubel, 1967).

In other words, to secure the vantage point that we need to consider the curriculum of the conventional school, we have to recognize that we live in a world which was largely created in the nineteenth century. The intellectual, social, and technological systems which dominate our lives were the creations of that century, and the school too was part of that creation, with the consequence that its intellectual world predates in a very real sense the intellectual and cultural achievements of our century. The English sixth form, for example, continues the ambience of such nineteenth-century foundations as Rugby and Winchester; its curriculum, history, science, mathematics, etc., was essentially fixed by 1910 and subsequent change has taken place *within* its original structures (Taylor *et al.*, 1974). The same is true of lower forms of the English school; while *some* schools offer film making, astronomy, seamanship and Urdu, the overwhelming majority offer their able students only English, history, geography, a foreign language, mathematics, religious knowledge, physics, chemistry and the like and their less able students English, history, mathematics, general science, biology, technical drawing, needlework, art, woodwork and social studies (Monks, 1968). These are the subjects of England's teacher training colleges of the 1850s (Sturt, 1967). Similar inertias mark the American school; indeed, the only major change that has taken place in the curricular categories of its schools since the turn of the century has been the addition of courses in such areas as driver education, typewriting, health and physical education (Osterndorf and Horn, 1976).

A different, although parallel and in some ways a more revealing persistence of forms occurs *within* the traditional subjects. Voege (1972, 1975) reports that it took twenty-five years for Keynesian principles and concepts to penetrate American high school texts and over ten years for these concepts to penetrate college texts. And older texts seemed, so Voege reports, to sell well even when there were newer texts to replace them. Hodgetts (1968) found that the Canadian history program that was common to schools in all of Canada's English-speaking provinces in the 1960s was in its essentials a course that had been developed in the 1920s to reflect the nationalist preoccupations of Canada in the years preceding the Statute of Westminster and the formal granting by Britain of an autonomous nationhood to its former 'dominion'. Needless to say, the course had been updated, but such revisions consisted of units added onto the program to bring it up to date and Hodgetts found that these units were, seemingly, rarely taught.

All of this suggests a way of looking at the curriculum that parallels the way of looking at classrooms I outlined above. Whether a mode of instruction, a subject, a collection of subjects, or all of these aspects of the curriculum together, a curriculum is an *idea* which becomes a *thing*, a social entity and/or social institution which exists in the world of the schools, an institution which was created at a specific time to deliver a conception of what knowledge was worth knowing, but an institution which has, in the course of time, become rooted in its own past and its own structures. This act of institutionalization casts, I believe, the most baneful pall over the present and the future that we must face, for it creates forms, procedures, and categories which become givens, ends in themselves that have their own momentum and their own directionality. This directionality is implicit in the motivations that lead young people into teaching as a career, and in the forces that lead some entrants to persist in the occupation and others to leave (Lortie, 1975). It is implicit in the classrooms that are offered teachers and it is a part and parcel of the training and experience we offer them as they learn their technologies. As important, these social forms, whether they be the forms of the classroom or the curriculum, become criteria which determine social and cultural achievement as the present movement towards the 'basics' makes clear. They become the negotiable currency of what Bernstein (1973, pp. 254–5) has called 'privileged meanings' and, as such, become a kind of symbolic property. Both for a society and for the schools change entails the discounting of investments in the acquisition of this symbolic property, and inevitably such discounting is resisted by a society which increasingly finds its common cultural meanings in the experiences which the schools offer and the distinctions which the schools create (Bourdieu, 1971; Lippman, 1928). For schoolmen it is this aspect of the curriculum that is most insidious. We are all captives, as I will argue in the next section of this paper, of our own socialization in those schools and our own investments in the learning of the knowledge systems, technologies and institutional forms that make up the world of these schools. And, as I suggested earlier and will suggest again in these next few pages, even when we *as individuals* have the will to change, the institution in which we work forces its terms and needs upon us.

The school as an institution for service delivery

For schoolmen the schools are *total* institutions in the explicit sense for not only have we been socialized by those schools but they at the same time are *our* institutions. We are the legatees of the ideals of our nineteenth-century founders: their ideals are our ideals and their institution is our institution. And, in the nature of things, we must recognize two aspects of the mission we accept and are given when we assume a place in the schools. We are committed, on the one hand, to what can be called the normative mission of the schools, to the idea of mass universal education, to the ideal of literacy and the like. We are committed likewise to the institution of the school, to the preservation of our interest in the school as an organization, to our colleagues who are our friends, to our jobs and to our economic well-being. It is not always clear whether when schoolmen think of improving schooling they are addressing the institutional or the normative aspects of their role incumbency: Are arguments for homogeneous grouping best seen as reflecting the interests of children or teachers? Are arguments against the development of voucher schemes or against state aid to parochial and non-governmental schools best seen as a defence of a long-established monopoly? Are assaults on elite schools, in the interests of 'social cohesion', a strategy to protect the 'mediocre' schools from competition? (Friedman, 1962; West, 1968, Kallós and Lundgren, 1977).

Questions of this kind about the motivations of schoolmen are now comparatively commonplace. Recently, however, there has been an increasing interest in driving the stance that underlies these questions into the curriculum itself. The implication, as I have been suggesting, is that many aspects of the classroom and the curriculum, and particularly the possibility of curriculum change, are determined less by a disinterested reflection on what 'education' should or might be than by the dynamics of the school as an organization.

Thus McKinney saw institutional facts writ large in a study of curriculum change that he undertook in one American city (McKinney, 1973; McKinney and Westbury, 1975). In 1956 the superintendent proclaimed that Gary, Indiana was fundamentally revising the district's science program to bring it up to date in the light of the nation's concerns over the successful flight of Sputnik; the best the science curriculum committee could do, however, was to copy the table of contents of a 1951 text into their new curriculum guide. And, although this committee did see the need for new laboratories, the city did not have the funds that such rebuilding required with the result that the city waited until the 1960s for the labs that they had planned in 1956, i.e. until Federal funds for such building were available. In 1942, 1954, 1955, and 1957 surveys of the Gary schools suggested that its vocational programs were quite inadequate. In 1942 the board changed the name of the shops at one of their schools to the Gary Trade and Vocational Center; in 1944 they reestablished this centre at this same school and, in anticipation of the opening of the centre, closed the shops at the city's other schools. By 1955 a vocational program barely existed in Gary and again in 1955 the board agreed to establish a new vocational educational facility—insofar as the operation of these centres entailed no cost to the city. And again in 1963 the board passed a resolution calling for the creation of the Gary Career Center, but this time federal funds were available for construction and program development with the result that in 1968 a vocational-technical school was opened in the district. A need which had been recognized in 1942 was at last met.

One point emerged very clearly in McKinney's study of Gary's schools. The history of the schools of the city reveal since the Second World War nothing that might be called a sustained concern for the enactment of any idea of education in the school; the history shows instead a constant (and, under the circumstances in which the city found itself, a proper) preoccupation with money, space, plant, student numbers, accrediting agencies and outside professional opinion and the task that the city's administrators found facing them was that of maintaining their school system in some semblance of equilibrium with both the local and the broader community's expectations about what school should provide. These expectations were narrowly conceived and narrowly presented: Gary's schools should provide desks and classrooms for all students who wanted to attend school, its programs should conform to 'professional' expectations about its breadth and scope, and, the set of 'oddities' that Gary inherited from the years of the much vaunted Gary Plan of the 1910s and 1920s when the city had been lauded as a pioneer of a new form of urban education should be eliminated from the city.

Gary is and was an unusual city and we must assume only that its history is somewhat typical of poverty-stricken school jurisdictions. However, there is a sense in which the relationship between resources and programs that is so clear in this one case is generalizable. The basic function of any organization is *maintenance* of its core functions; the possibility of *change* is predicated on securing and delivering its fundamental organizational mission. Change costs money and time: such money and time must be available before change is a possibility and schools do not have the resources for the rapid *en masse* training and retraining of their teachers. When we overlay these facts of cost on a conception of a school system as an organization whose primary task is maintenance we have, I believe, a powerful way of accounting for both the spasmodic nature of the school system's interest in curriculum change and the commonly observed correlation between such fiscal variables as tax base and per pupil expenditure and incidence of curricular innovation. The wealthier a school district, the more likely it is to have resources over and above those required for maintenance; these additional resources can be invested in plant, materials, and activities which produce change; these resources in their turn attract teachers who see themselves as innovators and respond to concerns of one kind or another that transcend a locality. There is, of course, a range of such socio-cultural communities with the result that the range of resources that are available within a jurisdiction produces a gradient of levels of innovativeness in which individual districts find themselves located as they face the consequences of choice between maintenance and change needs. Some districts become exemplars of what might be done in the schools while others struggle to stay afloat. Significant changes in the programs of such districts are, in a real sense, impossible (McKinney and Westbury, 1975). Unfortunately, curriculum planners tend not to see the true nature of the difficulty that most school districts face as they ponder change and have not explored the task of building social systems that might facilitate change by countering at least some of the steady-state aspects of the service delivery model that is the existing school.*

A speculative paper by Pincus (1974) pushes this kind of analysis of the curriculum as organizationally embedded still further and offers perhaps a way of closing this discussion of the agency that is schooling. Pincus neatly reverses the form of argument I have been outlining above by suggesting that the characteristics of the school itself, not the characteristics of the school's environment, determine how the educational system responds to both the idea of curricular change, demands for such change, and the form of change itself. He sees the school system as an industry with its own embedded technologies and structures and asks:

> How would we expect a self-perpetuating bureaucracy to respond to Research and Development findings if 1. it is not market-oriented; 2. it is widely considered to be socially necessary and therefore deserving of public protection—is, in fact, the captive servant of a captive clientele; 3. it is open to a good deal of public scrutiny on issues having to do with perceived equity, quality, and goals; 4. it cannot unambigously define its aims or clearly identify technologies that are dominant in the light of aims that might be specified; 5. its contribution to its clientele's life and learning is uncertain and also modest as compared to other societal influences; 6. its governance is highly decentralized, yet subject to a wide variety of influences, so that each unit perceives itself as facing a unique configuration of clients and masters? (p. 115)

Pincus's answers to these questions are sketchily argued but tantalizingly powerful in their appeal; and they complete in their thrust the circle I have been drawing in this essay. Schools, when compared with competitive firms, are

* Surprisingly little attention has been given to the institutional systems which support and surround the curricular system of the school. Where the curricular system had been explored it has been seen primarily from the point of view of curriculum *implementation* and *dissemination*; for recent reviews of such work, see Fullan and Pomfret (1977) and MacDonald and Walker (1976). Taylor *et al.* (1974) and Wirt and Quick (1975) are examples of studies of the curriculum system which keep institutional factors in the foreground. There is an increasing number of case studies of curriculum change which provide a base for further synthesis; see, for example, Dalin (1973) and Bermann *et al.* (1977). Westbury and Gaede (1975) report a case study of one unsuccessful US attempt to effect fundamental change in the curricular categories of the senior high school.

> more likely than the competitive firm to adopt cost-raising innovations...
> less likely than the competitive firm to adopt cost-reducing innovations...
> less likely than the competitive firm to adopt innovations that significantly change the resource mix . . .
> more likely than the competitive firm to adopt new instructional processes or wrinkles in administrative management that do not change institutional structure...
> less likely than the competitive firm to adopt innovations that change the accustomed authority roles and established ways of doing business...
> and... be equally unwilling as competitive firms to face large-scale encroachment on protected markets.... (pp. 117–18)

As Pincus suggests, 'The validation process for educational innovation is ultimately measured by bureaucratic and social acceptability—criteria that are far more tenuous than those of a competitive market, but no less important for actors in the bureaucratic marketplace' (p. 119).

We should expect, if the form of the analysis of the school that Pincus offers holds, that not only the innovation-selection behaviour of the schools, but also the kinds of demands which the schools make for change in the more general sense, will derive from their internal organizational dynamics. And, if we define change so liberally that it can include such factors as manning ratios and class size, we see fairly clearly the two-fold directionality of the conclusions that this form of analysis foreshadows. Smaller class size simplifies the teacher's work within conventional classrooms by decreasing the complexity of the coping decisions which the teacher must make—without necessarily improving student learning, and so productivity, in any way. But, of course, each time the student–teacher ratio is lowered the total costs of the educational system increase significantly. Each such increase in costs effects the proportion of a jurisdiction's budget that must be devoted to the maintenance function and so inhibits the possibility of program change (problems internal, in one sense, to the school system itself) while the sum of such charges on a tax base affects the distribution of national income between the state and private sectors. The source of the most significant demands for increased fundings is to be found in the classroom itself but the implication of these demands affects the scale of transfer between the private and the public sectors. Many commentators (e.g. Laqueur, 1974) believe that the scale of transfer between these sectors that the West has experienced for the past twenty-five or so years cannot be sustained. Curiously, therefore, the form of analysis for approaching classrooms that I outlined earlier may have a cosmic significance. Serious attempts must be made in the near future to increase the productivity of these classrooms but the kind of *ad hoc* discussion that has characterized such explorations of this problem as the British Great Debate on the curriculum and its relatives in the United States would not, from my vantage point, even begin to scratch the surface of the phenomena (see, for example, Reid, 1978; Spady and Mitchell, 1977; Wise, 1977). It would seem, if this line of thought has any merit at all, that we must get down to fundamental discussion of why the work of the classroom is structured in the way it is, what possibilities for changed structures might be at hand, and what organizational forms might support and/or inhibit the ready adoption of more productive technologies.

OECD (1966) has begun to use the term 'qualitative educational planning' and to suggest that such qualitative planning should be the focus of concern in western educational systems over the next few decades. Normative and economic dimensions have converged to create this demand for a new look at the schools and we would expect that some kind of new relationship between the normative and the institutional character of the schools as we know them should emerge from such an endeavour. Perhaps the approaches that we have suggested here for the analysis of the school and how it functions might be of service in the re-creation of that school that the times seem to be demanding. Let me conclude this essay with some remarks that flow from the argument I have been making and foreshadow some of the issues that might be pondered as we contemplate such re-creation.

Some concluding speculations

I have been arguing that, when we think about schools, we need to distinguish a domain of ideas about what education might be from an array of technological, institutional and organizational realities. Both of the domains, and they are both domains of value at least for some of the time, are in tension. There is at all times a tension between the ideal conception of the *work* that should be conducted in schools at any given time and the inadequate delivery of that form in the schools themselves; and there is a tension between the ideals for education embodied in the forms of the school at any given time and the possibility of other forms. Both of these tensions lurk behind any view of what the schools are at any time (Westbury, 1977). But, as I have been implying throughout this paper, they achieve their true force only when we see them in the context of the idea of schooling as work conducted within a structured organization, when, in other words, we connect an ideal with the idea of *agency*. Curiously, however, we in education tend to neglect and even ignore this nub of the question by refusing (at least tacitly) to think about agency in education. Perhaps this is inevitable when one is looking at a total institution from the inside, but this neglect of the hard question has led to an indifference on the part of practical men to the discussion of ends and purposes and a preoccupation on the part of those of us who are concerned with ends with chiliastic rumination (Reid, 1978). Both visionaries and practical men are in this sense victims of their place in history.

Can we escape this trap? I have been trying to suggest here that it is useful to distinguish between an ideal, a conception of what education might be from the variety of forms of embodiment of such ideals in institutions. I have been attempting this, however, while asserting the need to incorporate into our ideals notions of technology and structure, notions of agency. This qualification serves, I hope, to direct attention to the question of ways and means in the broadest sense, to the problem of how do we give meaning to our visions of what may be at the point of contact between a teacher and his students. This point of contact is in the classroom, in the technologies that actualize conceptions of ends-in-view in a pattern of work. What does this view of the tasks of educational theory imply for the ways in which we conceive of the schools?

Let us consider the implications of this kind of starting point for reflection on schooling in terms that we can derive from an exploration of some of the features of the church, an institution which is analogous in many ways to the schools as I see them. The core of the ministry of the church is the ritualized setting in which a people comes together to worship. When Catholics, Quakers, Anglicans or Jews assemble in their churches, meetings or synagogues, they enter a holy setting in which through re-enactment of liturgies they signify their adherence and belief and at the same time re-experience the essentials of their faith. It is the task of the liturgist to conceive of institutionalized ways in which mysteries might be enacted within secular contexts; I would suggest that the task of the curriculist is similar in all essential ways to the task of the liturgist for, just as different conceptions of the mysteries and differing conceptions of appropriate media have differing implications for worship, different conceptions of the proper nature and means of education have differing implications for the forms of the classroom. And just as a theology without a liturgy of some appropriate kind is inconceivable, so a conception of education without a concomitant articulation of implications for the classroom makes no sense (Westbury, 1973).

If we follow the line of thought suggested by this analogy, we have a way, I believe, of giving an appropriate connotation to the terms goals, technology and structure as Dreeben (1973) uses them. A given instructional pattern is a kind of liturgy and a given structural configuration in a classroom represents a conception of space, a conception as it were of a theatre, in which a liturgy might be enacted. And, just as in the context of a liturgy a priest is an agent for a form of worship, the dominant actor in a re-creation of a mystery, so a teacher is in the context of a school the re-creator for her 'congregation' of twenty-five or so pupils of the educational conceptions and meanings embedded in her classroom space and her methods*.

We can push this analogy still further. A conception of an appropriate liturgy, and a liturgy itself, has no meaning outside of the church which requires and sustains a given liturgy. A church is both an assembly of believers and an agency for sustaining and supporting those believers in their convictions. As such a church inevitably becomes a complex institution assuming a variety of relationships with the theologies that are its origin and the societies in which it is embedded. As O'Dea (1966) writes, there are

* For a view of the curriculum that is compatible with the argument being developed here see Meyer and Rowan (1978).

'reciprocal relationships between religious ideas and attitudes on the one hand and the forms of social relationship on the other... ideas affect action,... action leads to the emergence of stable social relationships, and those social relationships "feed back" and affect ideas' (p. 99). Religion is, as O'Dea notes, *integrative* in one sense inasmuch as it embodies and reflects many aspects of its surrounding milieu, but it is on the other hand *disintegrative* inasmuch as it seeks ultimates which transcend particular organizational forms and secular contexts. As a result of the inherent tension between these aspects of any religion, the history of all churches is one of schism and 'heresy' while at any one time in the history of a given church these aspects inevitably mingle and intertwine in the institution of the church, the body that brings a population of believers together in stable and predictable ways.

The fact of heresy and schism within churches has led to a preoccupation on the parts both of sociologists and theologians with the nature of the church as a peculiar kind of institution. Thus, if we focus only on the work of sociologists and sociologically-oriented theologians, we find such questions as Troeltsch's (1931) 'why do bureaucratically organized churches tend to break down?' and Niebuhr's (1929) 'why do charismatic groups tend to evolve into something else: bureaucratic churches?' (Coleman, 1968). As a result of the concern with issues of this kind there are theologies of the church which look at the nature and impact of routinization on faith, and its corollary, the effect of enthusiasm on stability. Likewise, there is a concern among sociologists of the church for the dilemmas which inhere in the fact of institutionalization of churches. O'Dea (1966, pp. 90–7), for example, has identified five such structurally inherent dilemmas which are 'characteristic of the development of specifically religious organizations, and from which derive many of the internal strains and functional problems of such religious bodies' (pp. 90–1): mixed motivation, objectification *vs* alienation, elaboration of administrative order *vs* alienation from such order, concrete definition of a religious message *vs* substitution of the letter for the spirit, and conversion to membership of the church *vs* coercion by social or secular power.

Education has not had to face questions of this kind many times in its recent history as a public mass institution, but as I have been suggesting here they are relevent and we can find in some of the recent literature, for example, specific critiques of the schools that are interpretable in all of O'Dea's terms. Heresy has become a commonplace and many calls for a new vision of the schools are being made—but somehow these calls and these critiques lack the feelings for context and for implications that similar analysis of the churches appears to have. I believe we can use this analogy to find our context for our concerns. Our nineteenth-century founders were churchmen in the best sense inasmuch as they were both theologians and founders of *a* church. Their ideals have been fully actualized only within the past twenty or so years. If we see this actualization as a reflexive test of the original conception there is much about their institution that must be judged as inadequate. I have implied one analysis of these inadequacies in this essay but I have not been able to articulate a mechanism by which corrective forces might be brought to bear on the schools. I can do no more than advocate the development of a market, a means that would permit our clients to choose what they might study and how they might be able to study it (Westbury, 1977).

But what does such a mechanism mean? The schools are like a church and for many of us, and our constituents, we must first find virtue in toleration and then seek to articulate what diversity means. As far as mass education is concerned, diversity clearly does not mean the proliferation of sects without organizational stability and an outward-looking mission. The forms of solution of the problems that religious sects have faced, charisma *vs* continuity, intangible goals *vs* tangible means, commitment *vs* recruitment, status *vs* dissident values (Demerath and Thiessen, 1966; Coleman, 1968), must be solved by any educational sect and the act of solution will probably turn them into denominations. The existing school must face the implications of O'Dea's 'paradoxes of institutionalization' and must undertake its most fundamental examination of itself in terms similar to those he suggests. Such an examination would seem to foreshadow a break down on the monolithic quality of the school as we have come to know it and the frank recognition of the possibility of alternatives with differing theologies, differing structures and differing clienteles, denominations perhaps (President's Science Advisory Committee, 1974).

I cannot foresee what the recognition of the possibility of such diversity means for the school, both in its philosophical and its practical senses. However, one thing is clear: such developments will challenge education insofar as it is an integrative institution and we must recognize that this is the rock upon which many reforms of the church have failed, and are still failing; it behoves us perhaps to ponder that fact for both its philosophical and practical implications. How, for example, do denominations co-exist and what are the consequences of co-existence? And what are the limits of rationality as we think about such questions? As Douglas (1970, p. 166) points out, 'Reforming bishops and radical theologians, to say nothing of utopian marxists, must eventually recognize that the generous warmth of their doctrinal latitude, their critical dissolving of categories and attack on intellectual and administrative distinctions are generated by analogous social experience.' How is social experience filtered and articulated so that it is called into the service of education as an ideal so that both the integrity of the ideal, the aspirations of our clienteles, and our traditions are honoured and directed? Clearly I cannot formulate the questions I am trying to articulate adequately, but I know they are the questions of our time. Perhaps, to follow the spirit of the argument I have been making here, we should do rather than ponder too hard, but, while clearly doing the major part of our task, it is, if it stands alone as *the* work, an unsatisfactory starting point. Clearly, we must begin an exploration of the topic of goals and set the conclusions of that analysis alongside the kind of analysis of schooling I have attempted here. I hope, however, that this paper can serve to show how the idea of agency might be related to the idea of education so that educational planning can find a way of fulfilling its primary task, that of actualizing ends in means.

Note: An earlier version of this essay was presented as part of a symposium, 'Towards Disciplined Inquiry in Curriculum: Breaking With Conventional Modes' at the annual convention of the American Educational Research Association, Chicago, 1974. I wish to acknowledge my debt to Edmund Short for organizing that symposium. The paper would not have been possible without the insight gained from many conversations with Jon Abrahamson, Robert Dreeben, Robert Kenny, W. Lynn McKinney, William A. Reid and Neil J. Wilkof.

*Appendix: Examination of Girls' Schools by Written Papers**

For Dictation

In time of summer, when animals are plagued with thirst, a lion and a wild boar came to a little spring to drink. But a dispute having arisen which of them should drink first, and a desperate fight ensuing, the affair seemed likely to end in murder. After they had fought a considerable time, stopping for a short space in order to take breath, they spied some vultures waiting to devour the one which should first fall. This circumstance induced them to dismiss their enmity, saying, 'It is better for us to become friends than to be a prey to vultures and crows.' The fable shows that it is wiser to put an end to strifes and contentions than to prolong them till they involve both sides in disgrace and ruin.

English Grammar

1. What do you mean by a noun substantive? Give the rules for the formation of the plural in substantives, with examples and exceptions.

Write down the plural forms of the following words:

Mouse	Penny	Hero	Child	Focus
Tooth	Shelf	Folio	Phenomenon	Walrus.

2. Decline the personal pronoun of the third person, and the possessive pronoun of the first person.

* From J. H. Hammond, 'General Report on the Counties of Norfolk and Northumberland,' [Great Britain], *Schools Inquiry Commission*, General Reports of Assistant Commissioners, VIII, London, Her Majesty's Stationery Office, 1868, pp. 615–28.

3. How is the past (preterite) tense of verbs formed? Give instances. Write down the preterite and past participle of the following verbs:

Ring Strike Smite Climb Glide Run Grind
Teach Clothe Strew.

4. Analyse the following passage, and parse the words printed in italics:

Now *fades* the *glimmering landscape* on the sight,
And all the air a solemn stillness holds,
Save where the beetle *wheels* his droning flight,
And drowsy *tinklings lull* the distant *folds*.

5. In the simplest form of sentence (proposition) what parts of speech must necessarily be found?

Write down any such sentence and then amplify it so as to introduce an article, adjective, adverb, a preposition followed by a pronoun, and a conjunction.

Explain the effect on the meaning of the original sentence of each part of speech so introduced.

Arithmetic

1. Express in figures

a One thousand and one
b One hundred million forty thousand seven hundred and six

In the number 658,457 how many times greater is the value of one 5 than that of the other?

2. Multiply 12,345 by 6,789 and divide 536,819,741 by 907.

3. Multiply £45. 19*s*. 9½*d*. by 88, and divide £15,942. 16*s*. 6*d*. by 108.

4. If the price of 3,000 copies of a book be £4,725, what sum will the sale of 1,937 copies produce?

5. A friend having lent me £1,035 for 45 days, for how many days should I lend him £2,025, so as to repay the obligation?

6. Find, by Practice, the value of 212 cwt. 3 qrs. 14 lbs., at £1. 13*s*. 2*d*. per cwt.

7. Add together 7/16, 2/3, 5/48, and 3 19/24.

8. Reduce 5/9 of 1*s*. 6*d*. to the fraction of 10*s*.

9. Divide 30 by 2/3 and by 3/2, and in each case explain, by some familiar illustration, the meaning of the quotient.

10. Convert 8·065 to a vulgar fraction; also divide 8·065 by 2·5 and by 0·00025.

11. Find the square root of 1521.

12. Explain the terms interest and discount. Are they the same in amount for the same sums at the same rates? Give the reasons for your answer.

13. Find the amount of £3,050. 10*s*. at 5 per cent per annum, for 3¼ years simple interest.

Geography

1. If I go from Edinburgh to Southampton by sea, what counties do I pass on the coast?

Name them in their order, and give their chief towns.

2. Name the principal islands in the Mediterranean, and the countries to which they belong.

3. If a telegraph were to be laid by land from Lisbon to St Petersburg what countries would it pass through, what rivers would it cross, and what towns might be conveniently selected as the most important stations?

4. Name the chief mountain ranges and rivers of Asia, and the countries in which they are situated or through which they pass.

5. Being at Quebec I wish to visit ten of the most important cities in the United States, and to return to Quebec from the westward.

Which towns would I select, and in what order should I visit them so as to make my journey as short as possible?

What States must I pass through, and what rivers must I see on my journey?

6. From what countries do we get tea, coffee, sugar, cotton, wool, flax, timber, hides, corn, gold, silver?

7. Explain *latitude, longitude, isthmus, North pole, basin* (of a river).

English History

1. Write down the list of Kings of England of the Norman line with the dates of their accession.

2. In what years and in whose reigns were the following battles fought? Mention the localities and the combatants on either side:

Agincourt	Bosworth	Flodden	Poitiers
Bannockburn	Camperdown	Hastings	Trafalgar
Blenheim	Culloden	Naseby	Waterloo

3. Give (with dates) the succession of Sovereigns from Henry VII, to James I, stating the relationship of each to his or her predecessor.

4. Under what circumstances did

a Cromwell become Protector?
and *b* William and Mary succeed to the Crown?

5. In whose reigns did the following persons flourish, and for what are they remarkable?

Lord Bacon	Cranmer	Sir Thomas More	Spenser
Burke	Dr Johnson	Sir Isaac Newton	Dean Swift
Caxton	Ben Jonson	Pitt	Sir Walter Scott
Chaucer	Milton	Sir Joshua Reynolds	Wycliffe

French

1. Compare the usage of the French and English languages in regard of *gender*. Which do you consider the more natural, and the more convenient? Give reasons for your opinion.

2. Translate the following sentences into French:

a I saw her there.
b The two ladies whom I had met yesterday.
c Give me some of them for him.
d I had just been walking.
e What o'clock is it? A quarter to four.
f How old is she? Twelve.
g Did he know nothing? / nobody?
h I have only twenty pounds.
i Charles II was restored to the Throne on the 29th of May 1660.

3. Write down the *first person singular* of the following tenses:

Present indicative	Pouvoir
Preterite indefinite	Sortir, Vivre
Preterite definite	Devoir, Naitre
Future	Valoir, Mourir, Savoir

4. Write down *in full* the following tenses:

Present indicative	Faire, Choisir, Vouloir
Future and Preterite definite	Retenir
Imperative Mood	Aller
Present subjunctive	Concevoir
Imperfect subjunctive	Etre

Basil Bernstein

8. Class and Pedagogies: Visible and Invisible

In this paper I shall examine some of the assumptions and the cultural context of a particular form of pre-school/infant school pedagogy, a form which has at least the following characteristics:

1. Where the control of the teacher over the child is implicit rather than explicit.
2. Where, ideally, the teacher arranges the *context* which the child is expected to re-arrange and explore.
3. Where within this arranged context, the child apparently has wide powers over what he selects, over how he structures, and over the time scale of his activities.
4. Where the child apparently regulates his own movements and social relationships.
5. Where there is a reduced emphasis upon the transmission and acquisition of specific skills (see Note I).
6. Where the criteria for evaluating the pedagogy are multiple and diffuse and so not easily measured.

Invisible pedagogy and infant education

One can characterise this pedagogy as an invisible pedagogy. In terms of the concepts of classification and frame, the pedagogy is realised through weak classification and weak frames. Visible pedagogies are realised through strong classification and strong frames. The basic difference between visible and invisible pedagogies is in the *manner* in which criteria are transmitted and in the degree of specificity of the criteria. The more implicit the manner of transmission and the more diffuse the criteria the more invisible the pedagogy; the more specific the criteria, the more explicit the manner of their transmission, the more visible the pedagogy. These definitions will be extended later in the paper.

If the pedagogy is invisible, what aspects of the child have high visibility for the teacher? I suggest two aspects. The first arises out of an inference the teacher makes from the child's ongoing behaviour about the *developmental* stage of the child. This inference is then referred to a concept of *readiness*. The second aspect of the child refers to his external behaviour and is conceptualised by the teacher as busyness. The child should be busy doing things. These inner (readiness) and outer (busyness) aspects of the child can be transformed into one concept of 'ready to do'. The teacher infers from the 'doing' the state of 'readiness' of the child as it is revealed in his present activity and as this state adumbrates future 'doing'.

We can briefly note in passing a point which will be developed later. In the same way as the child's reading releases the child from the teacher and socialises him into the privatised solitary learning of an explicit anonymous past (i.e. the text-book), so busy children (children doing) releases the child from the teacher but socialises him into an ongoing inter-actional present in which the past is invisible and so implicit (i.e. the teachers' pedagogical theory). Thus a non-doing child in the invisible pedagogy is the equivalent of a non-reading child in the visible pedagogy. (However, a non-reading child may be at a greater disadvantage and experience greater difficulty than a 'non-doing' child.)

The concept basic to the invisible pedagogy is that of play. This is not the place to submit this concept to logical analysis, but a few points may be noted:

1. Play is the means by which the child exteriorises himself to the teacher. Thus the more he plays and the greater the range of his activities, the more of the child is made available to the teacher's screening. Thus, play is the fundamental concept with 'readiness' and 'doing' as subordinate concepts. Although not all forms of doing are considered as play (hitting another child, for example) most forms can be so characterised.
2. Play does not merely describe an activity it also contains an evaluation of that activity. Thus, there is productive and less productive play, obsessional and free-ranging play, solitary and social play. Play is not only an activity, it entails a theory from which interpretation, evaluation and diagnosis are derived and which also indicates a progression. A theory which the child can never know in the way a child can know the criteria which is realised in visible pedagogy. Play implies a potentially all-embracing theory, for it covers nearly all if not all the child's doing and not doing. As a consequence, a very long chain of inference has to be set up to connect the theory with any one exemplar (a 'doing' or a 'not doing'). The theory gives rise to a total—but invisible—surveillance of the child, because it relates his inner dispositions to all his external acts. The 'spontaneity' of the child is filtered through this surveillance and then implicitly shaped according to interpretation, evaluation and diagnosis.
3. Both the means and ends of play are multiple and change with time. Because of this, the stimuli must be, on the whole, highly abstract, available to be contextualised by the child, and so the unique doing of each child is facilitated. Indeed, play encourages each child to make his own mark. Sometimes, however, the stimulus may be very palpable when the child is

invited to feel a leaf, or piece of velour, but what is *expected* is a *unique* response of the child to his own sensation. What is the code for reading the marks; a code the child can never know, but implicitly acquires. How does he do this?

4. The social basis of this theory of play is not an individualised act, but a personalised act; not strongly framed, but weakly framed encounters. Its social structure may be characterised as one of *overt* personalised organic solidarity, but covert mechanical solidarity. Visible pedagogies create social structures which may be characterised as *covert* individualised organic solidarity and *overt* mechanical solidarity. (See later discussion.)

5. In essence, play is work and work is play. We can begin to see here the class origins of the theory. For the working class, work and play are very strongly classified and framed; for certain sub-groups of the middle class, work and play are weakly classified and weakly framed. For these sub-groups, no strict line may be drawn between work and play. Work carries what is often called 'intrinsic' satisfactions, and therefore is not confined to *one* context. However, from another point of view, work offers the opportunity of symbolic narcissism which combines inner pleasure and outer prestige. Work for certain sub-groups of the middle class is a personalised act in a privatised social structure. These points will be developed later.

Theories of learning and invisible pedagogy

We are now in a position to analyse the principles underlying the selection of theories of learning which invisible pre-school/infant school pedagogies will adopt. Such pedagogies will adopt any theory of learning which has the following characteristics:

1. The theories in general will be seeking universals and thus are likely to be developmental and concerned with sequence. A particular context of learning is only of interest in as much as it throws light on a sequence. Such theories are likely to have a strong biological bias.

2. Learning is a tacit, invisible act, its progression is not facilitated by explicit public control.

3. The theories will tend to abstract the child's personal biography and local context from his cultural biography and institutional context.

4. In a sense, the theories see socialisers as potentially, if not actually, dangerous, as they embody an adult-focused, therefore reified concept of the socialised. Exemplary models are relatively unimportant and so the various theories in different ways point towards *implicit* rather than explicit hierarchical social relationships. Indeed, the imposing exemplar is transformed into a *facilitator*.

5. Thus the theories can be seen as interrupters of cultural reproduction and therefore have been considered by some as progressive or even revolutionary. Notions of child's time replace notions of adult's time, notions

of child's space replace notions of adult's space; facilitation replaces imposition and accommodation replaces domination.

We now give a group of theories, which despite many differences fulfill at a most abstract level all or nearly all of the five conditions given previously:

Piaget	1	2	3	4	5
Freud	1	2	3	4	5
Chomsky	1	2	3	4	5
Ethological theories of critical learning	1	2	3	4	5
Gestalt		2	3	4	5

What is of interest is that these theories form rather a strange, if not contradictory group. They are often selected to justify a specific element of the pedagogy. They form in a way the theology of the infant school. We can see how the crucial concept of play and the subordinate concepts of readiness and doing, fit well with the above theories. We can also note how the invisibility of the pedagogy fits with the invisible tacit act of learning. We can also see that the pre-school/infant school movement from one point of view is a progressive, revolutionary, colonising movement in its relationships to parents, and in its relationship to educational levels above itself. It is antagonistic for different reasons to middle class and working class families, for both create a deformation of the child. It is antagonistic to educational levels above itself, because of its fundamental opposition to their concepts of learning and social relationships. We can note here that as a result the child is abstracted from his family and his future educational contexts.

Of central importance is that this pedagogy brings together two groups of educationists who are at the extremes of the educational hierarchy, infant school teachers and university teachers and researchers. The consequence has been to professionalise and raise the status of the pre-school/infant school teacher; a status not based upon a specific competence, a status based upon a weak educational identity (no subject). The status of the teachers from this point of view is based upon a diffuse, tacit, symbolic control which is legitimised by a closed explicit ideology, the essence of weak classification and weak frames.

Class and the invisible pedagogy

From our previous discussion, we can abstract the following:

1. The invisible pedagogy is an interrupter system, both in relation to the family and in its relation to other levels of the educational hierarchy.

2. It transforms the privatised social structures and cultural contexts of visible pedagogies into a personalised social structure and personalised cultural contexts.
3. Implicit nurture reveals unique nature.

The question is, what is it interrupting? The invisible pedagogy was first institutionalised in the private sector for a fraction of the middle class—the new middle class (see Note II). If the ideologies of the old middle class were institutionalised in the public schools and through them into the grammar schools, so the ideology of the new middle class was first institutionalised in private pre-schools, then private/public secondary schools, and finally into the state system, at the level of the infant school. Thus the conflict between visible and invisible pedagogies, from this point of view, between strong and weak classification and frames, is an ideological conflict within the middle class. The ideologies of education are still the ideologies of class. The old middle class were domesticated through the strong classification and frames of the family and public schools, which attempted, often very successfully, cultural reproduction. But what social type was reproduced?

We know that every industrialised society produces organic solidarity. Now Durkheim, it seems to me, was concerned with only *one* form of such solidarity —the form which created individualism. Durkheim was interested in the vicissitudes of the types as their classification and framing were no longer, or only weakly, morally integrated, or when the individual's relation to the classification and frames underwent a change. His analysis is based upon the old middle class. He did not foresee, although his conceptual procedures make this possible, a form of organic solidarity based upon weak classification and weak frames; that is, a form of solidarity developed by the new middle class. Durkheim's organic solidarity refers to *individuals* in privatised class relationships; the second form of organic solidarity refers to persons in privatised class relationships. The second form of organic solidarity celebrates the apparent release, not of the individual, but of the person and *new* forms of social control (see Note III). Thus, we can distinguish *individualised* and *personalised* forms of organic solidarity *within* the middle class, each with their own distinctive and conflicting ideologies and each with their own distinctive and conflicting forms of socialisation and symbolic reality. These two forms arise out of developments of the division of labour within class societies. Durkheim's individualised organic solidarity developed out of the increasing complexity of the economic division of labour; personalised organic solidarity, it is suggested, develops out of increases in the complexity of the division of labour of cultural or symbolic control which the new middle class has appropriated. The new middle class is an interrupter system, clearly not of class relationships, but of the *form* of their reproduction. In Bourdieu's terms, there has been a change in habitus, but not in function. This change in habitus has had far reaching effects on the selective institutionalisation of symbolic codes and codings in the areas of sex, aesthetics, and upon preparing and repairing agencies, such as the family, school, and mental hospitals. In all these areas there has been a shift towards weak classification and frames (see Note IV).

This conflict within the middle class is realised sharply in different patterns of the socialisation of the young. In the old middle class, socialisation is into strong classification and strong framing, where the boundaries convey tacitly critical condensed messages. In the new middle class, socialisation is into weak classification and weak frames, which promote through the explicitness of the communication code far greater ambiguity and drive this class to make visible the ideology of its socialisation; crucial to this ideology is the concept of the *person* not of the *individual*. Whereas the concept of the *individual* leads to specific, unambiguous role identities and relatively inflexible role performances, the *concept* of the person leads to ambiguous personal identity and flexible role performances. Both the old and the new middle class draw upon biological theories, but of very different types. The old middle class held theories which generated biologically fixed types, where variety of the type constituted a threat to cultural reproduction. The new middle class also hold theories which emphasise a fixed biological type, but they also hold that the type is capable of great variety. This, in essence, is a theory which points towards social mobility—towards a meritocracy. For the old middle class, variety must be severely reduced in order to ensure cultural reproduction; for the new middle class, the variety must be encouraged in order to ensure interruption. Reproduction and interruption are created by variations in the strength of classifications and frames (see Note V). As these weaken, so the socialisation encourages more of the socialised to become visible, his uniqueness to be made manifest. Such socialisation is deeply penetrating, more total as the surveillance becomes more invisible. This is the basis of control which creates personalised organic solidarity. Thus the forms of socialisation within these two conflicting fractions of the middle class are the origins of the visible and invisible pedagogies of the school. We have a homologue between the interruption of the new middle class of the reproduction of the old and the interruption of the new educational pedagogy of the reproduction of the old; between the conflict within the middle class and the conflict between the two pedagogies: yet it is the conflict between and interruption of *forms* of transmission of class relationships. This point we will now develop. The new middle class, like the proponents of the invisible pedagogy, are caught in a contradiction; for their theories are at variance with their objective class relationship. A deep rooted ambivalence is the ambience of this group. On the one hand, they stand for variety against inflexibility, expression against repression, the inter-personal against the inter-positional; on the other hand, there is the grim obduracy of the division of labour and of the narrow pathways to its positions of power and prestige. Under individualised organic solidarity, property has an essentially physical nature, however, with the development of personalised organic solidarity, although property in the physical sense remains crucial, it has been partly psychologised and appears in the form of ownership of valued skills made available in educational institutions. Thus, if the new middle class is to repeat its position in the class structure, then appropriate secondary socialisation into privileged education becomes crucial. But as the relation between education and occupation becomes more direct and closer in time then the classifications and frames increase in strength. Thus the new middle class take up some ambivalent enthusiasm for the invisible pedagogy for the early socialisation of the child, but settle for the *visible* pedagogy of the secondary school. And it will continue to do this until the university moves to a weaker classification and a weaker framing of its principles of transmission and selection. On the other hand, they are among the leaders of the movement to institutionalise the invisible pedagogy in State pre-schools and often for its colonisation of the primary school and further extension into the secondary school. And this can be done with confidence for the secondary school is likely to provide both visible and invisible pedagogies. The former for the middle class and the latter for the working class.

The class assumptions of the invisible pedagogy

We can now begin to see that because the invisible pedagogy had its origins within a fraction of the middle class, it pre-supposes a relatively long educational life. Inherent within this pedagogy is a concept of time—middle-class time. Of equal significance because it originates within the middle class, it pre-supposes a communication code (an elaborated code) which orientates the child early towards the significance of relatively context-independent meanings, whether these are in the form of speech or of writing. Thus the development of specific educational competencies can either be delayed because of the longer educational life, or the child will achieve them early because of the focus of the communication code. But this does not complete the class assumptions of the invisible pedagogy. We have so far suggested two: a long educational life, and an elaborated code. There is a third.

The shift from individualised to personalised organic solidarity changes the structure of family relationships and in particular the role of the woman in the socialising of the child. Historically, under individualised organic solidarity, the mother is important as a transmitter of neither physical nor symbolic property. She is almost totally abstracted from the means of reproduction of either physical or symbolic property. The control of the children is delegated to others (nanny, governess, tutor). She is essentially a domestic administrator, and it follows that she can be a model only for her daughter. She was often capable of cultural reproduction, for often she possessed a sensitive awareness of the literature of the period. This concept of the abstracted maternal function perhaps re-appears in the concept of the pre-school assistant as a baby minder, and the governess as the teacher of elementary competencies. Thus individualised organic solidarity might generate two models for the pre-school or infant school:

1. The abstracted mother — Nanny—baby minder
2. The governess — teacher of elementary competencies.

Under personalised organic solidarity, the *role of the mother* in the rearing of her children undergoes a qualitative change. As we have noted earlier, with such solidarity, property has been partly psychologised and it arises out of forms of inter-active—forms of communication—which are initiated and developed and focussed by the mother very early in the child's life. Thus the mother under personalised organic solidarity is transformed into a powerful and crucial agent of cultural reproduction who provides access to symbolic forms and who shapes the disposition of her children so that they are better able to exploit the possibilities of education. Thus as we move from individualised to personalised organic solidarity so the woman is transformed from an agent of physical reproduction to an agent of cultural reproduction. There is, however, a contradiction within her structural relationships. Unlike the mother in a situation of individualised solidarity, she is unable to get away from her children. For the weak classification and weak frames of her child-rearing firmly anchor her to her children; for her interaction and surveillance is totally demanding and, at the same time, her own socialisation into both a personal and occupational identity points her away from the family. These tensions can be partly resolved by placing the child early in a pre-school which faithfully reproduces the ambience for her own child-rearing. Thus the middle class mother in a context of personalised organic solidarity provides the model for the pre-school infant school teacher. The pre-school, however, amplifies the messages, and wishes to extend them in time. Here we can see a second contradiction for such an amplification brings the middle class mother and the school into conflict. The public examination system is based upon a visible pedagogy as it is realised through strong classification and strong frames. It is this pedagogy which transmits symbolic property. If access to visible pedagogy is delayed too long, then examination success may be considered to be in danger.

We have now made explicit three assumptions underlying the invisible pedagogy. There is a fourth. The size of the class of pupils is likely to be small and the teacher-pupil ratio very favourable:

1. It pre-supposes a middle class conception of educational time.
2. It pre-supposes an elaborated code of communication.
3. It pre-supposes a middle class mother who is an agent of cultural reproduction.
4. It pre-supposes a small class of pupils.

Thus the social significance of the invisible pedagogy will be crucially different according to the social class of the child.

We started this section by abstracting the following points from our initial discussion of the invisible pedagogy:

1. The invisible pedagogy is an interrupter system both in relation to the home and in relation to other levels of the educational hierarchy.

2. It transforms the privatised social structure and cultural contents of visible pedagogies into a personalised social structure and personalised cultural contexts.
3. It believes that implicit nurture reveals unique nature.

We have argued that this pedagogy is one of the realisations of the conflict between the old and the new middle class, which in turn has its social basis in the two different forms of organic solidarity, individualised and personalised; that these two forms of solidarity arise out of differences in the relation to the division of labour within the middle class; that the movement from individualised to personalised interrupts the *form* of the reproduction of class relationships; that such an interruption gives rise to different forms of *primary* socialisation within the middle class; that the form of primary socialisation within the middle class is the model for primary socialisation into the school; that there are contradictions within personalised organic solidarity which create deeply felt ambiguities; as a consequence, the outcomes of the form of the socialisation are less certain. The contemporary new middle class are unique, for in the socialisation of their young is a sharp and penetrating contradiction between a subjective personal identity and an objective privatised identity; between the release of the person and the hierarchy of class.

Whereas it is possible for school and university to change the basis of its solidarity from individualistic to personalised, i.e. to relax its classification and frames, it is more difficult for those agencies to change their privatising function, i.e. the creation of knowledge as private property. It by no means follows that a shift to personalised organic solidarity will change the privatising function. Indeed, even the shift in the form of solidarity is more likely to occur in that part of the educational system which either creates no private property, as in the case of the education of the lower working class, or in the education of the very young. We are then left with the conclusion that the major effects of this change in solidarity will be in the areas of condensed communcation (sex, art, style) and in the form of social control (from explicit to implicit).

Transition to school

(*a*) *Class culture power and conflict*

The shift from visible to invisible pedagogies at the pre- and primary levels of education changes the relationships between the family and the school. We have already noted the ambiguous attitude of the middle class to such a shift. In the case of the working class, the change is more radical. The weak classification and the weak framing of the invisible pedagogy potentially makes possible the inclusion of the culture of the family and the community. Thus the experience of the child and his everyday world could be psychologically active in the classroom and if this were to be the case, then the school would legitimise rather than reject the class-culture of the family. In as much as the pacing of the knowledge to be transmitted is relaxed and the emphasis upon early attainment of specific competencies is reduced, then the progression is less marked by middle class assumptions. In the case of visible pedagogies early reading and especially writing is essential. Once the child can read and write such acts free the teacher but of more importance, once the child can read he can be given a book, and once he is given a book he is well on the way to managing the role of the solitary privatised educational relationship. The book is the preparation for receiving the past realised in the text-book. And the text-book in turn tacitly transmits the ideology of the collection code: for it epitomises strong classification and strong frames. The text-book orders knowledge according to an explicit progression, it provides explicit criteria, it removes uncertainties and announces hierarchy. It gives the child an immediate index of where he stands in relation to others in the progression. It is therefore a silent medium for creating competitive relationships. Thus socialisation into the text-book is a critical step towards socialisation into the collection code. The stronger the collection code, that is the stronger classification and frames, the greater the emphasis on early reading and writing. The middle class child is prepared for this emphasis, but not so in the case of the working class child. The weakening of classification and frames reduces the significance of the text-book and transforms the impersonal past into a personalised present. It would appear that the invisible pedagogy carries a beneficial potential for working class children. However, because the form we are discussing has its origins in a fraction of the middle class, this potential may not be actualised.

This point we will now develop. From the point of view of working class parents, the visible pedagogy of the collection code at the primary level is immediately understandable. The basic competencies which it is transmitting of reading, writing, and counting, in an ordered explicit sequence, make sense. The failures of the children are the children's failures not the school's for the school is apparently carrying out impersonally its function. The school's form of social control does not interfere with the social control of the family. The infant school teacher will not necessarily have high status as the competencies she is transmitting are, in principle, possible also for the mother. In this sense, there is symbolic continuity (or rather extension) between the working class home and the school. However, in the case of the invisible pedagogy, there is possibly a sharp discontinuity. The competencies and their progression disappear, the form of social control may well be at variance with the home. The theory of the invisible pedagogy may not be known by the mother or be imperfectly understood. The lack of stress on competencies may render the child a less effective (useful) member of the family, e.g. running errands, etc. However, there is a more fundamental source of tension. The invisible pedagogy contains a different theory of transmission and a new technology, which views the mother's own informal teaching, where it occurs, or the mother's pedagogical values, as irrelevant if not downright harmful. There are new reading schemes, new mathematics replace arithmetic, an expressive aesthetic style replaces one which aims at facsimile. If the mother is to be helpful, she must be re-socialised or kept out of the way. If it is the former or the latter, then the power relationships have changed between home and school: for the teacher has the power and the mother is as much a pupil as the pupil. This in turn may disturb the authority relationships within the home: this disturbance is further facilitated by the use of implicit forms of social control of the school. Even if the pedagogy draws its contents from the class culture, basic forms of discontinuity still exist. If the mother wishes to understand the theory of the invisible pedagogy, then she may well find herself at the mercy of complex theories of child development. Indeed, whichever way the working class mother turns, the teacher has the power: although the mother may well be deeply suspicious of the whole ambiance. (This does *not* mean that *all* teachers wish to have the power or use it.)

Where, as in the case of the visible pedagogy there are, for the working class, relative to the middle class, implicit forms of discontinuity and explicit forms of inequality in the shape of the holding power of the school over its teachers, the size of class and possibly streaming; in the case of the invisible pedagogy, there is also an *explicit* symbolic discontinuity which may well go with inequalities in provision and quality of teaching staff. The teacher also has difficulties, because the invisible pedagogy presupposes a particular form of maternal primary socialisation *and* a small class of pupils *and* a particular architecture. Where these are absent, the teacher may well find great difficulty. Ideally, the invisible pedagogy frees the teacher so that time is available for ameliorating the difficulties of any one child, but if the class is large, the socialisation, from the point of view of the school, inadequate, the architecture inappropriate, then such individual assistance becomes infrequent and problematic. Here again we can see that such a pedagogy, if it is to be successfully implemented in its own terms, necessarily requires minimally the same physical conditions of the middle class school. It is an *expensive* pedagogy because it is derived from an expensive class: the middle class.

From the point of view of the middle class, there is at least an intellectual understanding of the invisible pedagogy if not always, an acceptance of its values and practice. Further, if the middle class child is not obtaining the basic competencies at the rate the mother expects, an educational support system can be organized through private coaching or through the mother's own efforts. The power relationships between the middle class mother and the teacher are less tipped in favour of the teacher. Finally, the middle class mother always has the choice of the private school or of moving near a state school of her choice. However, because of the middle class mother's concept of the function of secondary education, she is likely to be anxious about the acquisition of basic competencies and this will bring her into conflict with the school at some point.

Finally, in as much as age and sex statuses within the family are strongly classified and ritualised, then it is likely that the acquisition, progression and evaluation of competencies obtained within the school will become part of the markers of age and sex status within the family. For example, there is a radical change in the status and concept of the child when he is transformed into a pupil. Now to the extent that the infant/primary school fails to utilise age and sex as allocating categories *either* for the acquisition and progression of competencies *or* for the allocation of pupils to groups and spaces, then the school is weakening the function of these categories in the family and community. Visible pedagogies not only reinforce age and sex classification, they also provide markers for progression within them. Invisible pedagogies are likely to weaken such classifications and in as much as they do this they transform the concept of the child and the concepts of age and sex status.

(*b*) *Class, pedagogy and evaluation*

Interesting questions arise over the system of evaluating the pupils. Where the pedagogy is visible an 'objective' grid exists for the evaluation of the pupils in the form of (*a*) clear criteria and (*b*) a delicate measurement procedure. The child receives a grade or its equivalent for any valued performance. Further, where the pedagogy is visible, it is likely to be standardised and so schools are directly comparable as to their successes and failures. The profile of the pupil may be obtained by looking across his grades. The pupil knows where he is, the teacher knows where he is and so do the parents. The parents have a yardstick for comparing schools. When children change schools they can be slotted into place according to their academic profile. Further, it is difficult for the parent to argue about the profile for it is 'objective'. Clearly, there are subjective elements in the grading of the children, but these are masked by the apparent objectivity of the grid. In the case of invisible pedagogies, no such grid exists The evaluation procedures are multiple, diffuse and not easily subject to apparently precise measurement. This makes comparison between pupils complex and also comparisons between schools. (Paradoxically, this situation carries a potential for increasing competitiveness.) Firstly, the invisible pedagogy does not give rise to progression of a *group*, but is based upon progression of a person. Secondly, there is likely to be considerable variation between infant/pre-school groups *within* the general form of the pedagogy. There is less difficulty in slotting a child into a new school because there is no explicit slot for him. Thus the mother is less able to diagnose the child's progress and as a consequence she cannot *provide specific educational support* (she can offer, of course, elements of a visible pedagogy). She would be forced into providing a general educational milieu in the home and this she might only be able to do if she had fully internalised the invisible pedagogy's theoretical basis. As we have previously argued, this is less likely to be the case where the parents are working class. Thus these parents are cut off from the evaluation of their child's progress. More, they are forced to accept what the teacher counts as progress.

Because an apparently objective grid exists for the evaluation of the visible pedagogies, then this grid acts selectively on those dispositions of the child which become candidates for labelling by the teacher. Clearly motivation and interest are probably relevant to any pedagogy, but their significance will vary with the pedagogy, and certainly their consequences. In the case of visible pedagogies, the behaviour of the child is focused on the teacher so that, in this case, attentiveness to, co-operation with, the teacher become relevant: persistence and carefulness are also valued by the teacher. Further, it is possible for there to be a conflict between the child's academic profile *and* the teacher's evaluation of his attitudes and motivation. These objective and subjective criteria may have different consequences for different class groups of pupils. Either criteria, irrespective of their validity, are likely to be *understood* by working class parents. In the case of invisible pedagogy, as more of the child is made available, and, because of the theory which guides interpretation, diagnosis and evaluation, a different class of acts and dispositions of the child become relevant. In the case of visible pedagogies we have argued that the attention of the child is focused on the teacher; however, in the case of invisible pedagogies the attention of the teacher is focused on the *whole* child: in its total doing and 'not doing'. This can lead to discrepancies between the teacher's and parents' view of the child unless the parents share the teacher's theory. Indeed, it is possible that the dispositions and acts which are subject to evaluation by the teacher may be considered by some parents as irrelevant or intrusive or inaccurate, or all three. Where this occurs, the child's behaviour is being shaped by conflicting criteria. From the point of view of the teacher, the child becomes an *innovating* message to the home. The invisible pedagogy is not only an interrupter system in the context of educational practice, but it also transforms the child, under certain conditions, into an innovating message to the family.

This pedagogy is likely to lead to a change in the school's procedures of evaluation, both objective and subjective. Where the pedagogy is visible, there is a profile which consists of the grading of specific competencies and a profile which consists of the grading of the child's motivation and work attitudes. It is likely that the latter will consist of rather short, somewhat stereotyped unexplicated judgements. In the case of invisible pedagogies, these highly condensed, unexplicated but *public*, judgements are likely to be replaced by something resembling a dossier which will range across a wide variety of the child's internal processes and states *and* his external acts. Further, the connection between inner and outer is likely to be made *explicit*. In other words, there is likely to be an explicit elaborated account of the relationships between the child's internal states and his acts. It is now possible that the school will have a problem of secrecy. How much is to go into the dossier, where is it to be kept, how much of and in what way are its contents to be made available to parents or to others in the school and outside of it? Thus invisible pedagogies may also generate *covert* and *overt* forms and contents of evaluation. Such a system of evaluation increases the power of the teacher to the extent that its underlying theory is not shared by parents *and* even when it is shared.

Finally, the major analysis in this section has been of idealised pedagogies. If, however, the argument is correct, that there may be a disjunction in the forms of socialisation between primary and secondary stages, *or* between secondary and tertiary stages, then behind weak classification and weak frames may well be strong classification and strong frames. Thus we can have a situation where strong Cs and Fs follow weak Cs and Fs, *or* where weak Cs and Fs follow strong Cs and Fs, as, possibly, in the case of the training of infant school teachers in England. It is important not only to understand continuity in the strength of classification and frames, but also *disjunction* and *when* the disjunction occurs. It is more than likely that if we examine empirically invisible pedagogies we shall find to different degrees a stress on the transmission of *specific* isolated competencies. Thus the 'hidden curriculum' of invisible pedagogies may well be, embryonically, strong classification, albeit with relatively weak frames. It becomes a matter of some importance to find out which children or groups of children are particularly responsive to this 'hidden curriculum'. For some children may come to see or be led to see that there are two transmissions, one overt, the other covert, which stand in a figure-ground relation to each other. We need to know for which teachers, and for which children, what is the figure and what is the ground. Specifically, will middle class children respond to the latent visible pedagogy, or are they more likely to be selected as receivers? Will lower working class children respond more to the invisible pedagogy or receive a weaker form of the transmission of visible pedagogy? The 'hidden curriculum' of invisible pedagogies may well be a visible pedagogy. However, the outcomes of the imbedding of one pedagogy in the other are likely to be different than in the case of the transmission of any *one* pedagogy. From a more theoretical standpoint, the crucial component of visible pedagogy is the strength of its *classification*, for in the last analysis, it is this which creates what counts as valued property, and also in so doing regulates mental structures. Frame strength regulates the modality of the socialisation into the classification. In the microcosm of the nursery or infant class, we can see embryonically the new forms of transmission of class relationships.

Let us take a concrete example to illustrate the above speculation. An infant school teacher in England may experience the following conjunctions or disjunctions in her socialisation:

1. Between socialisation in the family and between primary and secondary school.
2. Between secondary school and teacher training. The higher the qualifications required by the college of education, the more likely that the socialisation in the later years of the secondary school will be through strong classification and frames. On the other hand, the socialisation into the college of education may well be into classification and frames of varying strengths.

Transition between stages of education

We have examined aspects of the transition to school; there is also the question of transition between stages of education, from pre-school to primary, from primary to secondary. These transitions between stages are marked by three inter-related features:

1. An increase in the strength of classification and frames (initiation into the collective code).
2. An increase in the range of different teachers; that is, the pupil is made aware of the insulations within the division of labour. He also learns that the principle of authority transcends the individuals who hold it, for as teachers/subjects change his role remains the same.
3. The weak classification and frames of the invisible pedagogy emphasises the importance of *ways* of knowing, of constructing problems, whereas the strong classification and frames of visible pedagogies emphasise states of knowledge and received problems.

Thus there is a crucial change in what counts as having knowledge, in what counts as a legitimate realisation of that knowledge *and* in the social context.

Thus the shift from invisible to visible pedagogies in one phrase is a change in code; a change in the principles of relation and evaluation whether these are principles of knowledge, of social relationships, of practices, of property, of identity.

It is likely that this change of code will be more effectively made (despite the difficulties) by the new middle class children as their own socialisation within the family contains *both* codes—the code which creates the manifestation of the person and the code which creates private property. Further, as we have argued elsewhere, it is more likely that the working class children will experience continuity in code between stages of education. The class bias of the collection code (which creates a visible pedagogy) may make such a transmission difficult for them to receive and exploit. As a consequence, the continuation of the invisible pedagogy in the form of an integrated code is likely for working class children, and its later institutionalisation for the same children at the secondary level.

We can now begin to see that the conditions for continuity of educational code for *all* children, irrespective of class, is the type of code transmitted by the university. Simply expanding the university, increasing differentiation within the tertiary level, equalising opportunity of access and outcome will not fundamentally change the situation at levels below. We will only have expanded the size of the cohort at the tertiary level. From another point of view, although we may have changed the organisational structure we have *not* changed the code controlling transmission; the process of reproduction will not be fundamentally affected. To change the code controlling transmission involves changing the culture and its basis in privatised class relationships. Thus if we accept, for the sake of argument, the greater educational value of invisible pedagogies, of weak classification and frames, the condition for their effective and total institutionalisation at the secondary level is a fundamental change of code at the tertiary level. If this does not occur then codes and class will remain firmly linked in schools.

Finally, we can raise a basic question. The movement to invisible pedagogies realised through integrated codes may be seen as a superficial solution to a more obdurate problem. Integrated codes are integrated at the level of ideas, they do *not* involve integration at the level of institutions, i.e. between school and work. Yet the crucial integration is precisely between the principles of education and the principles of work. There can be no such integration in Western societies (to mention only one group) because the work epitomises class relationships. Work can only be brought into the school in terms of the function of the school as a selective mechanism or in terms of social/psychological adjustment to work. Indeed, the abstracting of education from work, the hallmark of the liberal tradition, or the linkage of education to leisure, masks the brutal fact that work and education cannot be integrated at the level of social principles in class societies. They can either be separated or they can *fit* with each other. Durkheim wrote that changes in pedagogy were indicators of a moral crisis; they can also disguise it and change its form. However, in as much as the move to weak classification and frames has the *potential* of reducing insulations in mental structures and social structures, has the potential of making explicit the implicit and so creating *greater* ambiguity but less disguise, then such a code has the potential of making visible fundamental social contradictions.

Note I

This raises a number of questions. We cannot consider skills abstracted from the context of their transmission, from their relationships to each other and their function in creating, maintaining, modifying or changing a culture. Skills and their relationship to each other are culturally specific competencies. The manner of their transmission and acquisition socialises the child into their contextual usages. Thus, the unit of analysis cannot simply be an abstracted specific competence like reading, writing, counting but the *structure* of social relationships which produces these specialised competencies. The formulation 'where there is a reduced emphasis upon transmission and acquisition of specific skills' could be misleading, as it suggests that in the context under discussion there are few specialised repertoires of the culture. It may be better to interpret the formulation as indicating an emphasis upon the inter-relationships between skills which are relatively weakly classified and weakly framed. In this way any skill or sets of skills are referred to the *general features of the socialisation*.

Note II

We regard the new middle class as being represented by those who are the *new* agents of symbolic control, for example, those who are filling the ever expanding major and minor professional class, concerned with the servicing of persons. We are not saying that all occupants are active members of the new middle class, *but* that there is a structural change in the culture which is shaping their transmissions. It is a matter of empirical research to identify specifically which groups, concerned with what symbolic controls, are active representatives. In earlier papers I suggested that there were two forms of an elaborated code, object/person, and that these were evoked by different class-based forms of family socialisation, positional and personal. It is now possible, at least theoretically, to show that such families vary as to the strength of their classification and frames and that such variation itself arises out of different forms of the transmission of class relationships and represents an ideological conflict *within* the middle class.

Note III

It is a matter of some interest to consider changes in emphasis of research methodologies over recent decades. There has been a shift from the standardised closed questionnaire or experimental context to more unstructured contexts and relationships. It is argued that the former methodology renders irrelevant the subjective meanings of those who are the object of study. In so doing, the researched offer their experience through the media of the researchers' imposed strong classification and strong frames. Further, it is argued that such a method of studying people is derived from a method for the study of objects and therefore it is an outrage to the subjectivity of man for him to be transformed into an object. These arguments go on to link positivist methods with the political control of man through the use of the technology of social science. The new methodology employs apparently weak classification and weak frames, but it uses techniques (participant observation, tape-recordings, video tapes, etc.), which enable more of the researched to be visible, and its techniques allow a range of others to witness the spontaneous behaviour of the observed. Even if these public records of natural behaviour are treated as a means of dialogue between the recorded and the recorder, this dialogue is, itself, subject to the disjunction between intellectual perspectives which will shape the communication. The self-editing of the researcher's communication is different from that of the researched, and this is the *invisible* control. On the other hand, paradoxically, in the case of a closed questionnaire the privacy of the subject is safeguarded, for all that can be made public is a pencil mark which is transformed into an impersonal score. Further, the methods of this transformation must be made public so that its assumptions may be criticised. In the case of the new methodology, the principles used to restrict the vast amount of information and the number of channels are often implicit. One might say that we could distinguish research methodologies in terms of whether they created invisible or visible pedagogies. Thus the former give rise to a total surveillance of the person who, relative to the latter, makes public more of his inside (e.g. his subjectivity) which is evaluated through the use of diffuse, implicit criteria. We are suggesting that the structural origins of changes in the classification and framing of forms of socialisation may perhaps also influence the selection of research methodologies. The morality of the research relationships transcends the dilemmas of a particular researcher. Research methodologies in social science are themselves elements of culture.

Note IV

It is interesting to see for example, where the invisible pedagogy first entered the secondary school curriculum. In England we would suggest that it first penetrated the *non-verbal* area of *unselective* secondary schools. The area which is considered to be the least relevant (in the sense of not producing symbolic property) and the most strongly classified: the area of the art room. Indeed, it might be said that until very recently, the greatest symbolic continuity of pedagogies between primary and secondary stages lay in the non-verbal areas of the curriculum. The art room is often viewed by the rest of the staff as an area of relaxation or even therapy, rather than a space of crucial production. Because of its strong classification and irrelevance (except at school 'show-off' periods) this space is potentially open to change. Art teachers are trained in institutions (at least in recent times) which are very sensitive to innovation and therefore new styles are likely to be rapidly institutionalised in schools, given the strong classification of art in the secondary school curriculum, and also the belief that the less-able child can at least do something with his hands even if he finds difficulty with a pen. We might also anticipate that with the interest in such musical forms as pop on the one hand and Cage and Stockhausen on the other, music departments might move towards the invisible pedagogy. To complete the direction in the non-verbal area, it is possible that the transformation of physical training into physical education might also extend to movement. If this development took place, then the non-verbal areas would be realised through the invisible pedagogy. We might then expect a drive to integrate the three areas of sight, sound and movement; *three* modalities would then be linked through a common code.

Note V

We can clarify the issues raised in this paper in the following way. Any socialising context must consist of a transmitter and an acquirer. These two form a matrix in the sense that the communication is regulated by a structural principle. We have suggested that the underlying principle of a socialising matrix is realised in classification and frames. The relationship between the two and the strengths show us the structure of the control and the form of communication. We can, of course, analyse this matrix in a number of ways:

1. We can focus upon the transmitter.
2. We can focus upon the acquirer.
3. We can focus upon the principles underlying the matrix.
4. We can focus upon a given matrix and ignore its relationship to other matrices.
5. We can consider the relationships between critical matrices, for example, family, peer group, school, work.

We can go on to ask questions about the function of a matrix and questions about the change in the form of its realisation, i.e. changes in the strength of its classification and frames. We believe that the unit of analysis must always be the matrix and the matrix will always include the theories and methods of its analysis (see Note II on research methodology). Now any one matrix can be regarded as a reproducer, an interrupter, or a change matrix. A reproduction matrix will attempt to create strong classification and strong frames. An interrupter matrix changes the *form* of transmission, but not the critical relationship *between* matrices. A change matrix leads to a fundamental change in the structural relationship *between* matrices. This will require a major change in the institutional structure. For example, we have argued that within the middle class there is a conflict which has generated two distinct socialising matrices, one a reproducer, the other an interrupter. And these matrices are at work within education for similar groups of children up to possibly the primary stage, and different groups of pupils at the secondary stage. However, in as much as the structural relationship between school and work is unchanged (i.e. there has been no change in the basic principles of their relationship) then we cannot by this argument see current differences in educational pedagogy as representing a change matrix. In other words, the form of the reproduction of class relationships in education has been *interrupted* but not changed. We might speculate that ideological conflict within the middle class takes the form of a conflict between the symbolic outcomes of reproduction and interruption matrices. If one takes the argument one stage further, we have to consider the reproduction of the *change* in the form of class relationships. In this case, the reproduction of an interrupter matrix is through weak classification and weak frames. However, it is possible that such a form of reproduction may at some point evoke its own interrupter i.e. an increase in either classification or frame strength, or both.

Appendix: A Note on the Coding of Objects and Modalities of Control

The coding of objects

The concepts of classification and frame can be used to interpret communication between objects. In other words, objects and their relationships to each other constitute a message system whose code can be stated in terms of the relationship between classification and frames of different strengths.

We can consider:

1. The strength of the rules of exclusion which control the array of objects in a space. Thus the stronger the rules of exclusion the more distinctive the array of objects in the space; that is, the greater the difference between object arrays in different spaces.
2. The extent to which objects in the array can enter into different relationships to each other.

Now the stronger the rules of exclusion the stronger the *classification* of objects in that space and the greater the difference between object arrays in different spaces. In the same way in which we discussed relationships between subjects we can discuss the relationships between object arrays in different spaces. Thus the stronger the classification the more the object arrays resemble a collection code, the weaker the classification the more the object arrays resemble an integrated code. The greater the number of different relationships objects in the array can enter into with each other the weaker their framing. The fewer the number of different relationships objects in the array can enter into with each other the stronger their framing.*

We would expect that the social distribution of power and the principles of control be reflected in the coding of objects. This code may be made more delicate if we take into account:

1. The number of objects in the array.
2. The rate of change of the array.

We can have strong classification with a large *or* a small number of objects. We can have strong classification of large or small arrays where the array is fixed across time *or* where the array varies across time. Consider, for example, two arrays which are strongly classified: a late Victorian middle-class living-room and a middle twentieth-century trendy middle-class 'space' in Hampstead. The Victorian room is likely to contain a very large number of objects whereas the middle-class room is likely to contain a small number of objects. In one case the object array is foreground and the space background,

* If the objects in the array can be called lexical items, then the syntax is their relationships to each other. A restricted code is a syntax with few choices: an elaborated code a syntax which generates a large number of choices.

whereas in the second case the space is a vital component of the array. The Victorian room represents both strong classification and strong framing. Further, whilst objects may be added to the array, its fundamental characteristics would remain constant over a relatively long time period. The Hampstead room is likely to contain a small array which would indicate strong classification (strong rules of exclusion) but the objects are likely to enter into a variety of relationships with each other; this would indicate weak framing. Further, it is possible that the array would be changed across time according to fashion.

We can now see that if we are to consider classification (C) we need to know:

1. Whether it is strong or weak
2. Whether the array is small or large (x)
3. Whether the array is fixed or variable (y)

At the level of frame (F) we need to know: Whether it is strong or weak (p); that is, whether the coding is restricted or elaborated.

It is also important to indicate in the specification of the code the context (c) to which it applies. We should also indicate the nature of the array by adding the concept realisation (r). Thus, the most abstract formulation of the object code would be as follows:

$$f(c, r, C(x, y), F(p))$$

The code is some unspecified function of the variables enclosed in the brackets.

It is important to note that because the classification is weak it does not mean that there is less control. Indeed, from this point of view it is not possible to talk about amount of control, only of its modality. This point we will now develop.

Classification, frames and modalities of control

Imagine four lavatories. The first is stark, bare, pristine, the walls are painted a sharp white; the washbowl is like the apparatus, a gleaming white. A square block of soap sits cleanly in an indentation in the sink. A white towel (or perhaps pink) is folded neatly on a chrome rail or hangs from a chrome ring. The lavatory paper is hidden in a cover and peeps through its slit. In the second lavatory there are books on a shelf and some relaxing of the rigours of the first. In the third lavatory there are books on the shelf, pictures on the wall and perhaps a scattering of tiny objects. In the fourth lavatory the rigour is *totally relaxed*. The walls are covered with a motley array of postcards, there is a various assortment of reading matter and curio. The lavatory roll is likely to be uncovered and the holder may well fall apart in use.

We can say that as we move from the first to the fourth lavatory we are moving from a strongly classified to a weakly classified space: from a space regulated by strong rules of exclusion to a space regulated by weak rules of exclusion. Now if the rules of exclusion are strong then the space is strongly marked off from other spaces in the house or flat. The *boundary* between the spaces or rooms is sharp. If the rules of exclusion are strong, the boundaries well marked, then it follows that there must be strong boundary maintainers (authority). If things are to be kept apart then there must be some strong hierarchy to ensure the apartness of things. Further, the first lavatory constructs a space where pollution is highly visible. In as much as a user leaves a personal mark (a failure to replace the towel in its original position, a messy bar of soap, scum in the washbowl, lavatory paper floating in the bowl, etc.) this constitutes pollution and such pollution is quickly perceived. Thus the criteria for competent usage of the space are both *explicit* and *specific*. So far we have been discussing aspects of classification; we shall now consider framing.

Whereas classification tells us about the structure of relationships in *space*, framing tells us about the structure of relationships in *time*. Framing refers us to interaction, to the power relationships of interaction; that is, framing refers us to communication. Now in the case of our lavatories, framing *here* would refer to the communication between the occupants of the space and those outside of the space. Such communication is normally strongly framed by a door usually equipped with a lock. We suggest that as we move from the strongly classified to the weakly classified lavatory, despite the potential insulation between inside and outside, there will occur a reduction in frame strength. In the case of the first lavatory we suggest that the door will always be closed and after entry will be locked. Ideally no effects on the inside should be heard on the outside. Indeed, a practised user of this lavatory will acquire certain competencies in order to meet this requirement. However, in the case of the most weakly classified lavatory, we suggest that the door will normally be open; it may even be that the lock will not function. It would not be considered untoward for a conversation to develop or even be continued either side of the door. A practised user of this most weakly classified and weakly framed lavatory will acquire certain communicative competencies rather different from those required for correct use of the strongly classified one.

We have already noted that lavatory one creates a space where pollution is highly visible, where criteria for behaviour are explicit and specific, where the social basis of the authority maintaining the strong classification and frames is hierarchical. Yet it is also the case that such classification and frames create a *private* although impersonal space. *For providing that the classification and framing is not violated the user of the space is beyond surveillance.*

However, when we consider lavatory four which has the weakest classification and weakest frames it seems at first sight that such a structure celebrates weak control. There appear to be few rules regulating what goes into a space and few rules regulating communication between spaces. Therefore it is difficult to consider what counts as a violation or pollution. Indeed, it would appear that such a classification and framing relationship facilitates the development of spontaneous behaviour. Let us consider this possibility.

Lavatory one is predicated on the rule 'things must be kept apart' be they persons, acts, objects, communication, and the stronger the classification and frames the greater the insulation, the stronger the boundaries between classes of persons, acts, objects, communications. Lavatory four is predicated on the rule that approximates to 'things must be put together'. As a consequence, we would find objects in the space that could be found in other spaces. Further, there is a more relaxed marking off of the space and communication is possible between inside and outside. We have as yet not discovered the fundamental principles of violation.

Imagine one user, who seeing the motley array and being sensitive to what he or she takes to be a potential of the space decides to add to the array and places an additional postcard on the wall. It is possible that a little later a significant adult might say 'Darling, that's beautiful but it doesn't quite fit' or 'How lovely but wouldn't it be better a little higher up?' In other words, we are suggesting that the array has a principle, that the apparently motley collection is ordered but that the principle is implicit and although it is not easily discoverable it is capable of being violated. Indeed, it might take our user a very long time to infer the *tacit* principle and generate choices in accordance with it. Without knowledge of the principle our user is unlikely to make appropriate choices and such choices may require a long period of socialisation. In the case of lavatory one no principle is required; all that is needed is the following of the command 'Leave the space as you found it'.

Now let us examine the weak framing in more detail. We suggest that locking the door, avoiding or ignoring communication, would count as violation; indeed anything which would offend the principle of *things must be put together*. However, in as much as the framing between inside and outside is weak then it is also the case that the user is potentially or indirectly under continuous surveillance, in which case there is no privacy. Here we have a social context which at first sight appears to be very relaxed, which promotes and provokes the expression of the person, 'a do your own thing' space where highly personal choices may be offered, where hierarchy is not explicit yet on analysis we find that it is based upon a form of implicit control which carries the potential of total surveillance. Such a form of implicit control encourages more of the person to be made manifest yet such manifestations are subject to continuous screening and general rather than specific criteria. *At the level of classification the pollution is 'keeping things apart'; at the level of framing the pollution is 'withholding'; that is, not offering, not making visible the self.*

If things are to be put together which were once set apart, then there must be some principle of the new relationships, but this principle cannot be mechanically applied and and therefore cannot be mechanically learned. In the case of the rule 'things must be kept apart', then the apartness of things is something which is clearly marked and taken for granted in the process of initial socialisation. The social basis of the categories of apartness is implicit but the social basis of the authority is explicit. In the process of such socialisation the insulation between things is a condensed message about the all-pervasiveness of the authority. It may require many years before the social basis of the principles underlying the category system is made fully explicit and by that time the mental structure is well-initiated into the classification and frames. Strong classification and frames celebrate the *reproduction* of the past.

When the rule is 'things must be put together' we have an *interruption* of a previous order, and what is of issue is the authority (power relationships) which underpin it. Therefore the rule 'things must be put together' celebrates the present over the past, the subjective over the objective, the personal over the positional. Indeed when everything is put together we have a total organic principle which covers all aspects of life *but* which admits of a vast range of combinations and re-combinations. This points to a very abstract or general principle from which a vast range of possibilities may be derived so that individuals can both register personal choices *and* have knowledge when a combination is not in accordance with the principle. What is taken for granted when the rule is 'things must be kept apart' is *relationships* which themselves are made explicit when the rule is 'things must be put together'. They are made explicit by the weak classification and frames. But the latter creates a form of implicit but potentially continuous surveillance and at the same time promotes the making public of the self in a variety of ways. We arrive finally at the conclusion that the conditions for the release of the person are the absence of explicit hierarchy but the presence of a more intensified form of social interaction which creates continuous but invisible screening. From the point of view of the socialised they would be offering novel, spontaneous combinations.

Empirical Note: It is possible to examine the coding of objects from two perspectives. We can analyse the coding of overt or visible arrays and we can compare the code with the codings of covert or invisible arrays (e.g. drawers, cupboards, refrigerators, basements, closets, handbags, etc.). We can also compare the coding of verbal messages with the coding of non-verbal messages. It would be interesting to carry out an empirical study of standardised spaces, e.g. local council housing estates, middle class suburban 'town' house estate, modern blocks of flats, formal education spaces which vary in their architecture and in the pedagogy.

I am well aware that the lavatory may not be seen as a space to be *specially contrived* and so subject to *special regulation* in the sense discussed. Some lavatories are not subject to the principles I have outlined. Indeed some may be casually treated spaces where pieces of newspaper may be stuffed behind a convenient pipe, where the door does not close or lock, where apparatus has low efficiency and where sound effects are taken for granted events.

Acknowledgments: This paper was written on the suggestion of Henri Nathan for a Meeting on the effects of scholarisation, itself, a part of the International Learning Sciences Programme, C.E.R.I., O.E.C.D. I am grateful to Henri Nathan for his insistence on the need to understand the artefacts of learning. The paper appeared originally as No. 2 in the series *Studies in the Learning Sciences*, CERI/OECD, Paris, 1975.

The basis of this paper was written whilst I was a visitor to the Ecole Pratique des Hautes Etudes (Centre de Sociologie Européenne under the direction of Pierre Bourdieu). I am very grateful to Peter Corbishley, graduate student in the Department of the Sociology of Education, for his help in the explication of the concept of an 'interrupter system'. The definition used in this paper owes much to his clarification. Finally I would like to thank Gerald Elliot, Professor of Physics at The Open University, who whilst in no way ultimately responsible assisted in the formal expression of an 'object code'.

Daniel Kallós

9. On Educational Phenomena and Educational Research

Introduction

Scientific research has been regarded as a

> . . . sequence of transformations of complexes composed by knowledge, problems, and instruments. The term 'instrument' refers to hardware tools used in laboratories, and to software tools such as mathematical and statistical techniques. It will be assumed that research is concerned with a part of the real world. Knowledge may then be described as an authorized map over a territory. (Törnebohm, 1971, p. 2)

If we look upon Education as a discipline we may state that it is concerned with a part of the real world. It is concerned with activities like teaching, training and child-rearing. The production of knowledge within a discipline aims, according to Törnebohm (*op. cit.*), at the creation of an increasingly refined map of its territory. The production of knowledge is regarded as governed by certain scientific ideals or perspectives expressed in terms of acceptable research strategies and methods, and is furthermore also governed by the organizational forms in which the scientific efforts take place.

In recent years knowledge production within the discipline of Education has been criticized. Thus, e.g. Shulman (1970) advocated a necessary reconstruction of educational research, which in his opinion had failed in producing workable theories and had made only small contributions to the improvement of the daily practice of e.g. teaching. In his paper he argued that researchers

> . . . must step back, regain perspective and then identify clearly the most fruitful routes toward development of an empirically based discipline of education. (*ibid.*, pp. 371–2)

Shulman, however, did not question the basic scientific ideals or perspectives underlying educational research. His criticism was well within the limits of an established paradigm (Kuhn, 1970). Other critics have gone beyond such limits. Dunkel (1972) questioned what he labelled as a 'narrow view of science'. He argued that if scientific research in education primarily had to be descriptive, value-free, nomothetic and furthermore mainly deal with statistical manipulation of quantified data it would leave '. . . largely untouched some areas of major concern to education.' (*ibid.*, p. 80)

Dunkel called for 'new' paradigms and a 'normative base for educational research'. In a somewhat similar vein Gowin (1972; 1973) also attacked the dominant philosophy of science as the only acceptable basis of educational research. He, however, suggested that researchers should start with an analysis of what is distinctively educational rather than discuss only what is and is not scientific. In their discussions both Dunkel and Gowin identified serious shortcomings of the narrow view of science when applied to the study of educational phenomena. They did not, however, identify or seriously discuss alternatives to the dominant philosophy. In a recent book of readings in *Philosophy of Educational Research* sponsored by the American Educational Research Association (AERA) and edited by Broudy, Ennis and Krimerman (1973) at least one such alternative is identified by the inclusion of excerpts from Dilthey. It is rather ironical that hermeneutics (and critical theory) are being introduced today as alternatives for educational researchers in the United States. In Germany (and subsequently in the Federal Republic of Germany) Education was looked upon as a '*Geisteswissenschaft*' and thus it was the adherents of a narrow view of science who had to fight for recognition within the discipline in the fifties and sixties (*cf.* Klafki, 1971; Ulich, 1972).

In Great Britain it is perhaps first and foremost educational sociologists who have advocated a break with traditional views, and tried to introduce a 'new sociology of education' (e.g. Young, 1971). It is indeed not difficult to share much of the critique against structural functionalist approaches and/or the empiricist tradition as

> . . . engaged in a series of 'fact finding' and 'head counting' missions producing a great deal of statistical information about, for example, differential class chances for educational attainment, but offereing little by way of theoretical or conceptual breakthroughs for interpreting such data. (Sharp and Green, 1975, p. 2)

But it is not as easy to accept the claims of the new sociologists when it comes to suggestions concerning what ought to be done and how, because as e.g. Sharp and Green note, these 'new' developments seem to hold in common a

> . . . heritage in German Idealism, developed in social science in the work of G. H. Mead, M. Weber and A. Schutz, and second, their substantive concern with the problem of subjective meaning as basic for an understanding of the social world. (*ibid.*, p. 3)

In a paper on current trends in Swedish educational research tendencies similar to those mentioned above were discussed. The 'new' Swedish trends were labelled as a 'rose coloured wave' in educational research and practice (Callewaert and Kallós, 1976).

A study of educational research within the capitalist countries thus reveals an attempt to break with (or at least a critique towards) the dominant philosophy of science ('the narrow view') often accompanied by a proposed 'new' set of 'models', 'paradigms' or theories borrowing heavily from e.g.

symbolic interactionism, ethnomethodology, hermeneutics, phenomenology, existentialism etc. The picture emerging is a seemingly blurred one. In this paper I will try to analyse some of the tendencies, using as a starting point the perspectives and ideals adopted by the 'new critics'. In my analysis I will furthermore use examples from various areas of educational research, thus attempting to cover not only various 'new' tendencies on the theoretical level but also different problem areas within the field of educational research.

For the sake of convenience I will define the task of education as a science to describe the educational practices prevailing in the society in question and to work out theories that can explain the casual relationships giving rise to such practice. The immediate causes are, in their turn, rooted in the overall structure of the society.

Educational phenomena and educational research

An advantage of the older logical empiric research tradition, now under trendy attack, was that it bore a rather uncomplicated relationship to the question of whether educational research is a normative or a theoretic-explanatory endeavour. The matter of concern was to be able to make predictions on the basis of empirical data. When the goals of educational practice had been defined by politicians for example, the results of research were useful because researchers could say something about the means which should be utilized to achieve the goals. In this way the discipline could function both theoretically-explanatory and normatively. The issue of selection of objectives (goals) is, within this tradition, not a scientific issue. The only aspects of this issue that may be studied scientifically have to do with the possibility of reaching a certain objective at a certain age level and with given resources. Research may accordingly rule out some objectives (goals).

At one level the dilemma confronting educational researchers might be described in terms of the relations between explicit aims of schooling and its observable effects. When it became obvious that the high hopes pinned on education were not fulfilled this was also regarded as a scientific failure. The rational view of educational planning embedded in the dominant tradition implies that decisions concerning schooling, curricula and instruction are to be based on scientific research. When and if schools are malfunctioning this is considered as an abnormal state of affairs that in principle may be corrected by rational decisions based on educational research. The task of the educational researcher is not only to detect and describe the state of affairs but also to provide the remedy. The educational researcher as a critic assumes and argues that schools have failed in carrying out their mission and that they are in need of radical change. It is assumed that reform (or change) will alter the situation and that reforms (or changes) with such an effect are possibly within present-day capitalist society. Judging from the size of the literature trying to reconstruct educational research and educational practice, there seem to exist almost endless possibilities within present day society. There is always at least one classroom, one group of teachers, or one particular school which can be offered as proof that change is possible.

Several issues have emerged from the current debate on educational research. One of the key issues concerns the problem arising from attempted analyses of the relations between society, state and the educational apparatus. Gintis (1972) wrote that educational reformers commonly err in treating education as if it existed in a social vacuum. Educational research takes place within a social context: educational researchers commonly err in not recognizing this fact. But educational researchers often err also by only paying lip service to the acknowledged fact that there exists 'some kind of relation' between society and education. When directing the research efforts towards the classroom or the teachers the discussion about state and society seem to be almost forgotten.

The issue of the relations between society, state and schooling have traditionally been dealt with using one or another variant of an equilibrium theory of society as opposed to what has been labelled a conflict theory (*cf.* Collins, 1971; Paulston, 1976). Another way of presenting a dichotomy would be to confront Marxist and non-Marxist theories. In my opinion it is quite obvious that the renewed interest in Marxism-Leninism during the sixties and seventies has provided powerful analyses also of the educational apparatus in the capitalist societies of today.

But if answers to the problems of the relations between society, state and education are to be sought within Marxist theory and discussed within the discipline of education a somewhat strange set of problems emerge. Judging from the literature in education it seems that two preliminary steps need to be taken before it is possible to discuss the relations between society, state and schooling within a Marxist frame of reference. The first of these two steps would involve an account of Marxism-Leninism and the second a discussion of the differences between Marxist and non-Marxist theories of society. This is in a way symptomatic. Educational literature often contains references to society as well as discussions about the effects of various educational reforms upon society. But these discussions only rarely take into account the Marxist tradition[1].

At the same time another tendency may be noted. This tendency was clearly observed and attacked by Lenin (1918) in his important analysis of 'The State and Revolution'. Lenin vigorously attacked the distortions, corruptions and misrepresentations of Marxism. Current variants on this theme are the attempts to reconcile historical materialism with e.g. symbolic interactionism, or the attempts to reduce Marxism to a theory of society in desperate need of a theory of the Person. On the other hand the educational literature of today, especially in the area of teaching (i.e. the literature directed towards what is commonly referred to as the 'micro level') deals very perfunctorily with non-Marxist theories of society. Therborn (1973) noted a similar tendency in sociology, and coupled it to the emergence of what he labelled as a 'sociology as a middle strata experience'. Within the domain of pedagogical practice Bernstein (1975, 1977) has described a corresponding trend which he called an 'invisible pedagogy'. What I have elsewhere described as a 'rose coloured wave in Swedish pedagogical research' is another example (Callewaert and Kallós, 1976).

It is, of course, impossible within the scope and limits of this paper to deal with what I mentioned as the preliminary steps. The purpose was primarily to point to some of the difficulties confronting the writer who on the one hand attempts to use a Marxist theory and at the same time on the other hand is aware of the fact that he addresses an audience which may (or may not) be familiar with Marxism-Leninism.

The discussion concerning the relations of society, state and the educational sector within the Marxist tradition follows at least two major lines in so far as the capitalist societies are studied. On the one hand a number of economists and educationalists in the Federal Republic of Germany tried to re-establish a critical political economy which also included an attempted analysis of the educational sector. This school which has sometimes been called 'state interventionist' has produced numerous books and papers directly dealing with education (e.g. Altvater & Huisken, 1971; Huisken, 1972; Heinrich, 1973; Masuch, 1973; Rolff *et al.*, 1974; Thien, 1976). These approaches tell us something about the general economic reasons which underlie expansion, reform and crises within the educational apparatus. They also represent a powerful challenge to the dominant mode of reasoning within the field of economics of education[2]. But the educational apparatus also fulfils 'crucial functions on the symbolical-ideological level, that serves to support the reproduction of economic and legal-political power relations in the society.' (Berner *et al.*, 1977, p. 12. My translation.) This notion illustrates the second perspective, developed mainly in France and associated with the writings of Althusser (1971) and Poulantzas (1974, 1975). The direct analyses of education by Baudelot and Establet (1971, 1975) should also be mentioned in this context.

In a now famous and often quoted paper Althusser discusses the school as an ideological State apparatus playing a central part in the reproduction of the relations of production[3]. Althusser advances the thesis that

> . . . the ideological State apparatus which has been installed in the dominant position in mature capitalist formations as a result of a violent political and ideological class struggle against the old dominant ideological State apparatus, is the educational ideological apparatus. (Althusser, 1971, p. 152)

Although Althusser notes that this thesis may sound paradoxical he still holds, that

> . . . behind the scenes of its political Ideological State Apparatus, which occupies the front of the stage, what the bourgeoisie has installed as its number-one, i.e. as its dominant ideological State apparatus, is the educational apparatus, which has in

> fact replaced in its functions the previously dominant ideological State apparatus, the Church. One might even add: the School-Family couple has replaced the Church-Family couple. (*ibid.*, pp. 153–4)

As an ideological State apparatus the educational apparatus inculcates the ideology of the ruling class in such a way that two objectives are reached. First, all pupils must 'learn' this ideology and its modes of expression and conceptualisation. Secondly, the contents and effects of a proletarian ideology are suppressed wherever they appear. According to Baudelot and Establet (1971) the educational apparatus divides and selects the students *and* inculcates ideology (i.e. an explicit transmission of bourgeois ideology and the distortion and repression of a proletarian ideology). But this process is not a smooth one that takes place without effort. The educational apparatus is characterized by its contradictions and within it struggle and various forms of opposition are clearly visible, if not always analysed in terms of class and class struggle[4].

The analyses of Baudelot and Establet (1971) try to demonstrate that the unified school system in fact is comprised of two separate systems that correspond to the two antagonistic classes in French society—the bourgeoisie and the working class. The division, which the authors tried to verify both empirically and theoretically, in their view is clearly related to the division between mental and manual labour. The two systems reflect this separation, which furthermore is visible in the contents and in the pedagogy within the systems. Poulantzas (1975) regarded the reasoning about the two systems as basically correct, but added that

> . . . the 'bipolar' division involved here is a tendential one, and takes specific forms for the various social classes affected. This is where the argument of these writers seems to fall short. Their conclusion directly leads them to obscure the specific place of the new petty bourgeoisie in the educational apparatus. (*ibid.*, p. 260)

Poulantzas maintains that a whole series of indices point to a quite specific education of the new petty bourgeoisie[5]. His argument leads him to the conclusion that the educational apparatus

> . . . plays quite a specific role for the new petty bourgeoisie, directly contributing to reproducing its place in the social formation. This is directly reflected in the role that this apparatus plays in distributing agents among places of the social classes, a role which is very important for the new petty bourgeoisie, while it remains a secondary one for both the bourgeoisie and the working class. The agents of these two basic classes, or alternatively their children, are not themselves distributed by the educational system in any literal sense, or rather they are distributed while remaining in the same place, everything happening as if they were bound to these places, with the school simply sanctioning and legitimizing this connection. The petty-bourgeois agents, on the other hand exhibit . . . a quite remarkable shift, directly bound up with the educational apparatus. These are real processes with considerable repercussions on the ideology of the new petty bourgeoisie, an ideology directly bound up with its special relationship to 'knowledge', 'instruction', 'culture' and the educational apparatus. (*ibid.*, p. 269)

Althusser (1971) as well as Baudelot and Establet (1971) argued that the educational apparatus is the dominant ideological apparatus. This is a questionable position within the capitalist mode of production as far as the reproduction, distribution and training of agents is concerned (Poulantzas, 1975, p. 269). Poulantzas notes that the dominance of any one ideological state apparatus is dependent on the class struggle in specific social formations. He furthermore states that the dominant apparatus may vary even within a particular social formation. The education apparatus is according to him the dominant apparatus for the petty bourgeoisie in France, but it is not so '. . . for the working class, either in France or in the other capitalist countries. It would seem in fact that for the working class, this dominant role falls directly to the economic apparatus itself, to the "enterprise"' (*ibid.*, p. 270). This does, of course not imply, that schools are 'unimportant' from the point of view of the working class. On the contrary. The capitalist school emphasizes and qualifies mental labour, while at the same time it disqualifies manual labour. To the majority of the working class the school teaches '. . . the veneration of a mental labour that is always "somewhere else"' (*ibid.*, p. 266). While the school cannot even provide the worker with sufficient technical or professional skills (manual labour) it is fully equipped to train the new petty bourgeoisie.

I have briefly (perhaps too briefly) outlined a few elements in the theory of the educational apparatus as an ideological State apparatus. In my opinion the propositions put forward in the analyses mentioned here provide educational research and theory with powerful instruments. To apply them would mean to analyse concretely the existing situation within different societies.

A common misunderstanding is that it is the school that creates ideology, and that the school therefore might change the ideology[6]. This is a view strongly refuted by all of the writers referred to here. Poulantzas accordingly states:

> In referring to ideological apparatuses, we must recognize that these apparatuses neither create ideology, nor are they even the sole or primary factors in reproducing relations of ideological domination and subordination. Ideological apparatuses only serve to fashion and inculcate (materialize) the dominant ideology. (*ibid.*, p. 31)

Ideology is thus not invented by the school or by any other ideological apparatus. It is concrete processes and power relations at all levels in the society that determine how ideology and symbolical relations are formed, maintained, and changed. It is thus, to repeat, a misunderstanding that it is the schools that bear the responsibility for the origin, shaping, and upholding of existing ideals and values in society as such.

In the following section I will try to use the perspective outlined here, and thus at a more concrete level contribute to the discussion of educational research.

Comments on the issues of the tasks of educational research

In the introductory section of this paper I stated that the task of education as a science was to describe educational practices in the society and to work out theories that can explain the causal relationships giving rise to such practice. I noted that the immediate causes were rooted in the overall structure of the society. In the foregoing section I advanced the explanation of educational practices in terms of regarding the educational apparatus as an ideological state apparatus. I used the ideas put forward by Althusser (1971), Baudelot and Establet (1971) and Poulantzas (1975) to illuminate that perspective.

A common critique towards the position developed by these authors is that they do not provide teachers and pupils with advice for action (*cf.* note 2). Thus Erben and Gleeson (1977) argue that the analysis by Althusser (1971)

> ... inhibits teachers and students from considering the possibility that they may be concerned with struggle and change. Its message not only leaves teachers completely flattened and speechless, but it is likely to reinforce the idea that radical change is beyond their frames of reference. (Erben and Gleeson, 1977, pp. 74–5)

Firstly, it may of course be asked if this statement corresponds with the position adopted by Althusser. Secondly, it seems appropriate to ask how teachers and students are chosen as the primary agents for change. Thirdly, it may be asked if teachers and students can be treated like teachers and students if radical change is discussed. Enter the concepts of class, and class struggle (curiously missing in the Erben and Gleeson paper). Fourthly, it may be asked if it is the task of the educational researcher to propose blue-prints for radical action. Questions like these may be asked not only in conjunction with the paper by Erben and Gleeson, but seem relevant after reading several allegedly radical texts, including the volume where the Erben-Gleeson text is presented (Young and Whitty, 1977) [7].

It seems quite evident that neither Althusser nor Poulantzas deny the possibility for change. Althusser thus explicitly states: '... Ideological State Apparatuses may be not only the *stake*, but also the *site* of class struggle, and often of bitter forms of class struggle' (Althusser, 1971, p. 147). Althusser even explicitly mentions the school in this context, e.g. in noting '. . . the class struggle in the ISAs is indeed an aspect of the class struggle, sometimes an important and symptomatic one: e.g. . . . the "crisis" of the educational ISA in every capitalist country today' (*ibid.*, p. 185). Thus, the educational apparatus is not only regarded as the site of struggle, but, indeed, viewed in direct relation to the ongoing struggle within the capitalist societies. But to mention class and class struggle is something else than to mention 'teachers' and 'pupils'[8].

The second question concerned how teachers and students are chosen as the primary agents of radical change. The radical potentiality of teachers as a group is highly questionable. What is involved here is the issue of a possible conjunctural alliance between a certain group of teachers and the working class. Such an alliance is by no means certain as history has proven. This does not imply that there are no teachers who have joined e.g. the Communist Party in past times or at present[9]. But it implies that the whole issue of involvement of teachers in the class struggle is a matter that cannot be solved individually[10].

The third question is already touched upon. Any discussion about the potentiality for radical change within the schools via teachers and pupils must take into account the differences between teachers, and the differences between pupils. That is, the problem must be treated in terms of class, class struggle, and conjunctural class alliances.

The fourth question concerns the task of educational research in connection with radical action within the schools. This question is in a way similar to the questions asked and answered above concerning teachers. But, a couple of important additional remarks may be made. It should be realized that neither researchers nor research itself initiates or realizes system-related or radical change. Instead it is the large social forces in the society which contribute to this with certain degrees of freedom and within certain limitations. The task of the educational researcher is to describe and explain this reality, which also implies to define the scope for action which actually exists. But this scope for action is not identical with that of the State apparatus, nor is it the same for different social classes. Analyses of this kind may very well reveal that the changes that are taking place are all but radical (*cf.* Kallós and Lundgren, 1977, 1978). In its turn that would point to a conclusion which is more seldom mentioned in the educational literature. An important task for the radical teacher may very well be the fight against reactionary tendencies. But such a struggle is perhaps less appealing to the teacher who has read in the educational literature that he might be engaged in aiding the working class child by exposing oppression and by the application of the famous new methods.

It should furthermore be pointed out that in our society research work takes place within the framework of the prevailing social distribution of work. This means that research is carried out by academically trained people with access to economic and intellectual resources and institutionally more or less clearly related to the State apparatus and, thereby, to the ruling class. Even Marxist researchers cannot in the present-day situation avoid these institutional conditions and the existing distribution of work[11]. The space open for genuinely critical research is not large. In Sweden approximately 60 per cent of all the funding to educational research is administered by the National Board of Education (NBE). According to two liberal and prominent Swedish professors of education this means

> . . . that assignments are mainly given to researchers who agree with the basic view of the NBE. . . . Research which is critical of the NBE's basic view is not supported, it is very soon checked. This is certainly not done intentionally—there have been

> cases of support being awarded to critical research. The main impediment lies in the fact that critical research cannot be integrated with the top priority problem areas, and also in the fact that there are so few bodies apart from the NBE which can provide financial resources for research of this kind. (Ahlström and Wallin, 1976, pp. 84–5)

One of the prime functions of educational research has been (and still is) to legitimate existing practice and suggested change. Research furthermore serves the purpose of upholding the myths of schooling and today also the illusions about possible radical change within the educational apparatus. In an era when signs of crisis within the society are constantly visible also as crises within the schools, educational researchers have had little success in providing the solutions asked for. The legitimating capacity of the educational research community is being questioned (decrease in funding, etc.). Even the very rationale of linking research to decisions concerning organization, curricular change etc. is being questioned. Irrationalism is visible also within the field of education (*cf.* Balibar, 1978). But what is supplied is still an ideological defence for the established society.

Acknowledgement: An earlier version of this paper was written with the support of a grant from the Department of Educational Research and Development of the National Board of Universities and Colleges, as a part of a research project concerning the 'Relative Merits of Various Teaching Methods in Higher Education'.

Notes

1. The situation in this respect obviously differs between countries. E.g. Paulston (1976, p. 26) notes that 'In the United States . . . Marxist perspectives on social and educational change have been largely rejected and/or ignored.'
A study like that by Bowles and Gintis (1976) is perhaps more of an exception than an indicator of change in this respect. The situation in Sweden is rather similar to that in the United States (*cf.* Kallós and Lundgren, 1977). The situation seems somewhat different in the Federal Republic of Germany and in France. At the same time the increasing repression in the Federal Republic of Germany (Ban of Professional Employment—*'Berufsverbot'* and similar measures) has been effective in curtailing the debate as well as experimentation within the schools (*cf.* Alff *et al.*, 1975).
2. The school of thought represented by e.g. Altvater and Huisken has been very influential on educational research in Denmark, whereas it has had comparatively less influence in Sweden. To the best of my knowledge none of the important papers or books within this tradition as it refers to education has been translated into English. Although sceptical towards a number of conclusions contained in the books mentioned I would hold that any serious Marxist scholar in education ought to study also this literature. I will return to some of the critical issues in a later section of this paper.

3. In this rather long note I will take up three issues.

Firstly, it is important to note that the main distinction that Althusser (1971) makes is between the Repressive State Apparatus and the Ideological State Apparatuse*s*. He thus argues that it is '. . . necessary to distinguish between State power (and its possession by . . .) on the one hand, and the State Apparatus on the other. But I add that the State Apparatus contains two bodies: the body of institutions which represent the Repressive State Apparatus on the one hand, and the body of institutions which represent the body of Ideological State Apparatuses on the other.' (*ibid.*, pp. 147–8)

The ideological State apparatuses function predominantly by ideology, but they also function secondarily by repression. Poulantzas (1975) has 'developed' the propositions made by Althusser (1971). He makes the following distinctions relevant to the issue of Ideological State Apparatuses: 'The principal role of the state apparatuses is to maintain the unity and cohesion of a social formation by concentrating and sanctioning class domination, and in this way reproducing social relations, i.e. class relations. Political and ideological relations are materialized and embodied as material practices, in the state apparatuses. These apparatuses include, on the one hand, the repressive state apparatus in the strict sense and its branches: army, police, prisons, judiciary, civil service; on the other hand, the ideological state apparatuses: the educational apparatus, the religious apparatus (the churches), the information apparatus (radio, television, press), the cultural apparatus (cinema, theatre, publishing), the trade-union apparatus of class collaboration and the bourgeois and petty-bourgeois political parties, as well as in a certain respect, at least in the capitalist mode of production, the family. But as well as the state apparatuses, there is also the economic apparatus in the most strict sense of the term, the "business" or the "factory" which, as the centre of appropriation of nature, materializes and embodies the economic relations in their articulation with politico-ideological relations.' (Poulantzas, 1975, pp. 24–5)

He furthermore adds that the '. . . apparatuses are never anything other than the materialization and condensation of class relations; in a sense, they "presuppose" them, so long as it is understood that what is involved here is not a relation of chronological causality (the chicken or the egg). Now according to a current of bourgeois ideology in the "social sciences", which might be loosely referred to as the "institutionalist-functionalist" current, it is apparatuses and institutions that determine social groups (classes), with class relations arising from the situation of agents in institutional relationships. This current exhibits in specific forms the couple idealism/empiricism, in the specific form of humanism/economism, both of which are characteristic of bourgeois ideology.' (*ibid.*, pp. 25–6)

Secondly, it should be noted that the original distinctions, definitions and propositions made by Althusser (1971), which he himself considered as nothing 'more than the introduction to a discussion' and as 'notes towards an investigation' have triggered off a heated debate (*cf.* also Althusser's comments on this debate in Althusser, 1977). The discussion has also reached the educational research community in Great Britain. Thus Erben and Gleeson (1977) published a critical examination of Althusser's position. They incorrectly state that Althusser fails to take into account '. . . the possibilities for dynamic changes within situations themselves.' (*ibid.*, p. 89)

They add, in a similar vein, that 'It is one thing to describe education as reproduction, but it is another to explain this phenomenon as transcendable.' (*ibid.*, p. 89)

I will return to this issue in a later section of the paper. But it should be made clear, that it is by no means self-evident, that an analysis of the educational apparatus as an

Ideological State Apparatus, must include a blue-print for social action, which in a way is what Erben and Gleeson demand.

Thirdly, I would like to point out that several of the issues that Althusser touches upon in his paper are debatable. His concept of ideology, has recently been discussed by Hirst (1976a; 1976b), and his discussion is helpful to clarify some of the problems. I have already noted, that Poulantzas (1974, 1975) has made critical remarks which directly bear on the position outlined by Althusser in his paper on Ideological State Apparatuses. These discussions—as well as others—transcend the rather simplistic notions made by Erben and Gleeson (1977). Although the essay by Althusser may be somewhat overrated it still has been extremely powerful in stimulating Marxist debate concerning the State and ideology.

4. It is interesting to note that the general works of Poulantzas and Althusser have been rapidly translated into English. More specialized books, dealing with education in a specific country and trying to analyse that education in a concrete fashion (a necessary step) is perhaps not regarded as sufficiently 'interesting' to merit translation. To my knowledge only a small excerpt of the book by Baudelot and Establet (1971) has been translated into English and included in a collection of papers edited by Gleeson (1977).

5. Poulantzas (1975) identifies the 'new petty bourgeoisie' and the 'old petty bourgeoisie' as forming a class. This is a highly debatable point. Other Marxist analyses would identify 'the new petty bourgeoisie' as belonging to the middle strata (*cf.* e.g. Therborn, 1971; 1976). The class analysis by Poulantzas (1975) has been criticised by Wright (1976). Several of the essays in Hunt (1977) also take up Poulantzas' position, and he himself comments on the critique in the same volume.

The discussion by Poulantzas (1975) concerning the 'old' and the 'new' petty bourgeoisie is somewhat similar to the distinction made by Bernstein (1975) between the 'old' and the 'new' middle class, although Bernstein does not undertake the endeavour of presenting a class analysis of Great Britain (*cf.* Bernstein, 1977).

For the purpose of this paper, it is sufficient to note the controversy concerning the identification of the 'new' petty bourgeoisie (or the 'new' middle class) as belonging to a separate class. I have argued elsewhere (Kallós, 1978) that the position adopted by Therborn (1971; 1976) is more tenable.

6. I have already noted that the concept of ideology as defined by Althusser has been critically examined (*cf.* note 3). I could also have referred the reader to the critical presentations in the volume coordinated by Schwarz (1977).

7. I particularly mention this volume since it in a sense is self critical. It contains a cautious critique of the positions advanced in an earlier volume edited by Young (1971). Several of the contributions to that volume are criticised in the new volume. For an additional and important critique of the earlier volume I refer the reader to Simon (1974).

8. The issue of struggle within the ISAs and the relation between the ISAs and class struggle is also dealt with by Poulantzas (1974, pp. 229–309) as well as in Poulantzas (1975). It is furthermore also clearly present in Baudelot and Establet (1971) and in their small book 'L'Ecole Primaire Divise . . .' (Baudelot and Establet, 1975) they even attempt to present guidelines for the struggle within the school (e.g. in chapter 9, significantly enough entitled 'Mettre l'école au service du peuple').

9. Thien (1976) has presented a careful attempt to analyse the position of the teacher and his function in the process of reproduction of capitalist society. He also discusses the position of teachers in the class struggle. The important point to make is

that the whole issue of teacher participation in class struggle in any alliance with the working class must be analysed concretely, i.e. with specific reference to the social formation in question. It is thus probable that the situation in Great Britain in this respect is different from that in France or in Sweden. Secondly, the group of teachers is by no means homogenous, a fact that also has to be taken into consideration.

10. Again it must be stressed that what is at stake here is organized class struggle, not the tasks of an individual teacher or an isolated group of teachers.

11. This does not imply that all research necessarily takes place within the universities or at R and D centres. But the main body of educational research is carried out within such institutions.

David Hamilton

10. Educational Research and the shadows of Francis Galton and Ronald Fisher

Since its emergence educational research in Britain has been guided by problems, methods and standards of solution derived from mainstream psychology. Indeed, William Taylor (currently Director of the University of London Institute of Education) has contended that 'at times . . . [before 1940] the psychologists came close to making claims that their concerns and research interests constituted the sole basis of educational practice' (Taylor, 1973, p. 12). Despite the post-war proliferation of research and the associated annexation of educational sociology, the steering influence of psychology has remained. In particular it has been exerted through the dual agencies of mental testing and field-experiment research. Recently, however, the traditional authority of psychological reasoning has been challenged.

While the merits of empirical studies in education have always been the subject of debate, many of the doubts have arisen beyond the conventional boundaries of research. They have come from philosophers (e.g. Bantock, 1965), from historians (e.g. Simon, 1953) or from those—often the object of research—who felt its activities were clumsy, dehumanising or just plain irrelevant (see Brehaut's review, 1973). Since much of this criticism originated from 'outsiders' (e.g. Hudson, 1966), it tended to be ignored. There was little or no debate. Those researchers who acknowledged the criticisms tended to justify the retention of the *status quo* on the pragmatic grounds that nothing more efficient was available.

Today the climate has changed. A subtle shift in the locus of debate has had major repercussions. The research community has begun to take the criticisms seriously. The worth, nature and scope of educational research have all become legitimate topics for books, journal articles and conference papers. While much of the disputation has been couched in technological terms and concerned, for example, with the interpretation of test scores, a significant element has focused on the taken-for-granted assumptions that underpin current practice. This critical stance (see, for example, Shaw, 1971; Brehaut, 1973; and Parlett, 1972) represents a new and vigorous departure—a sustained effort to search out and examine the 'deep structures' of educational research.

This short paper is conceived in the same tradition. It has two aims. First, to discuss the origin of the mental measurement and the experimental movements in educational research; and second, to consider their current methodological influence. The mental measurement movement began in the nineteenth century with Francis Galton's work on individual differences; the experimental movement 'took off' in the 1930s with the impetus offered by Ronald Fisher's research with agricultural botanists. In Britain both these educational research traditions were imported from psychology where they developed side by side in relative isolation (see Shulman, 1970, p. 327 ff.). Indeed, certain writers (e.g. Cattell, 1966; Cooley and Lohnes, 1971; and Cohen, 1971) have argued that mental testing and field experimentation are fundamentally different research styles. It is maintained that Galtonian methods are concerned with the inductive generation of hypotheses through the survey analysis of natural situations, whereas Fisherian ideas relate more to the deductive testing of hypotheses by means of controlled experimentation. Whether or not these traditions are analytically distinct—Neyman (1971) and Rao (1964), for example, stress their mathematical unity—it remains the case that their past and present impact upon educational research has been profound.

This paper begins by locating the work of Galton and Fisher within the intellectual and social debates of their epoch. It then examines the incorporation of their ideas into the research models of that time. Finally, it relocates the contributions of Galton and Fisher in the current fabric of educational research. Throughout, the issues raised by this analysis are regarded as symptomatic of a deep-seated (and largely uninvestigated) disjunction between the common-sense knowledge held by the educational community and the operational framework currently used by educational research.

Francis Galton and the Age of Correlation

In any history of educational research the name of Francis Galton (1822–1911) would feature prominently. Though his work has proved seminal, Galton cannot claim to be a founding father. This honour falls more accurately upon the associationist psychologist Alexander Bain (1818–1903). author of *Education as a Science* (1879). Associationism stood in contrast to Galton's ideas. It was a theory of mental life which maintained that sense impressions derived from the external world set off vibrations (or sensations) in the mind. Associationist ideas provided not only a psychological explanation for memory images but also a theoretical basis for educational doctrines which argued that experience formed the basis of human development. Despite the advocacy of John Stuart Mill and Herbert Spencer, the crudely mechanistic and environmentalistic ideas of associationism were replaced towards the end of the nineteenth century by a set of hereditarian ideas which drew their empirical support from the work of Francis Galton. From that time the influence of associationist ideas in educational research has been negligible.

(For discussions of the link between associationist psychology and the ideas of Francis Galton, see Simon. 1956; and Hearnshaw, 1964.)

Inheriting a sizeable fortune from his Quaker father, Galton abandoned his mathematical and medical studies at Cambridge and took up an amateur interest in science and foreign travel. For more than sixty years he pursued the study of geography, meteorology, anthropology, psychology and heredity. The culmination of these endeavours came when Galton used the ideas generated by his research to found the science of eugenics. While only part of his intellectual output, Galton's investigations into psychology would guarantee him a place in the history of ideas. His particular claims to fame relate to the following: he was one of the first people to develop quantitative methods for analysing mental attributes; he went on to pioneer a range of statistical procedures (e.g. ranking, percentiles, correlation) to codify the results of such analyses; and finally, he helped to provide an empirical rather than a theological basis for the belief that individual differences were innate and inherited.

It was the last of these that occupied his mind first. In 1869 Galton published *Hereditary Genius*, an analysis of the reputations of eminent men. Its opening lines provide not only a précis of the book's contents but also a synopsis of Galton's intellectual career:

> I propose to show in this book that a man's natural abilities are derived by inheritance, under exactly the same limitations as are the form and physical features of the whole organic world. Consequently, as it is easy, notwithstanding those limitations, to obtain by careful selection a permanent breed of dogs or horses gifted with peculiar powers of running, or of doing anything else, so it would be quite practicable to produce a highly-gifted race of men by judicious marriages during several generations. (p. 1)

Galton used Darwin's theory of heredity (Pangenesis) to support his ideas. Darwin held that every organism contained a multitude of elementary particles ('gemmules') which circulated in the blood and developed and reproduced independently of each other. Galton realised that these 'germ cells' could provide a hereditary mechanism and account for the persistence of ancestral 'peculiarities' in an 'unchanged' form from generation to generation (Galton, 1869; p. 371). This theory was, as Galton readily acknowledged, based 'on pure hypothesis' (p. 364). Nevertheless it enabled him to overturn associationist thinking and substitute biological for social determinism.

The exact provenance of these ideas is obscure, since, with the exception of his cousin Charles Darwin, Galton makes scant reference to other thinkers of the period. However, it is clear that, like Darwin, Galton drew his social inspiration from Malthus (the struggle for existence) and his methodology (observation, measurement and number) from the positivism of J. S. Mill (see Willer and Willer, 1973).

Galton's interest in quantitative procedures developed alongside his hereditary studies. Following Darwin's precept that natural variation (i.e.

variation within the species) held the key to evolution, Galton began to systematise his early observations on *Homo sapiens*. He gradually turned from the conjoint study of exotic races and Anglo-Saxon family trees towards the analysis of physical and psychological data collected directly. In 1883 he published *Inquiries into Human Faculty and its Development*—a popular résumé of his anthropological, hereditarian and psychological work over the previous decade. The culmination of this period of Galton's research was the establishment of the Anthropometric Laboratory at the London Health Exhibition in 1884. Members of the public were invited to submit themselves to a series of bodily measurements. These ranged from height and weight, through strength of pull to colour vision and acuity. Later versions incorporated more and more psychological measures (e.g. sensory discrimination and word association). Besides supplying Galton with sufficient material to establish a National Register of Anthropometric Data, the laboratory also facilitated his own research into human heredity. Throughout this period Galton extended his research into the psychometric domain since, in common with many of his peers, Galton believed that mental attributes ('moral faculties') and physical characteristics had homologous properties.

To codify his anthropometric data Galton used the ideas of the Belgian astronomer turned demographer, Adolphe Quetelet (1796–1874). Upon examining the graphical distribution of human heights and weights, Quetelet had noted their isomorphism with the well-studied pattern produced by errors of observation. Both distributions were bell-shaped in form. This observation led Quetelet to the belief that all physical and mental characteristics would exhibit equivalent natural properties. Furthermore he argued that the similarity of curve-shape was not co-incidental but arose from a common mechanism: the operation of a large number of small but independent causes (see Lazarsfeld, 1961, p. 164ff.).

Galton fused Quetelet's 'normal' distribution law with Darwin's theory of gemmules and produced a satisfactory explanation for both the shape and the origin of the observed patterns. Thus, following Quetelet, Galton accepted the 'constancy and continuity with which objects of the same species are found to vary' and, following Darwin, believed that the individual differences were 'caused by different combinations of a large number of minute influences' (1883, pp. 33 and 34).

Galton then extended the argument by making two additional assumptions. First, he accepted the universality of Quetelet's law and used it to establish the 'true' nature of a given distribution. Any cases that did not fit were treated as exceptional: 'whenever we find on trial that the outline . . . is not a flowing curve, the presumption is that the objects are not all of the same species. . . . This presumption is never found to be belied' (p. 34). By reversing Quetelet's logic and arguing from statistical law to empirical data, Galton inevitably vouchsafed the analytic purity of its assumptions. Certainty and circularity became confused. Second, Galton resurrected the central theme of faculty psychology. He assumed that although the individual variations were a function of 'minute causes' the distributions were composite evidence of underlying unitary phenomena. As a result he was able to argue that 'there is no bodily or mental attribute . . . which cannot be gripped with a smooth outline and thenceforward be treated in discussion as a single object' (p. 36).

Given the intellectual climate of the time (i.e. the emergent 'cult of science', see Webb, 1926, p. 146, and the belief that psychology and education were merely subdivisions of biology, see Young, 1970, *passim*), Galton's propositions were simple and self-evident. The above quotations, taken from a passage of less than 800 words, illustrate the dramatic conceptual advances that Galton was able to make. By merging mental and physical phenomena; by compounding statistical and empirical artefacts; and by reducing the complexity of observed phenomena to a series of one-dimensional 'faculties', he provided the psychological and educational sciences with a set of easily-used but powerful tools. Psychometrics (the behavioural measurement of mental states); norm-referenced testing (the allocation of individual rank on the basis of an assumed population distribution); and factor (or faculty) analysis can all be traced back to the imaginative links forged by Galton in the 1870s and 80s. However, as shown, Galton's ideas were also mutually interpenetrating and logically self-confirming. Thus, in practice, the methodological foundations of British educational research were built by Galton on the unstable premises of an epistemological quicksand. For nearly 100 years large sections of the research community have struggled to keep themselves afloat.

The unfolding of Galton's ideas did not stop with *Inquiries*. They were further extended by his research on the concept of correlation. According to Karl Pearson, his biographer, Galton initially sought a numerical measure to compare, say, the heights of a group of fathers with that of their sons. Galton subsequently realised that the problem was analogous to describing the covaration of characteristics (e.g. height with weight) within the same individual. (The term correlation had already been used in this sense.) This connection provided the key. Galton took the idea of intra-individual correlation and applied it to the characteristics exhibited by different generations of the same family. His early analyses were conducted with cress and sweet pea seeds rather than with human beings. In 1875 he had plotted the diameters of a group of mother sweet pea seeds against those of the daughter group and produced the first 'regression line' (see Figure 1).

Galton realised by inspection that the slope of the regression line was a function of the intensity of resemblance between the mothers and the daughters but was unable to develop the necessary mathematics. Later, following the publication of *Natural Inheritance* (1889), Pearson and F. Y. Edgeworth took up Galton's work and developed the statistical index we now know as the correlation coefficient. While Galton's insight generated a 'new calculus' for statistics, his genetic ideas—notably on regression—have proved less influential. Nevertheless they are worth reporting since they provide a clear demonstration of the confusions that can arise when the statistical and

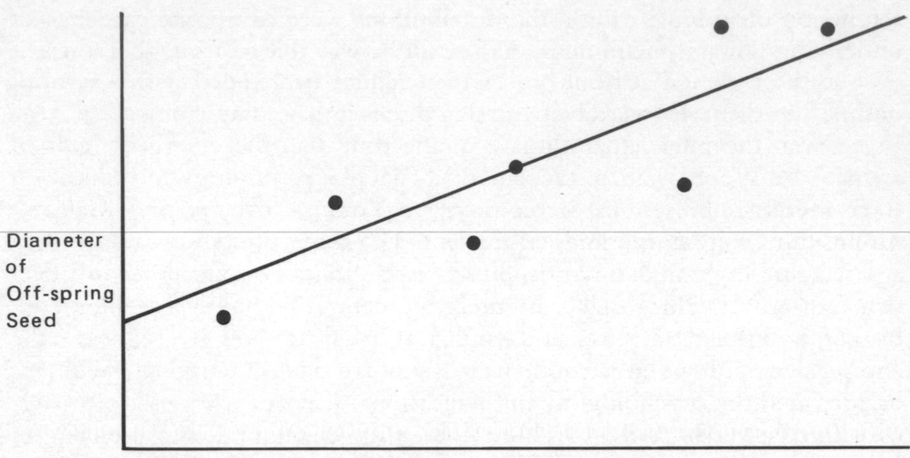

FIGURE 1 *The first 'regression line' (redrawn from Pearson, 1914, Vol. IIIa, p. 4)*

observed properties of a phenomenon are confounded. For Galton, the fact that tall fathers have shorter sons indicated an evolutionary trend towards the population mean. However, Galton did not realise that this 'natural law' of 'regression towards mediocrity' was a direct result of his measurement procedures. It occurs in any system which contains inherent 'error' in the initial (i.e. independent) variable. In this case, for example, Galton had ignored the genetic contributions of the mothers. Had he chosen sons with tall mothers as well as tall fathers the results would have been more 'progressive'. By doing so he would have eliminated one further source of error.

One final episode in Galton's life relevant to educational research concerned a controversy over the evolutionary significance of biological variation. The issue related to the question: is natural selection based on the 'continuous' variation found among species or is its raw material to be found among the discontinuous variations known as 'sports' or mutants? The intellectual differences that gave rise to this controversy were not only theoretical but methodological. Pearson and W. F. R. Weldon (later Professor of Comparative Anatomy at Oxford) advocated the continuous position and appealed to Galton's statistical theory of regression for their evidence. The opposition (led by William Bateson, Professor of Biology at Cambridge) felt the issue was more likely to be resolved by 'experimental breeding' than by the 'actuarial', biometric methods used by Galton, Pearson and Weldon (see Pearson, 1914, vol. IIIa, p. 260). In 1900 Pearson sent a paper to the Royal Society. Before it appeared, however, the Society circulated a paper by Bateson (one of the original referees) which sharply criticised Pearson's views. Not surprisingly, Pearson was offended by this action. He gathered support from his colleagues and in 1901 founded the journal *Biometrika* with Weldon as co-editor and Galton as consulting editor. (Galton declined a more active role—he was then in his eightieth year.) For more than forty years *Biometrika* remained a stimulus, an outlet and a platform for the biometric viewpoint in psychology.

In the 1900s the advancement of Galton's statistical and psychometric ideas fell to his pupil and 'lieutenant' Karl Pearson. In 1905 Pearson became Professor of Applied Mathematics at University College London and remained there until his retirement in 1933. While Pearson was developing the mathematics of the bell-shaped normal curve, the chi-square test and the multiple correlation coefficient, Galton spent the remains of his active life and most of his money proselytising in favour of 'human improvement' and eugenics (his term). Thus, after a long period of incubation and development his science emerged as his creed.

Throughout his life Galton's work was directed to achieve the 'status and dignity' of the natural sciences. Like many of the scientific community he took a relatively undifferentiated view of science. He saw it more as a world-view (cf. Thomas Paine's 'true theology') than, say, as a body of knowledge or a set of procedures. As Pearson described it:

> Modern science does much more than demand it shall be left in undisputed possession of what the theologian and the metaphysician please to term its 'legitimate field'. It claims that the whole range of phenomena, mental as well as physical—the entire universe—is its field. (Pearson, 1892, p. 24)

At the end of the nineteenth century the natural sciences included psychology and sociology as well as physics and biology. In such a climate it was widely accepted that not only the methods but also the processes and causal mechanisms were common to the different disciplines of knowledge. Thus, Beatrice Webb, a pupil of Spencer and an acquaintance of Galton, notes in her autobiography that one of the most characteristic assumptions of those decades was that 'physical science could solve all problems' (Webb, 1926, p. 78). Galton's position was, therefore, intrinsically more valid than it would be today where few would accept nineteenth-century 'physics' (or natural philosophy as it was then known) as the theoretical paradigm for the educational sciences. Yet, in many respects it has been retained intact as the methodological paradigm.

Francis Galton's intellectual life encompassed an epoch of rapid social change. Plotted against these historical developments—from laissez-faire individualism to state intervention—Galton's ideas shifted very little. Throughout, his viewpoint remained hierarchical. Galton began with a stratified, static view of society, used it to fashion his methods and statistics, and then reversed the process to establish his new-found eugenic view of mankind. The connection between Galton's statistics and his social theories is very close. For instance, to present his ideas and observations concerning the distribution of mental and physical attributes, Galton preferred the ogive to the normal curve (see Figure 2). One reason for this preference was that the shape of the ogive—'upwards towards genius and downwards towards stupidity'—provided a better idealisation of his hierarchical views (Galton,

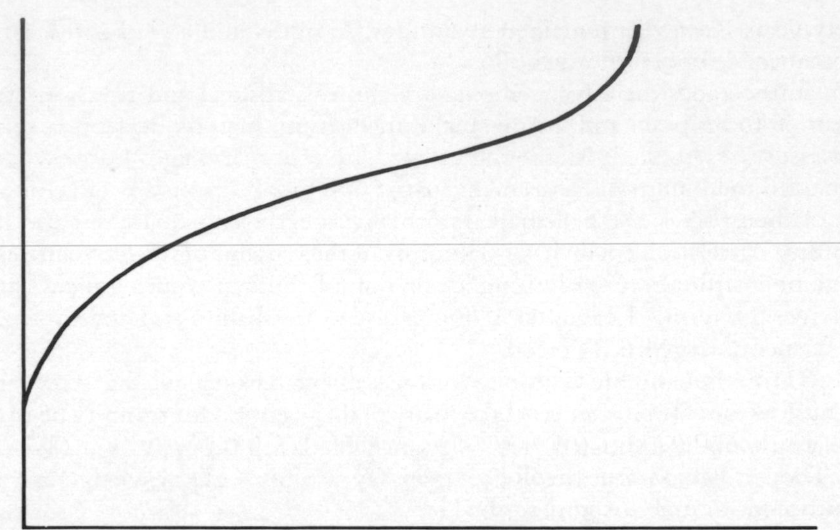

FIGURE 2 *The shape of the ogive curve (redrawn from Galton, 1883, p. 35) If a random sample of adult males are stood side by side in order of increasing height, the resultant profile is in the form of an ogive*

quoted in Pickens, 1968, p. 25). Likewise, Lee J. Cronbach has commented with reference to distribution-based measures (cf. Galton's use of percentiles) that 'comparison (competition) is a theme straight out of John Stuart Mill and Charles Darwin' (Cronbach, 1969, p. 36, parentheses in original).

Compared with those of Charles Darwin and Herbert Spencer, Galton's ideas are virtually absent from discussions which focus on the development of nineteenth-century social theory (see, for example, Greene, 1962; Burrow, 1968; and Young, 1970). At his death, however, the part they were to play in framing an epistemology for the psychological and educational sciences had hardly begun.

Ronald Fisher and the Age of Field Experiments

As already noted, the intellectual links between Galton and Fisher are problematic. On the one hand Fisher spent his early life working on correlation problems and also succeeded Pearson to the Galton Professorship of Eugenics at University College. On the other hand much of Fisher's work in the 1920s and 30s was in direct opposition to Pearson's ideas. Indeed, according to Fisher's biographers the intellectual 'conflict' between them eventually became 'irreconcileable' (Yates and Mather, 1963, p. 94).

Ronald Aylmer Fisher (1890–1962) entered Cambridge to study mathematics eighteen months before Galton died. In 1919 he declined an offer to become chief statistician under Pearson and, instead, entered a newly created post at Rothamsted Agricultural Experimental Station near London.

His task was to re-examine 'by modern statistical methods' the data that had accumulated from the station's long-term field trials. After fourteen years at Rothamsted and ten years at University College, Fisher moved in 1943 to a Chair of Genetics at Cambridge—a post he held until his retirement in 1957. His last years were spent as a Research Fellow at the Commonwealth Scientific and Industrial Research Organisation in Adelaide, Australia.

While Fisher made equally important contributions to the study of heredity, genetics and evolution (notably in providing a mathematical resolution of the Bateson-Pearson debate and in unravelling the genetics of rhesus-factor blood grouping), it is his contribution to statistics and experimental design that are remembered most in education and psychology.

By the end of the First World War correlation research had begun to drift aimlessly with the 'futile elaboration of innumerable measures of correlation' (Cornish, 1970, p. v). Besides Pearson's product-moment coefficient, other proposals had included coefficients of association, colligation, mean square contingency, tetrachoric correlation and equiprobable correlation. All these measures had been developed for specific, often limited, circumstances. Their proliferation took place in the absence of a coherent theory of statistical association which could be applied uniformly to different types of data (categorical, continuous etc.). For similar reasons little effort had been devoted to assessing the statistical significance of the associations revealed by correlation techniques. By the mid-1920s Fisher had made major advances in this area. He strengthened Pearson's chi-square test by introducing the concept of 'degrees of freedom'; he provided a rigorous mathematical proof of Student's *t*-test; he identified and formalised the *z*-distribution (which allowed significance tests to be performed with correlation coefficients derived from small samples); and finally, he developed the technique known as analysis of variance as a means of separating the effects of different 'causes'.

When Fisher confronted the Rothamsted data for the first time a major theoretical lacuna existed in the understanding of experimental error. Whenever a result deviated from the expected or hypothesized value it was appreciated that the deviation could be apportioned between 'error' and 'true' deviation, but no formal understanding had been reached. Clearly, a knowledge of the distribution of error was a pre-requisite to the formulation of significance tests which identified 'true' deviation. Although it was realised that the scatter of results from a series of replicated experiments might form the basis of such an analysis, few procedures had been evolved which could sort out more than two treatments at a time. Soon, however, Fisher saw that he could separate the sources of variation in field trials by using analysis of variance. In essence, this required him to compare the patterning of results within and between different treatments (cf. 'causes'). Success with these methods, which were reported in *Statistical Methods for Research Workers* (1925), led to the elaboration of a series of experimental procedures (e.g. Latin Square and Factorial designs) which, by their increased sophistication (i.e. intrinsic replication and the randomisation of extraneous factors) helped to identify previous sources of experimental 'error'. The logical principles underlying these methods and their more complex analogues appeared in *The Design of Experiments* (1935). Fisher's major contribution to research technique was to establish the basic requirements of an efficient agricultural experiment as randomisation and simultaneous replication.

While adequate to the requirements of agricultural-botany, these methods were, as shown below, not strictly applicable to other spheres. Their immediate appeal, however, was in the procedural rigour they brought to the techniques of experimentation. According to Hearnshaw (1964, p. 226), the first psychological reference to Fisher's work came in 1932 in a paper by R. H. Thouless, Psychology Lecturer at the University of Glasgow. Despite this early intervention, the major expansion of Fisherian methods did not begin in Britain (and in the USA) until a decade later. After the Second World War the growing status of Fisher's ideas was confirmed by their appearance in the standard psychology and education textbooks.

At that time Fisher made little or no claim for his methods outside the biological sciences. It remained necessary for other workers to make the connection with psychology and education. With hindsight, some recent commentators in the social sciences have noted the tardy diffusion of Fisher's ideas and attributed the delay to their mathematical complexity (see, for example, Hearnshaw, 1964, p. 226; and Stanley, 1966). In relative terms this explanation may be correct but it tends to ignore the mathematical expertise shown at that time by factor analysts such as Godfrey Thomson and Cyril Burt. However, given the intellectual antipathy between Fisher and Pearson it is understandable that the initial acceptance came not from factor analysts (who worked on correlation problems) but from psychologists like Thouless who shared Fisher's interest in the development of experimental procedures. Nevertheless it is still not sufficient to ascribe the take-up purely to the methodological predilections of the proponents. Other, more subtle issues were involved. The prevalence of biological explanations for human actions (e.g. behaviourism) and the popularity of biological models for social theorising (e.g. naturalism) can also be cited. Both facilitated the adoption of Fisher's ideas. For instance the rise of behaviourism in the 1920s was based on the idea (derived from Pavlov's research) that human psychology could be reduced to biological principles and mechanisms (see, for example, O'Neill, 1968, p. 138; and Murphy and Kovach, 1972, p. 251). Similarly, naturalism maintained that human behaviour could be interpreted using the findings of biology. The most enduring influence of naturalism in education is the philosophical tradition which stresses education as a process of 'natural growth'. (The biological underpinning of this movement is equally well illustrated by its reverence for the kindergarten or child-garden.) A major pedagogical text during the 1920s and 30s was *Education: Its Data and First Principles* (1920) by Percy Nunn, the (then) Principal of the University of London Institute of Education. Nunn was heavily influenced by naturalism. He derived his data and principles from a biological standpoint and paid little attention to the specifically human aspects of social reality. As Tibble (1966, p. 14) pointed out, Nunn was 'dominated by biological conceptions . . . regarding cultural facts and values as belonging to the same order as the biological'.

Within such an intellectual climate the biological sciences were seen to subsume rather than complement the social sciences. As a result, terms were often interchanged without implying any shift in meaning. Thouless provides an example. (By this time he was a Lecturer in Education at Cambridge.) In a contribution to a volume entitled *The Study of Society* (1939) he outlines his views on 'Scientific method and the use of statistics'. In particular he discusses the difficulty of achieving full 'control' in educational experiments. His conclusion demonstrates the super-ordinate status of biology: 'If this is a defect in the conditions of the social scientist's observations, it is a defect which he could only avoid by becoming a research worker in physics instead of in the biological sciences' (p. 151).

If Fisher's methods were, indeed, slow to enter the psychological and educational literature, there is clear evidence that they were not only methodologically but also philosophically acceptable to many research workers at that time. Thus, like Galton, Fisher offered a set of procedures to the research community that not only agreed with the current definitions of science but also resonated harmoniously with the prevalent educational ideologies. They were, in Gouldner's apt usage, 'affectively laden, cognitive tools'. Through time the ideas of Galton and Fisher have been handed down shorn of their social trappings. Little attention is now paid to the intellectual contexts which conceived and fostered them. Despite widespread dissatisfaction with their utility, they have rarely been the object of critical analysis. As a result they have remained central to our contemporary images of educational research.

The past in the present

Besides influencing the day to day methodology of educational research Galton and Fisher have also exerted a pervasive influence in the area of research strategies. Their work is reflected in the search for culture-free tests; the assumption that causal relations are linear and additive; the nature/nurture controversy; the use of control and experimental groups; the interpretation of change scores; and the generation of pedagogical theory. Each of these is considered below.

Galton's empirical studies laid the basis for analyses of educational phenomena that play down the importance of historical and societal influences. His conception of heredity and his naturalistic views of society proved sufficient, in Galton's terms, to account for the substance of history. Social or cultural facts played no part. Instead he explained the dominance of 'Anglo-Saxon and other civilised races' in terms such as the 'survivorship (sic) of the fittest', the inferiority of 'bohemian habits' and the 'impulsive and uncontrollable nature of the savage' (Galton, 1869, Chapter 20). Further,

Galton's predilection for 'measurement and number' reinforced this ahistorical slant. The quasi-objectivity of his numerical procedures masked the elements of cultural dependency upon which they were founded. Finally, Galton followed the example of faculty psychology and believed that external appearances were the reflection of a true, unchangeable 'essence'. Thus, much of his work attempted to isolate mental phenomena in pure form. Like the physical scientist he sought to eliminate the impurities which contaminated his experiments and which produced the unwanted error in his results. Inevitably Galton's theory became ecologically invalid—it disregarded the contexts which articulated the phenomena he sought to explain. (For a discussion of this problem and its relation to theories of childhood socialisation, see Bronfenbrenner, 1973.)

The most potent consequence of these ideas in education has been the search for a 'culture-free' intelligence test. By attempting to divorce mental tests from the world they were meant to reflect, psychometricians have implicitly denied the existence of culture and, as a result, have short-circuited any examination of its relationship with human thought and human physiology. (For a psychometrician's view of this debate see Pilliner, 1972.) A further consequence has been the assumption that empirical theory need not take account of social or historical phenomena. Thus, for example, educational research has regarded 'attitude' as a psychological attribute rather than as a social relationship (see Swift, 1973); and 'teaching style' as an individual characteristic rather than as a time or culture-based function of the classroom setting (see Hamilton and Delamont, 1974).

As already noted, Galton's early work on psychometrics and correlation embodied certain assumptions which he took to be correct. In one important instance, however, Galton compromised his position: he deliberately based the measurement of individual differences on an equal interval rather than an ordinal scale. (An ordinal scale assumes that the measurements differ in magnitude along a particular dimension, but does not assume that the differences between successive points on the scale are necessarily equal.) He explicitly retained this assumption because it allowed him to make comparisons between intervals on different parts of the scale. (For example, 'The average ability of the Athenian race is, on the lowest possible estimate, very nearly two grades higher than our own—that is, about as much as our race is above that of the African negro', Galton, 1869, p. 342.) Although Galton realised that different types of measuring scale admit different types of interpretation, his caution was largely vitiated by his eagerness to build an elaborate social theory upon such 'off-hand results' (Galton, 1889, p. 337; see also Jensen's re-use of the same data, 1973, p. 70).

A century later the problem of scaling and its interpretation is still central to educational research. In particular it raises itself whenever attempts are made to compare results within or between measurements (e.g. I.Q. or test scores) which appear to be based on an interval scale but which, in fact, are more correctly described as ordinal measures.

A domain assumption underlying Galton's correlational research is that there is a linear relationship between the co-varying measures. (A linear relationship, when plotted on a graph, appears as a straight line.) If, in fact, there is a curvilinear relationship (as for example, between age and body weight) the derived correlation will give a conservative estimate of the relationship. More important, it may fail to indicate the presence of a relationship when a significance test is applied. Thus, unless the results are displayed graphically, the relationship may be lost from the analysis.

Following Galton, correlation research also assumes that the variables make an independent additive contribution to the observed effect. In theoretical terms an additive model attempts to explain the overall effect by the cumulative impact of a series of independent minor causal mechanisms. For example, mathematical equations can be derived from a theoretical model which link an individual's 'success at university' with a series of contributory additive factors like secondary school grades, social class, sex, age and personality. In this respect, the whole is treated as if it were the sum of its parts. There is, however, no reason to assume that this additive model holds for every observed case. For instance, 'threshold' effects can be seen as the outcome of non-additive causal mechanisms. Similarly the behaviour of catalysts in chemical reactions and the consequences of multi-drug therapy are two other effects which are difficult to explain using a simple additive model.

One corollary of the additive assumption is that the variables under review are independent. Thus quasi-additive statements like 'attitude contributes sixty per cent of the variance in I.Q., and social class a further twenty per cent' are misleading if not meaningless since attitude and social class only make independent contributions if they are themselves uncorrelated (see the cautionary comments of Darlington, 1971, p. 393; and Burroughs, 1971, p. 187). Although, in this example, they are presented in cumulative terms their effects are certainly not additive. The biometric controversy between Bateson and Pearson provides another illustration. Bateson argues that the additive model did not fit the breeding ratios obtained by Mendel. Later it became apparent that the ratios could be explained if the assumption of gene independence was over-ruled and replaced by notions of gene interaction (e.g. dominance, gene-linkage).

A number of these problems are brought to a head in the fashionable device known as path analysis. It was used, for example, by Jencks *et al.* (1973) in their 'reassessment of the effect of family and schooling in America'. Path analysis attempts to establish causal relationships between antecedent and consequent variables. To do so it requires that a number of assumptions are sustained: 1. that all the relevant variables are included; 2. that the relationships among the variables are linear and additive; 3. that reciprocal causality does not take place; and 4. that an interval scale is used to measure the variables.

As a statistical procedure this is perfectly valid but as a mode of conceptual analysis it comes into conflict with analyses of social processes derived from other sources (e.g. child development studies). Such a procedure may, in fact, rule out components which other researchers feel are more important. Either way, the discrepancy between the model and its application provides plenty of opportunity for debate (see, for example, Kerlinger and Pedhazur, 1973, p. 305ff.; H. F. Taylor, 1973; and Allan, 1974).

Further difficulties using additive procedures occur in 'nature/nurture' studies. (Here the link with Galton is direct—the terminology is his.) As with path analysis, many of the arguments are necessarily inconclusive since they depend on an acceptance of Galton's assumptions. Thus Jensen's contention in *Educability and Group Differences* (1973) that we should 'stick to the additive model' because it 'better comprehends the existing data' (p. 51) is fallacious. Jensen is not alone in this respect. The widespread retention of linear, additive models (see, for example, Digman, 1966; and Jencks *et al.*, 1973, p. 266ff.) typically rests upon a similar argument: that the data and the model are logically distinct. This is not true. As with Galton's research, both are inextricably linked. For example, the construction of standardised intelligence tests implicitly supports the additive model—items with high intercorrelations are deliberately pruned. The use of standardised tests to study sex differences provides a further illustration. The original blue-print for the tests usually assumed that there were no differences between males and females. Thus, during the development of the tests, the items which differentiated were systematically eliminated. Inevitably, therefore, the data of sex-difference studies are contaminated by this *a priori* assumption. As in Jensen's case the model guarantees the validity of the data. It is hardly surprising that they exhibit 'the closest fit'. Ironically, the tone and substance of the nature/nurture controversy are very similar to those in the debate that engaged Pearson, Bateson and the Fellows of the Royal Society.

Fisher's major contribution to experimental design was the development of self-contained experiments that were sufficiently 'large and complex' to answer the maximum number of questions at any one time. They were, therefore, essentially one-shot trials. Fisher was fully aware that even in the case of agricultural botany, intrinsic replication was more effective than a series of logically equivalent but repeated trials. In fact he always argued against unnecessary long-term investigations (i.e. those which could be redesigned in terms of intrinsic replication): 'in agricultural plot work, the experiment cannot in practice be repeated upon identical conditions of soil and climate' (1925, p. 272). Not only did Fisher try to avoid long-term trials, he was also very circumspect about using groups matched on assumed but unmeasured criteria. He cited the problems that had arisen with the assumption that the variation in the number of plants from plot to plot was irrelevant to the analysis of treatment. (An educational equivalent would be those experiments which control for sex, social class and intelligence but take no account of class size.) As far as agricultural experimentation was concerned, Fisher believed that controlled methods were 'troublesome, inexact, and unnecessary' (1935, p. 166). He felt the uncontrolled variables should be eliminated by the process of randomisation or 'equalised' using the technique of analysis of covariance. Both techniques are difficult to use in education. Covariance analysis, for example, requires that subjects be randomly assigned to groups and that groups are randomly assigned to treatments. Whenever these conditions are violated the results can be 'dangerous and misleading' (Hope, 1968, p. 141). Even if such conditions can be obtained (e.g. in a laboratory-type setting), the ecological validity and 'field' status of the experiment is likely to be undermined.

While Fisher did not discount the use of 'control' and 'experimental' groups he was very careful to demonstrate the interpretative difficulties that can arise. The general problem is as follows: are the observed effects due to the treatment or are they, in fact, due to some other variable which has not been successfully controlled? To illustrate his point Fisher discussed experiments used to determine the efficiency of animal feed-stuffs: is the 'true' gain, with respect to an individual animal, the weight increase measured absolutely (i.e. the final weight minus the initial weight) or is it the increase expressed as a percentage of the original weight? (E.g. if a 100 kg pig and 150 kg pig both increase by 15 kg, the absolute increase is the same but the percentage increase is different.) In other words, is the gain due to the feed-stuffs or to some other variable (in this case initial weight) which may not have been controlled?

By this demonstration Fisher also points to the interpretative difficulty of using change scores. This problem is peripheral to agricultural-botany (most analyses are based on a single measurement—the cropping yield grown from seed), yet it is central to educational assessment. For instance, the evaluation of attitude change and the measurement of achievement are closely connected with 'before-and-after' measures. Even if abilities and attitudes can be measured using procedures derived from Galton, the problem pin-pointed by Fisher cannot be avoided. (It emerges, essentially, because the growth of pigs is neither linear nor additive.) Indeed, as Fisher's example shows, the common-sense interpretation of change scores may not always be correct. The educational implications of this state of affairs are more than merely technical. For example, performance contracting and teacher accountability in the USA—modern examples of 'payment by results'—both rely for their implementation on the analysis of change scores. Despite efforts to augment or update Fisher's experimental designs (e.g. Campbell and Stanley, 1966; and Hotelling, 1963), psychometricians are still 'floundering' (Roebuck, 1972) and the lay public are still confused. (For a critical review of performance contracting see Stake, 1973.)

One final aspect of educational research that can be linked to the ideas of Fisher and Galton is the tendency to identify theory with method. Factor analysis, for example, is both a psychological theory and a mathematical procedure. As such it pre-selects data which are consonant with its theoretical and methodological assumptions. (Much the same criticism could be made of cluster analysis (see Sneath and Sokal, 1973) and classroom interaction analysis (see Flanders, 1970).) Hence the empirical generation of new theory is difficult because potential discrepancies between observation and theory have already been reduced to a minimum. The most advanced theoretical 'concepts' that can be derived in this manner are merely empirical constructs (i.e. the factors) or statistical generalisations (i.e. extrapolations from sample to population). Since the data are so theory-laden they can do little more than complete a circle: the methods reinforce the theory and both become self-perpetuating. (Indeed, should internal reliability take over as the sole criterion of validity, theory and method become indistinguishable.) In practice the circle cannot be broken simply by the application of a method. Ultimately, its dissolution requires the intervention of theory, not data.

Summary and conclusions

The purpose of this paper has been to review a variety of core-assumptions that have become deeply rooted in educational research. By using a historical frame of reference it has been possible to identify the philosophical origins and the logical nature of these ideas. At the same time their contemporary importance has been considered. Overall, an attempt has been made to articulate some of the doubts and uncertainties that are currently widespread in British educational research. Certainly, many of the historical, philosophical and methodological issues deserve further exploration, elaboration and emendation. But, clearly, the effort is more than an exercise in the archaeology of ideas. The substance of many of these debates is as real today as it was 100 years ago. To take one example: the relationship in Britain between 'payment by results' (1862–1897) and Galton's eugenic ideas has many parallels with the twentieth-century link in the USA between teacher accountability and meritocratic social theories (e.g. Herrnstein, 1973).

In a narrow sense, then, the topics considered in this paper have implications for the development and teaching of educational research. To be sure, most statisticians and many research workers are aware of the concerns that have been expressed. Nevertheless, in so far as these issues are also relevant to the educational community at large, they deserve much wider currency. In a broad sense they are equally pertinent to the understanding of educational practice and to the generation and validation of pedagogical (rather than psychological) theory. This essay is dedicated to those tasks.

Acknowledgment: For their comments on earlier drafts I should like to thank Mike Cannon, David Oldman, Hamish Paterson, Margaret Reid, Iris Robertson, Graham Thorpe, Rob Walker, Eric Wilkinson and participants in an Education department seminar at Stirling University.

Margaret Martlew, Peter K. Smith and Kevin Connolly

11. A Perspective on Nursery Education

Science like most human activities is subject to fashions. There are fashions in concepts, methods and problems, though the fashion in problems is often determined by new concepts, developments in methodology, and sometimes by the availability of financial support.

The interaction between education, psychology and child development is clearly subject to fashion and to certain emphases. Some of these are ephemeral, whilst others are more enduring. These concerns are of course linked quite closely to those aspects of education which our society values at any given time. In general one could say of education in Britain (and of many other highly developed technology based societies) that it is academic, almost scholastic. This broad orientation is reflected in our educational psychology by a concern with learning theories, with stages of cognitive growth and with the psychometric evaluation of abilities, primarily intellectual abilities. While these are by no means the exclusive concerns of educational psychology they serve to provide a vignette of the principal preoccupations. What follows is a preliminary attempt to consider educational issues from a somewhat different standpoint. The empirical data that are presented and their discussion will be concerned only with preschool children but the approach may have value in other age ranges.

Education in evolutionary perspective

If a species is to survive it must adapt to the demands of its environment. The adaptedness of an organism is accomplished by a multiplicity of means and in man it is a consequence not only of genetic evolution but also of cultural evolution (Connolly, 1971). The technological developments and innovations of the past 100 years or so have given rise to a rapid acceleration in the rate of cultural change which is now manifest in an increasing rate of sociological change. To prosper members of our society must not only be numerate and literate. They must also be able to fulfil varying and often highly complex social roles, and able to cope with a variety of stresses. To meet these demands they require cognitive skills and they require too social skills and the ability to communicate in subtle ways with others. On top of this the most difficult and demanding requirement is flexibility itself; the power to cope with and master those exigencies which we have not so far met.

At the risk of appearing trite the purpose of education is to enable an individual to meet various and changing demands throughout his life. This is a very general aim that few would quarrel with, but if it is to serve as a useful guide then it is necessary to translate it into more specific sub-goals. Since our culture is changing so rapidly it is enormously difficult to specify what will be needed at some future date. At this stage most utility is perhaps gained by developing a broad theoretical framework of development rooted in the social biology of man. Cognitive growth, the acquisition of skills and competence, including communicative skills, form principal landmarks, as does the importance of the social context in which the child operates.

From birth onwards the context in which the child lives, grows and matures has profound effects on his behaviour. Life itself can be described as a process of interaction with the environment during which the organism undergoes various alterations. Changes which result from this process of interaction may result in part at least from previous changes, thus some aspects of behavioural development are a consequence of, or greatly affected by, previous changes. If development is seen as a process of changing patterns of organisation through time then a significant question is whether such changes proceed according to some schedule or programme. There are general age trends and chronological correlates for both physical and psychological development and these are well attested in the literature. In broad terms we can find examples where the appearance of one form of behaviour is certainly dependent upon the prior appearance of another. Development is a hierarchical process where the patterns of interaction which the organism displays as a function of a changing organisation can be studied at the biological, psychological and social level.

An attempt to link the view of development outlined above to education and in particular to nursery education would give rise to a family of questions. Paramount in this grouping will be questions concerning the functional utility of various behaviours. To ask what function various behaviours and psychological attributes have for a child could be very revealing in terms of identifying features towards which education might usefully be directed. For an educationalist this is not a new question but rarely has it been asked of specific behavioural attributes with an adequate degree of analytic rigour. Linked with this quest for functional explanations is the need to maximise at all times the individual's potential flexibility for meeting as yet unspecified environmental demands.

Along with the need to acquire various specific cognitive skills such as literacy and numeracy other essential and perhaps more basic features can be identified. The ability to communicate effectively is one, yet we know little about the growth of communicative competence in the preschool years. Our culture demands a wide variety of social skills and the individual must appreciate subtle differences and attune his behaviour to the required role.

Cutting across intellectual and social skills but central to education are factors such as motivation. Our understanding of motivation in infancy may be greatly extended by the study of that most ubiquitous characteristic of infancy and childhood, play. For the young child play provides a major vehicle for his behavioural and psychological growth. Play and communication whilst not exclusively important features of infancy may provide a major focus on which to mount an educational programme for the nursery school child. Play provides a means whereby the child can learn about the world of objects and people in relation to himself and his own actions. The social context of play requires a child to adjust repeatedly and irregularly to changes produced by others. He must modulate his activities so as to produce a reciprocity with others. It thus has social and communicative attributes deeply embedded within it and has many properties in common with communication.

Methodological considerations

Methods are related to questions and are in large measure dictated by the specific question which is asked. Our concern in this essay is to point out the particular value of direct observation in natural settings in studying the psychological development of children. This approach was used extensively in the 1930s and 1940s (Smith and Connolly, 1972) and is beginning to attract wide interest again. In the intervening period there have been many technical, conceptual and analytical sophistications and this approach is now much more powerful.

Much of the sophistication which has entered into the direct observation of behaviour stems directly from the work of the animal ethologists. Whilst the ethological approach is now broadly very similar to that adopted by the experimental psychologist, and is in some respects identical, certain differences are also apparent. Ethologists do perform experiments, they do seek for antecedent causes and they do formulate reductive explanations. However, two primary concerns are the study of behaviour in the natural habitat and the adaptive significance or survival function which any pattern of behaviour has for the organism.

The observation of behaviour in a natural environment serves to help establish what is to be explained in 'real life' occurrences and it also aids in generating new hypotheses. The problems associated with direct observation have been laid out elsewhere (Smith and Connolly, 1972; Connolly, 1973) and will not be discussed in detail here.

What constitutes the natural habitat for our own species may prove more difficult to determine than it appears at first sight. More than any other animal man has shaped his environment, to a very great degree at least. His social structures are of his own devising and they serve to alter and steer his actions. For the child, institutions which prescribe to a great extent the behavioural context, are significant environmental determinants. For our purpose therefore the nursery school and playgroup are part of the preschool child's natural habitat. How that habitat should be designed and the ways in which it might beneficially be changed are other questions which we believe research should have a major bearing upon.

What follows in the remainder of this paper are reports on two quite different investigations. Each of these has involved the direct observation of behaviour in a natural setting and both seek to explore the function of certain aspects of the behaviour of preschool children. The investigations are preliminary, not definitive, and should be evaluated in that way. They are here offered partly because of the findings which emerge, preliminary though these are, and partly because they reflect methodological developments.

The educational significance of fantasy play in young children

The nature of fantasy play

The fantasy play of young children is one of the most complex forms of behaviour seen in a nursery class or playgroup, and interest in its nature and functions has recently increased (Smilansky, 1968; Singer, 1973). Although this kind of play has been described by a variety of adjectives—dramatic, thematic, symbolic, make-believe, imaginative—they all mean essentially the incorporation of fantasy or make-believe elements into a play sequence. For example, play objects may substitute for real objects (e.g. torn paper as bus tickets); play vocalisations and movements may mimic real activities (e.g. bus noises, arm movements as if turning a steering wheel). Often, though not necessarily, these fantasy actions imply that the child is accepting a role and acting out some of its implications (e.g. the bus driver). In this case we can talk of imaginative role play. Fantasy play can be carried out by a child alone, or with an adult or with other children. The latter kind has been called sociodramatic play by Smilansky (1968).

Piaget (1962) suggests that 'symbolic' play represents a universal and inevitable stage in a child's development (from about 3 to 6 years), gradually superseding the 'practice play' of infancy, and to be superseded by games with rules in later childhood. However, the amount of fantasy play seen in children seems to vary widely according to the cultural background; for example, it was seldom seen in children of the Gusii, a pastoralist tribe in Kenya (LeVine and LeVine, 1963), nor in an Egyptian village community (Ammar, 1954). This may reflect the lack of variety of adult work roles, and the relatively early pressure on children to help directly in subsistence activities. Feitelson (1959) and Smilansky (1968) have drawn attention to a paucity of fantasy play in children of Jews recently immigrated to Israel from the Kurdish mountains of other middle eastern areas. Smilansky (1968, p. 59) ventures so far as to state that 'culturally deprived children, aged from three to seven years, ... do not develop the ability to engage in symbolic play'. In fact Smilansky adopted very strict criteria for assessing sociodramatic play (including a minimum length of 10 minutes for a play episode), and her evidence seems to suggest that fantasy play is poorly developed, rather than absent, in 'culturally deprived' children. Other studies in American urban centres such as New York (Freyberg, 1973) and Boston (Feitelson and Ross, 1973) have also suggested that children from lower socio-economic groups may engage in little fantasy play. Findings such as these have led to renewed consideration of the importance of fantasy play in connection with Headstart programmes and the educational handicap of underprivileged communities.

One already well-established finding is that when children show a low level of fantasy play, it can be increased by means of adults who act as 'play-tutor' or encourage and participate in fantasy play sequences (Marshall and Hahn, 1967; Smilansky, 1968; Feitelson, 1972; Freyberg, 1973). The supposed beneficial effects of the training, and more specifically of any increased level of fantasy play, are more difficult to demonstrate (Feitelson and Ross, 1973; Rosen, 1974). Some attempts have been made to show that fantasy play does have some of the broad competence-enhancing functions postulated for example by Smilansky, but as with any study of the function of play the problem of control groups is a crucial one. Almost all tutoring or training programmes offer a considerable amount of cognitive and linguistic stimulation from an adult, in addition to the more specific effect of increasing fantasy play for which they were intended. The problem is to arrange control groups who receive a comparable amount of general stimulation from adults, without receiving the specific training for fantasy play.

The few studies which have attempted this are reviewed in Smith (1977). In general, they suggest that tutoring in fantasy or sociodramatic play does help to develop creative and social skills in children; but it still cannot be inferred with confidence that these results are due to the play, rather than to the adult interaction.

Even if fantasy play does have competence-enhancing functions we should not necessarily assume that all types of fantasy play can be considered together, as having the same developmental impact. There are considerable individual differences in the amount of fantasy play which children exhibit (Singer, 1973) and sex differences have been reported though not very consistently (Brindley *et al.* 1973; Markey, 1935). The study reported here was designed to describe the different kinds of fantasy play seen in a playgroup and forms part of a larger set of investigations.

Structure and content of fantasy play in a playgroup

One part of the project carried out in Sheffield was a comparison of the effects of a child-centred or free play regimen with an adult-centred or organised activity regimen in a playgroup. Amongst other things, this enabled us to compare the incidence of fantasy play in the two conditions. Since detailed records of fantasy play were obtained it was possible to examine differences in the structure and content of episodes in greater detail than has previously been reported. This was done in order to throw more light on sex differences in fantasy play, and on the criteria which might usefully be employed to assess the complexity of spontaneous fantasy play. In addition, different types of fantasy play might evoke different reactions from staff under a free play or an organised activity setting.

The playgroup

The investigation, which extended over two terms from September to April, was carried out at an experimental playgroup run by the Department of Psychology at the University of Sheffield. The children attending the group were drawn from a socioeconomically mixed catchment area. The playgroup was equipped with the usual range of toys and apparatus and run by three experienced paid staff.

Two groups of children, each attending two mornings a week from 9.00 a.m. to 12 noon, were involved. One, the structured activities (SA) group, experienced mostly organised activity conditions in which the staff encouraged the children to join in various activities. The structured activities group also experienced a few free play sessions at the beginning and at the end of the project, for comparison.

The second, free play (FP) group experienced only free play conditions throughout the project. The same staff had a caretaking rather than an educational role with this group. They were instructed that their interactions with the children should be minimal, allowing the children to choose their own play activities and intervening only when they judged essential (e.g. prevention of injury to children or property, helping a distressed child). The material and equipment provided was exactly the same for the free play (FP) group and the structured activities (SA) group on corresponding weekdays.

Each group comprised 22 children aged between 2½ and 5, matched for age and sex. Both groups had been formed a year previously.

Data collection

Observations were made in the playgroup by an observer who dictated notes into a small portable tape recorder. The records were subsequently transcribed. Both activity scans, and incident sampling, of fantasy play were utilised in data collection. For both kinds of sampling, eight corresponding blocks of data were obtained for each group of children, each observation block consisting of a 45 minute period during one morning's play. During activity scans the observer scanned the room at two-minute intervals, stating the choice of play activity of each child as rapidly as possible. If a child was engaged in fantasy play this was noted. A reliable measure was thereby obtained of the amount of time spent by children in fantasy play. During incident sampling the observer scanned the room frequently, looking only for instances of fantasy play. In describing incidents the observer concentrated on recording the identities of the children in the fantasy episode and the nature of the sequence (objects used or pretended, apparatus utilised, gross motor patterns, roles assigned or accepted). The time was noted every minute so that the duration of sequences could be estimated.

Analysis and results

The results from the activity scan data showed much less fantasy play in organised activity conditions compared to free play. For the structured activity (SA) group, each child spent on average only 2·2 minutes in fantasy play in a 45 minute observation period; but this increased to 7·0 minutes in the initial and final observation periods when free play was allowed. This difference is significant, across children, at $p < \cdot 002$ (Wilcoxon test). For the free play (FP) group, on corresponding sessions (but always in free play) the means were 3·6 and 5·4 min respectively, a non-significant difference. No sex differences in fantasy play were found for either the SA or FP group on the basis of the activity scan data.

To examine further the kinds of fantasy play seen, and the reactions of staff in the different conditions, the data from incident sampling were studied. A tentative classification of the content and structure of fantasy episodes was produced. The usefulness of the classification can be assessed in terms of independent characteristics such as the duration of episode, number of play participants, sex differences, and intervention by playgroup staff. It seemed possible and perhaps likely that different kinds of fantasy play might show sex differences, and be differentially affected by organisational factors. They may indeed have different developmental functions.

Examination of the incident sample data suggested a fourfold classification both by content and by structure. One clear difference in content of fantasy play episodes is that between rough-and-tumble based episodes (R play) and episodes based primarily on object manipulation (O play). Some fantasy episodes, however, contain an appreciable amount of both rough-and-tumble and object manipulation. In these mixed forms a further distinction was made as to whether the R and O elements were sequenced in a disjointed fashion (S play) or integrated (I play). An example of S play is a tea party (O play) which is interrupted and becomes monster play (R play), perhaps as another child joins the group. Examples of I play are a glove puppet show, where manipulation of the puppets may be combined or rapidly alternated with chasing episodes.

Structure was classified as being at levels 1, 2, 3, or 4. Level 1, or simple structure, characterises an episode where essentially one kind of role is acted out using one set of closely related behaviours (use of objects or apparatus, motor patterns). Examples are daleks chasing (R1) or mother has tea party (O1). An R1 and an O1 episode connected in a disjointed way would be classified as S1, and the puppet show episode as I1.

Levels 2 and 3 exemplify different ways of producing changes on a given simple structure. Level 2 episodes are characterised mainly by changes in roles assigned or acted, without substantial changes in the kinds of action observed. For example, 'monster' play changes to 'dalek' play changes to 'spaceman' play, all based on chasing and hiding. Level 3 episodes are characterised mainly by changes in the kinds of action observed, without substantial changes in the roles assigned or accepted; for example mother and baby, acting out bedtime, breakfast, then shopping.

Finally, level 4 episodes are characterised by having both substantial role changes and substantial action changes. For example, a sequence in which two boys played first at having a picnic in the park (under a climbing-frame), then at monsters and using the climbing-frame as a boat to jump into the 'water', then at mother and baby reading a story and going to the 'bookshop' (Wendy house), was classed as type S4.

The type of episode was assessed for each child separately if need be, depending on his activities while participating in a fantasy play sequence. Summing over children, the number of occurrences of each type of episode for the structured activities and free play groups separately, are shown in Table 1.

TABLE 1 *The number of occurrences of each type of fantasy play episode, summed over children. SA, structured activities; FP, free play*

			CONTENT			
			R rough-and-tumble based	O object based	S mixed-sequenced	I mixed-integrated
STRUCTURE	1 simple	SA	31	61	16	4
		FP	100	77	16	8
	2 role change	SA	21	0	1	0
		FP	25	0	7	0
	3 action change	SA	0	32	3	5
		FP	5	14	7	2
	4 role and action change	SA	7	0	9	0
		FP	0	2	8	0

The most common types of fantasy play were either simple rough-and-tumble (R1), simple object based (O1), rough-and-tumble with mainly role change (R2), and object based with mainly action change (O3). In addition there is a fair sprinkling of mixed episodes at various structural levels (S1 to 4, I1, I3). In the subsequent analyses there appeared to be little discrimination between the S and I type of mixed episodes, so these were added together. Because of the small numbers, structural levels 3 and 4 were also added together. This gave a revised, three by three classification.

The duration of each episode was measured to the nearest minute, and the mean duration for each type of fantasy play is shown in Table 2. The mean duration of episodes varies with the structure of the episode much more than with the content. Simple structure episodes (level 1) tend to last some 2 to 3 minutes on average, whereas episodes involving changes in action (levels 3, 4) generally last around 10 minutes or so. Episodes involving role change without action change (level 2) come in between. It is interesting to note that at a given level of structural complexity, there is little difference in duration between rough-and-tumble, object-based or mixed forms of fantasy play; however the many R2 episodes tend to be shorter than the many O3 episodes.

TABLE 2 *The mean duration of each type of fantasy play episode in minutes. SA, structured activities; FP, free play*

			CONTENT		
			R	O	S+I
STRUCTURE	1	SA	1·7	2·7	2·7
		FP	2·8	2·8	5·1
	2	SA	6·0	—	2·0
		FP	7·6	—	6·0
	3+4	SA	8·3	9·2	13·9
		FP	18·2	10·3	11·4

While the duration of a sequence might be considered as one criterion for validating the structural criteria used, an alternative measure of the complexity of a play sequence is the number of participants in the sequence. This was calculated for each episode, including only children who were present for at least half the total duration of the sequence. The mean number of participants in each type of fantasy episode is shown in Table 3.

By this criterion the mean number of participants for most types of fantasy play was 2 to 3, with a usual range of 1 to 4. For object-based and mixed content episodes there is little variation with structural level, though the mixed content episodes tend to have more participants than the purely object-based forms. The simple structure rough-and-tumble based episodes also average around 2 participants. The more complex rough-and-tumble

TABLE 3 *The mean number of participants in each type of fantasy play episode. SA, structured activities; FP, free play*

			CONTENT		
			R	O	S+I
STRUCTURE	1	SA	1·7	1·4	3·3
		FP	2·4	2·6	2·8
	2	SA	4·5	—	—
		FP	4·7	—	2·5
	3+4	SA	3·0	1·9	2·4
		FP	4·0	2·0	2·5

forms have an appreciably larger number of participants. Summing R2 with R3 + 4 episodes, the means are 4·0 for the structured activities group and 4·6 for the free play group. These are significantly different from R1 episodes (both groups), O3 + 4 episodes (both groups), or mixed content episodes (FP group only), Mann-Whitney test.

The importance of this becomes clearer when sex differences are examined. No significant sex differences in overall fantasy play were obtained in terms of number or length of episodes, or number of participants. There were non-significant tendencies in both groups however, for boys to play in more fantasy episodes, of shorter duration, and with a larger number of participants. These tendencies are brought into sharper relief by considering the different types of fantasy play. Table 4 shows the number of times boys, and girls, participated in each kind of episode. The differential participation by the two sexes is clearly affected by the content but not directly by the structure of fantasy play. Boys more often take part in R episodes; on Wilcoxon tests across boy–girl pairs matched for age, this is significant at $p < \cdot 05$ for the FP group, and at $p < \cdot 05$ for both groups combined. Girls more often take part in O episodes; significant at $p < \cdot 05$ for the SA group, and $p < \cdot 05$ for both groups combined. There is no clear sex difference for mixed content episodes; $p < \cdot 05$ for the SA group, but non-significant for the FP group or for both groups combined.

TABLE 4 *The number of times boys and girls participated in each type of fantasy play episode. SA, structured activities; FP, free play*

			CONTENT					
			R		O		S+I	
			Boys	Girls	Boys	Girls	Boys	Girls
	1	SA	22	9	18	43	17	3
		FP	66	34	25	52	11	13
STRUCTURE	2	SA	17	4	—	—	0	1
		FP	19	6	—	—	5	2
	3+4	SA	5	2	8	24	13	4
		FP	5	0	6	10	7	10

The distinction between R and O content episodes thus seems a useful one in terms of differential preference by the two sexes in our groups of children. In terms of duration, R and O type episodes of a given structural level seem comparable. In terms of frequency of occurrence, however, many R episodes exhibit primarily variation in roles, often of a rather repetitive nature, rather than substantial variations in action. These R episodes are of shorter duration than the many O episodes which show sequences of action variation maintained within a given role structure. This might suggest that many O episodes are more complex in their structure than many R episodes. In contrast, R episodes average an appreciably greater number of participants than O episodes. Subgroups of 4 or 5 children playing together, as found in all but the simple structure of R play, are large for children of this age range

(Parten, 1932). The mean size of subgroups in which a child plays increases steadily through the primary school age range, and is an indicator of the social-cognitive level that a child has reached (Eifermann, 1970). R episodes may thus be considered more complex than O in this alternative sense of maintaining play episodes with a large number of other participants. There is perhaps a reciprocal relationship; the more stereotyped and predictable nature of the behaviour patterns in R type play may allow greater scope for coping with the potential unpredictability involved in having a larger number of other children in the play episode.

The higher level R episodes, involving a large number of children, usually boys, are often very noisy and sometimes distracting to other activities. Besides being highly salient they also often contain elements, such as gun play, of which some nursery staff or teachers disapprove. Further, some teachers seem to confuse the play fighting episodes in rough-and-tumble with real fighting, and will tell children to 'stop fighting'. For these various reasons, R episodes of fantasy play are probably quite frequently interrupted by staff in nurseries and infant classes. In the two playgroups we observed, children in R episodes were interrupted by staff in 31 per cent of cases in the SA group and 10 per cent of cases in the FP group. Equivalent figures for mixed content episodes were 18 per cent and 10 per cent respectively. No cases of O episodes were observed to be interrupted.

The interruptions of R episodes are greater in the structured activities (SA) group than in the free play (FP) group because much of the time of the former was in organised activity conditions. When in this more 'educational' type of setting, as many as 50 per cent of the children in R episodes were interrupted; nearly 80 per cent of these children were boys.

Discussion

Two questions of educational importance are raised by these and by previous researches on fantasy play. One relates to the overall importance of fantasy play, the other to the different types of fantasy episode proposed above. The two questions interrelate, since it should not be assumed that different types of fantasy play have the same function or developmental significance.

Firstly, there is evidence that fantasy play has an important role in the development of certain skills in childhood. Social skills and creativity have been most directly implicated, though it may well turn out that language skills are also fostered by fantasy play. The available experimental evidence points more firmly to the beneficial effects of training in fantasy play, rather than to the spontaneous occurrence of fantasy play. Taken together with our broader knowledge of the development of competence and the importance of play in early development (Connolly and Bruner, 1974), the available evidence suggests that the emergence of fantasy play in young children should be encouraged.

This may be particularly important for children whose home backgrounds do not facilitate the development of fantasy play, indeed perhaps inhibit it. In the USA and in Israel this seems to be true of children from certain minority groups, or from very low socioeconomic status families. While comparable research evidence is lacking for children in Britain, there is informal evidence that a similar paucity of fantasy play is to be found in children in underprivileged communities (such as in the Educational Priority Areas). While the possible dangers of intervention by a dominant culture into the affairs of a less dominant one must be borne in mind (e.g. Tulkin, 1972), nevertheless positive steps to tutor and develop fantasy play may be both successful and educationally valuable.

This brings us to a consideration of the different contents and structures of spontaneous fantasy play suggested by our own research. Clearly the results of our investigations are only known to apply to the population of children from which our playgroups were drawn, though we believe they are reasonably representative of urban middle- and working-class children, but not including children of 'problem' families. For these children, boys on the average preferred to play in large groups in rough-and-tumble types of fantasy play, while girls on the average preferred to play in smaller groups in object-based episodes. These results say nothing directly about the relative importance of biological or cultural factors in their causation. It is possible that the preference for role changes rather than action changes in the fantasy play of some boys may be due to a paucity of knowledge about the actions appropriate to adult male roles in modern urban society. A little girl knows what mother does in the home, from observation. A little boy may not know what his father does, and draws his models instead from TV programmes which themselves present generally restricted and stereotyped aspects of role models. This is a possible explanation for sex differences in the structure of fantasy play. So far as content is concerned, it is likely that a preference of boys for rough-and-tumble or gross motor fantasy episodes would be found in most cultures, as is the case for rough-and-tumble play generally (Smith, 1974).

If these sex differences in type of fantasy play are more than a transient cultural phenomenon, or a localised effect specific to our groups, then the developmental and educational significance of fantasy play will need to be considered afresh. In particular, do rough-and-tumble based episodes have the same, different, fewer or additional functions as object-based episodes? Perhaps they are less important in developing language skills, but more important in relation to certain social skills; but this is speculation. Possible functions of rough-and-tumble play itself also need to be considered. What does seem likely is that a policy to encourage spontaneous fantasy play in the preschool and infant school will be easier to implement for object-based episodes than for rough-and-tumble based episodes. Short of noticeable changes in school organisation and attitudes, the latter are likely to be discriminated against. This may mean that for certain boys in particular, fantasy play will be discouraged. Whether this matters, or whether alternative forms of fantasy play will be substituted, are matters for investigation.

Patterns of speech in the nursery

Few would dispute the central part played by language in both the cognitive and the social development of the child. Language is the medium through which the child can encode his perceptions of the world and communicate meaningfully with those around him. The extent to which a child is affected by what he hears and can himself utilise words appropriately, is likely to have enormous implications for his present competence and future development.

There are numerous methodological difficulties and many unanswered, even unformulated, questions relating to the study of language. Problems in investigating how children use language lie largely in conceptualising the questions to be asked which, through appropriate formulation and exploration, can lead to useful insights. Great diversity is apparent in the *modus operandi* of language investigators, manifest in methods employed for data collection, variety of sample size or techniques used for analysis. Three approaches can be identified: diary studies, experimental procedures and the sampling of speech in natural settings. Diary studies have the longest history where investigators, frequently parents with psychological or linguistic interests, have conducted detailed and systematic examinations of the emerging grammars of a small number of children, often their own child (Taine, 1877; Leopold, 1939–49; Bloom, 1973; Brown, 1973).

Experimental procedures have also been used to explore a range of different questions such as the child's underlying knowledge of the rules of grammar (Berko, 1958; Chomsky, 1969). There are however problems attendant on using contrived experimental situations with young children. Artefacts can arise from the child's comprehension of what is expected of him, how motivated he is to respond and what unconsidered individual constraints there are on responses. For these and other reasons the child may adopt strategies in an experimental situation which can give misleading results.

A number of investigators have examined the language used by children in natural settings. Work in the thirties and forties provided valuable normative studies using these techniques (McCarthy, 1954). More recently similar methods have been used for testing grammatical theories (Menyuk, 1969) or looking for the rules underlying communicative situations (Geest *et al.*, 1973; Sinclair and Coulthard, 1975).

All three methods have been used to study conversations of young children; diary studies (Keenan, 1974), experimental methods (Glucksberg, Krauss and Wiesberg, 1966; Flavell *et al.*, 1968) and spontaneous speech recorded in natural environments (Mishler, 1975). The study reported here combines the two latter methods, creating experimental situations which provide natural settings for recording children's conversations.

The wide spectrum of questions explored through these research strategies has important implications when considering the relationship of language to the young child's cognitive achievements and social integration.

Much research has been inspired by the poor achievement of children from low income groups. Many American studies have pointed to deficiencies (Hess and Shipman, 1965; Bee *et al.*, 1969) or differences (Labov, 1970; Baratz, 1970) in the language used by disadvantaged as compared with advantaged children. In Britain, Bernstein and his colleagues have found cultural differences reflected in the structure of speech (Bernstein, 1961; Brandis and Henderson, 1970; Hawkins, 1969; Robinson and Rackstraw, 1972). Tough (1974), interested in describing the ways in which children use language, suggests it is the range of functions rather than complexity of structure that differentiates children from disadvantaged homes.

Questions posed by environmental effects and modes of analyses have been approached in other ways. A different facet of environmental effects relates to speaker and respondent roles in a conversation and this has inspired research in education and psychology. Seminal work by Bellack *et al.* (1966) and others (Barnes, 1969; Flanders, 1970) has been concerned with ways of analysing the structure of teacher/child interactions in the classroom. Other studies have investigated speech adaptation to the needs of the listener showing that, for instance, adults modify their speech when talking to children as opposed to other adults (Snow, 1972) and that children as young as four simplify their speech when talking to younger children (Shatz and Gelman, 1973). These studies, and those referred to earlier, mark a growing interest in the communicative functions of language and the importance of looking at language in context.

Nevertheless, the processes of communication are by no means understood. An awareness of the subtle effects that different communicative situations can create is of enormous relevance for all interested in the education of the young child. Some of these have been touched upon in the preceding discussion. It would seem that the school's concern with language should be both social and cognitive. An environment is needed in which a child can communicate with adults and peers within a social framework and yet be able to extend the use of language for elaborated analysis and explanation. The way in which teachers structure verbal interchanges can be as important as the content of the message. While conveying information the teacher can encourage turn taking, develop the perceptions of other points of view and extend the ways in which a child can comprehend and develop his use of language.

The patterning of verbal interactions between adults and young children brings another dimension to the consideration of language usage. Despite its obvious importance, very little is known about discourse or its development. In order to better understand some of the complex integrations that must take place and what strategies these involve, a study was designed to investigate some of the processes which make up discourse. The aim of the study was to provide a comprehensive description of conversations between adults and children to consider the effects of depriving children of any immediate shared referents and to relate the findings from this to other aspects of language use.

Methods

Children from the playgroup described in the previous section have been involved in a series of investigations designed to compare their ways of speaking in different environments. Children were observed talking to peers, mothers and playgroup staff in a variety of situations within the playgroup and at home. The work reported here is concerned with the speech exchanges between children and a familiar adult in a familiar environment. Two groups of children, balanced for age and playgroup experience were selected. They were the four oldest children in each group, with a mean age of 4 years 4 months, and they had all attended the playgroup for one year and one term. All three members of the playgroup staff were well known to the children. They each talked, individually, to a group of four children, in two different situations. The difference between the two situations lay in the presence or absence of table activities for the children to play with, which could serve as contextual referents in conversation (activity and no activity conditions).

Fifteen minute recordings were made of each conversation, twelve recordings being made in all. Each of the three adults talked to both groups of children in the activity and no activity conditions. An observer, using a Sony stereo-cassette tape recorder, recorded all the speech produced by the adults and children into one microphone while relating a simultaneous account of ongoing events into the other. Both staff and children were accustomed to the observer's presence and no noticeable account was taken of her being in the room. All the recordings made were subsequently transcribed and analysed.

Categories

The essential components of discourse, which any description must take account of, are the speaker, the topic and the listener. Discourse then is a process involving the exchange of messages and the inter-changing of the role of the speaker and respondent. There are two points to be made about appraising a conversation. Speech exchanges take place between the people involved, and these exchanges contain messages (the topic of the conversation). Although these two features are interrelated they may be considered independently. A speaker can introduce several topics without involving another speaker's participation. On the other hand a single topic can be maintained over several interchanges between different speakers and respondents. During such events, speakers can initiate participation, by deliberate invitations to respondents. There are then, two forms of initiation: the introduction of a new topic, or the invitation to another to take over. One is connected with content and the other with reciprocity of roles.

The manner in which discourse is maintained also differentiates speech exchange and topic. Conversations are maintained by the introduction of new ideas, new material and new themes. To sustain interest by the extension and elaboration of a single topic, while maintaining the interchanges of speaker and respondent, is a complex process.

The initiation and maintenance of discourse illustrates ways in which topics are exchanged between speakers. A speaker can initiate or open conversations, or he may respond. There are different strategies for these functions. The classification devised to study the conversation exchanges between adults and children examines these features. The categories are divided into opening and response modes and a bias to topic or to speech exchange is contained within the subdivisions of these two main categories. The discourse categories and their definitions are given in Table 5.

Certain words and phrases, such as, 'well', and 'now then' are used to engage the listener's attention or delineate one part of a conversation from another. These words and phrases could be attached to many of the categories listed so a separate assessment of them was made.

The basic unit of measurement was the utterance. This was defined as the smallest meaningful group of words linked together by a speaker, and generally demarcated by a pause. All that a speaker said in his turn in the

TABLE 5 *Classification of discourse categories*

These categories were developed to differentiate between opening and response modes in speech and to relate these to speech content and speech exchanges.

Opening modes	
Initiate:	The introduction of a new topic into the conversation. This new topic might arise out of an existing one or be unrelated to any previous discussion.
Starter:	An utterance referring back to a previous topic.
Invite:	A deliberate invitation for verbal participation. The speaker requests a verbal response.
Interpolate:	An inappropriate or mistimed intrusion into a conversation. Either the topic is irrelevant or the bid for a place is out of turn.
False start:	An utterance which is begun but fails to reach completion.
Response modes	
Acknowledge:	Brief remarks which acknowledge and accept the previous speaker's utterance and show the role of speaker has been adopted.
Yes/no:	Simply yes or no responses. This and the answer category classify minimal verbal responses.
Answer:	Brief, generally one word responses, often involving labelling and attributive functions.
Comment:	An extended answer, less redundant and containing more information than the preceding category.
Repetitions:	Three types of repetition are classified below;
	Partial: The repetition of a word or phrase from the previous speaker's utterance.
	Whole: The repetition of the whole of the preceding utterance which generally involves syntactic reformulation.
	Extension: The repetition of the preceding utterance with additional information.
Sustain:	The maintaining of a topic or theme by the addition of new information.
Extend:	The drawing out of new themes from the existing topic.

conversation, whether it was one utterance or more, was termed a discourse segment.

The language used by adults and children was described in other ways which were related to the categories devised for discourse. The form of utterances was defined by adopting the mood system so that formally utterances could be imperatives: 'Come here', interrogatives: 'Can I have the bike now', or 'Where is my doll', indicatives: 'This is a very big house', or exclamations: 'What a mess'. Elliptical utterances which avoided giving redundant information ('The red one' as opposed to 'I want the red one') and negatives were also differentiated.

Utterances were classified broadly into three principal functional types each of which was further elaborated to provide a more precise description. The three principal functional types related to, 1. behaviour or actions, 2. to the giving or receiving of information, or 3. to affective expressions. The speaker's effectiveness in talking to others was also assessed; this was done on the basis of whether they received an anticipated appropriate response, a non-verbal appropriate response, no response because none was expected, or were ineffective as a response was required but was not given.

An interrelated picture of the speech patterns of adults and children can be reconstructed from a combination of these descriptions.

Analyses and results

In both situations adults talked more than the children; the total number of utterances for adults being greater than the combined utterances of all the children. However, an increase in adult speech did not necessarily produce a decrease in the amount spoken by the children; when adults talked more the children also tended to talk more. The mean number of utterances and the range for adults and children is given in Table 6. The data presented in Table 6 indicate that the absence of any immediate and obvious contextual referent does not lead to any reduction in the amount of speech produced by the adults or by the children.

Each participant in a conversation can produce one or more utterances before someone else adopts the speaker's role. We shall refer to this utterance or sequence of utterances as the discourse segment. Adults show proportionately fewer occasions on which they make only one utterance before another person takes over. Typically adults produce longer sequences of

TABLE 6 *Mean number of utterances, and the range, recorded for adults and children in activity and no activity conditions, based on 6 × 15 minute samples*

	Activity	*No activity*
Adult	279·3 (range 215–330)	254·5 (range 212–287)
Child	181·0 (range 111–221)	188·5 (range 157–218)

TABLE 7 *The mean number of utterances in discourse segments for adults and children recorded in the two conditions.*

Number of utterances in discourse segment	Activity		No activity	
	Adult	Child	Adult	Child
1	51·0	32·0	62·5	31·0
2	31·5	5·0	35·5	5·5
3	19·0	1·0	16·5	1·0
4	9·0	·5	7·0	·5
5	9·3	·2	3·5	·3
6	2·5	—	1·3	—
7	1·0	—	·5	—
8	·5	—	1·0	—
9	1·0	—	·5	—
10	·5	—	·5	—
10+	·5	—	·5	—

utterance within a discourse segment. No child produced a segment of discourse which was longer than five utterances, Table 7. When children did string pieces of information together they were inclined to create one long 'and then' type of structure rather than break it down into two or more utterances. For example, 'I took a football game in a big box and its got one of those pressers about that big and you go press and this leg moves and kicks the ball'. This was produced without any demarcation pause to justify splitting it into separate utterances.

The opening modes employed by adults and children in the two situations show interesting similarities as well as differences, Table 8. The initiation of a new topic is as much the prerogative of the child as of the adult, if not more so. The form which the initiation takes, however, radically differentiated adults from children, implying a certain amount of egocentricity in children's initiations compared with those of adults. Rarely did the children initiate a topic or reintroduce a previous one in any other form than a statement. Adults tended to use question forms or occasionally statements with tags attached, as in 'You can swim, can't you, Anthony?'. Such forms tend to encourage a response. As well as asking for information the adult is drawing the child into the conversation. The child's use of the question form may well be restricted to the more obvious and less redundant function of asking for help or information. Its functional use in discourse for eliciting

TABLE 8 *Means for the opening modes of adults and children. Comparisons between the data from the two conditions were made using the Mann–Whitney test*

	Activity			No activity		
	Adult	Child		Adult	Child	
Initiate	5·5	6·2	n.s.	8·0	9·9	n.s.
Restart	24·5	25·5	n.s.	17·5	24·5	$p < \cdot 05$
Invite	69·4	8·7	$p < \cdot 001$	66·9	3·5	$p < \cdot 001$
Interpolate	·6	14·9	$p < \cdot 001$	—	11·0	
False start	4·2	15·4	$p < \cdot 01$	4·2	18·5	$p < \cdot 005$

participation and involvement is perhaps not so well developed.

In the no activity condition, no toys made available, adults reintroduced topics ('start' category) less frequently than in the activity condition, $p < \cdot 05$. They also returned to previous topics less frequently in the no activity condition than did the children, $p < \cdot 05$. Maintaining group interest in the task and sustaining continuity led adults to take control of the topic when engaged in playing with the children. This was not so when there was no activity to engage in. In the no activity condition children readily returned to topics which were of special interest to them, often related to their own personal experiences.

The involvement with idiosyncratic concerns is reflected in the invite category. This includes all utterances where a deliberate invitation is given to another to take part in the conversation. There is a highly significant difference in such invitations between adults and children. Adults encourage the children to talk, to take the speaker role. Generally, each segment of adult discourse ended with an invitation to a child to say something. On the occasions when children deliberately requested a verbal response they were asking for help or information whereas adults tended to evoke responses in order to sustain the conversation. In this way invitations had a supportive function aimed at ensuring continued discourse.

Interpolations and false starts are category descriptions for the occurrence of inappropriate timing or the inadequate formulation of utterances. Interpolations reflect attempts to enter the conversation at inopportune moments; because the topic may be out of place, or because another person is speaking. False starts are utterances which are begun but not completed and have to be reformulated or abandoned. They occur more in the speech of children than that of adults, and interpolations are more frequently used by children when there is an ongoing activity. It is possible that when children want assistance immediately or the attention and admiration of others they are more likely to cut across what someone else is saying. If this is the case it may also account for the quite large number of false starts which occur in both conditions. The finding that false starts occurred rather more in the no activity condition could indicate a greater complexity in the processing and production of speech when the group is deprived of an obvious contextual referent (the play materials). Similarly the finding that more semantic and syntactic errors occurred in the no activity condition may also be a reflection of the greater difficulties in structural organisation which children encounter in the absence of a clear and obvious contextual referent.

The analysis of the opening modes suggests that adults are concerned with speech exchanges and with encouraging children to join in the conversations. Children, on the other hand, are concerned with content. When they have something they want to say, they say it. There is little to show they appreciate the possibilities of sharing discourse by using the strategies which the adults adopted.

Response modes can be divided into those which are immediate

TABLE 9 *Means for the response modes of adults and children. Comparisons made by the Mann–Whitney test*

	Activity			*No activity*		
	Adult	Child		Adult	Child	
Acknowledge	14·5	·8	$p < ·005$	17·2	1·2	$p < ·001$
Yes/no	5·7	13·7	$p < ·01$	6·4	27·9	$p < ·001$
Answer	3·2	21·7	$p < ·001$	8·0	24·8	$p < ·01$
Comment	35·4	44·0	$p < ·06$	22·3	39·0	$p < ·05$
Partial repeat other	2·9	1·5	$p < ·05$	10·0	1·5	$p < ·001$
Whole repeat other	17·0	4·4	$p < ·001$	11·0	2·0	$p < ·001$
Extend other	7·2	—		8·0	1·5	$p < ·001$
Sustain topic	34·5	15·5	$p < ·001$	24·5	12·0	$p < ·001$
Extend topic	26·2	8·5	$p < ·001$	22·4	16·0	$p < ·1$

responses to the previous utterance or responses which sustain or extend a topic. The results from the analysis of response modes are given in Table 9. The immediate response to an utterance can serve various functions. It may accept or acknowledge what has just been said. 'That's right', 'Very good' are throwaway phrases used for reassurance rather than their information content. These acknowledgements show that one person's turn to speak has been replaced by another and are indications that the role has been accepted. The analyses illustrate that this element of verbal recognition is hardly present in children's speech, especially when compared with the adults. It is a redundant element which suggests again that children are non-redundant in their use of discourse. Conversely, short immediate responses giving a brief one word, yes/no reply occur much more frequently in children. This results in part from the questions asked, and the demands made upon the children. In the activity situation a child may frequently be asked to give, or affirm, the names or attributes of what is being played with. There were fewer inversions and more 'Wh?' type questions asked by adults in this situation compared with the no activity condition. This probably accounts for the greater frequency of one word responses in the no activity condition. However, the children's responses are still noticeably different from those of the adults, for when giving the single direct answer they do so without including a throwaway acknowledgement. The tendency for adults is to include it.

Comments are extended immediate responses which have an information content lacking in the previous categories. Elliptical utterances, 'That brick', as opposed to 'that', are included. Comments comprised the largest number of children's responses, similarly invitations formed the larger part of adult speech. Although children initiate topics as often as adults, conversations are maintained by adults directing initiations to children. These initiations are accepted by children who take the speaker role, but they do not tend to return it. The pattern of a child's discourse segment is to give either a yes/no response, a brief answer or a comment, and leave it at that. Adults tend to adopt two or more immediate responses, such as an acknowledgement and a comment, before going on to sustain or extend the discourse, releasing it then with an invitation to someone else to participate and take their turn. As in:

Adult: 'Yes, that's right. You have got very fierce ones.
The fierce ones ought to go together in there.
What's the one with spots called?'

There are still other ways of taking up a turn in discourse apart from those listed already. Repetitions play a noticeable role, especially in adult speech. We have classified repetitions into three types. There can be a partial repetition, as in:

Child: 'I've got a dog'.
Adult: 'A dog'.

or a whole repetition which generally involves syntactic reformulation, as in:

Adult: 'You've got a dog'.

or, there can be an extension of the utterance giving additional information, as in:

Adult: 'I've got a dog as well.'

The extent to which adults use repetitions, and their increased use of them in the no activity condition, which lacked any immediately obvious contextual reference suggests that they are used supportively. When children used repetitions it tended to be for emphasis or the gratification gained from repeating a name, or attribute of an object of interest to them.

When an immediate response has been made to a previous utterance, the speaker has the choice of continuing or handing the speaker role over to someone else. Adults frequently sustained and extended topics and they did this in both of the conditions. Children showed a propensity for introducing new information into the conversations in the no activity condition, $p < \cdot 05$. The children, talking about their own experiences and not confined by an immediate task, extended topics by talking about themselves and their particular interests.

Response modes of adults also emphasise the relational aspects of their discourse. They acknowledged and often repeated what the children had said. This reciprocity was not apparent in children. Their responses were topic centred in that they generally gave immediate answers to questions and then the speaker role passed to another person.

The effectiveness of speakers was assessed and the results of the analyses are given in Table 10. Success or failure in being given the appropriate

TABLE 10 *The means for effectiveness in discourse for adults and children*

	Activity		*No activity*	
	Adult	Child	Adult	Child
Not answered	14·3	19·8	5·7	10·3
Answer not required	41·0	27·0	29·7	13·6
Answered	161·3	95·0	218·0	126·3

response was assessed from discourse segments, not utterances. In the course of the conversations all interchanges were between adults and children apart from three which were child–child exchanges. On two of these occasions the same child expressed disagreement with another child. On the third occasion a different child offered reasons why wild pandas came to her friend's house for milk. In each case the adult took up the conversation. A high proportion of appropriate answers were given and there were few occasions when answers were expected but not given. To a certain extent the situation affects the number of answers required. When there is a specific shared referent there is less need to give an answer because it is probably obvious from the context. There is no need to make it verbally explicit.

Discussion

The sheer flexibility of language forms the basis of its power as a communication system. Appropriate combinations of words can convey messages of enormous functional diversity. A child first encounters the institutionalised transmission of culture in the context of a school and here language plays a major part. The way in which teachers and other adults use language is likely to have significant consequences for the child's integration into school and into certain other environments. Extending the cognitive functions of language by encouraging children to explore the interpretations, projections and explanatory possibilities of language has become a major objective of many educational programmes. Language communicates not only information but also attitudes; it can be used supportively and so facilitate the child's social interactions. By showing acceptance and sustaining the interest and involvement of the child language provides a means whereby the child is able to participate fully in the activities of the nursery. This in turn will enhance his cognitive and social development.

Each situation makes its own demands which will affect the pattern of language used. The topic of the conversation, the individual concerns of those engaged, their status and role all play some part in determining the structure and function of the discourse. The results presented above show that the adults utilised certain strategies for engaging and maintaining the participation of the children. The adult's technique of using 'invitations' to elicit a verbal response was not a feature of the children's utterances, they would give the required response but not follow it with an invitation. Children showed no evidence of deliberately sustaining the flow of the discourse. Their invitations served to bring topics but rarely speakers into the conversation. When considered in the light of a child's preverbal interactions with his mother the ability to introduce and restart topics is not surprising. The human infant goes through a lengthy period of relative helplessness which necessitates some form of signalling to communicate his needs, desires and affections, thus he must be able to initiate interchanges with his mother. This ability to initiate is also apparent in the preschool child communicating with an adult who is not the mother. It seems probable that it is less demanding to initiate a topic and talk about one's own immediate concerns than it is to enter into another's area of interest.

The discourse patterns of the children and adults show differences in their awareness of the devices for maintaining and sharing discourse. Adults acknowledge utterances addressed to them and create opportunities for others to participate to a much greater extent than do children. This may result in part from the supervisor role held by the adults. But it may also reflect a general adult view of what is required in talking to children of this age and it may be supported by cues which young children provide. The children for their part may not realise the relevance of existence of strategies for maintaining and sharing discourse, their interest being predominantly in topics, not in speech exchanges. As the results indicate when a child wanted verbal recognition from an adult and requested a response from her the adult acknowledged and complied with the request. This pattern of reciprocity appears to be difficult for the children to maintain. They do formulate utterances which show an ability to take another's point of view and they can introduce such utterances appropriately into a conversation. However, preschool age children may be unaware of the supportive elements which can be used to sustain and sequence discourse. They tend therefore to be more direct and non-redundant, focussing on immediate message value rather than discourse involvement or showing concern for the involvement of others.

The two conditions in which observations were made, activity and no activity situations, gave rise to few differences in the discourse patterns. In the absence of any play activities the adults showed an increase in the frequency with which they partially repeated previous utterances, these were used for emphasis in the case of non-contextual referents. In the same condition the adults showed a decrease in the extent to which they restarted topics. The tendency to return to previous topics in the activity condition reflects the adults bringing the conversations back to the play activities which were engaging the children. The results from the comparison of the two conditions revealed little difference between the structure of the discourse produced. This interesting finding has educational implications since it suggests that the physical environment has less effect than some have supposed. The discourse pattern is very largely a function of the adult who plays a dominant and directing role.

A deeper understanding of the intricacies of language as it is used in a social context is extremely important for educational theory and practice. The importance of language for the child's intellectual and social development is appreciated but much remains to be discovered about the mechanisms involved. The study of discourse by the methods described provides a promising level of analysis which remains to be fully exploited.

Note: The work reported in this paper was supported by a grant from the Social Science Research Council. Dr Martlew was in receipt of a research studentship from the Council.

References

Educational Research: The State of the Art

ASHBY, E. (1958) *Technology and the Academics*. London: Macmillan.

BAIN, A. (1879) *Education as a Science*. London: Kegan Paul.

BURT, C. (1921) *Mental and Scholastic Tests*. London: King and Staples.

BUTCHER, H. J. and PONT, H. B. (eds) (1968, 1970, 1973) *Educational Research in Britain*, Vols 1, 2 and 3. London: University of London Press.

CONRAD, A. (1960) See Radford (1973) footnote, p. 6.

CUNNINGHAM, C. (1972) 'A research policy for economics', *SSRC Newsletter*, 14 March 1972.

FLEMING, C. M. (1946) *Research and the Basic Curriculum*. London: University of London Press.

HALSEY, A. H. (1972) *Educational Priority*, Vol. 1. London: HMSO.

HOLMES, E. (1972) Book review in *Br. J. educ. Psychol.*, **42**, 92.

NISBET, J. D. and ENTWISTLE, N. J. (1966) *The Age of Transfer to Secondary Education*. London: University of London Press.

NISBET, J. D. and ENTWISTLE, N. J. (1969) *The Transition to Secondary Education*. London: University of London Press.

RADFORD, W. C. (1973) *Research into Education in Australia, 1972*. Canberra: Australian Government Publishing Service.

RICHARDSON, E. (1975) *Authority and Organisation in the Secondary School*. London: Macmillan.

RUSK, R. R. (1913) *Introduction to Experimental Education*. London: Longmans Green.

SANFORD, N. (1964) *The American College*. New York: Wiley.

TAYLOR, W. (1972) 'Retrospect and prospect in educational research', *Educ. Res.*, **15**, 3–9.

TAYLOR, W. (ed.) (1973) *Research Perspectives in Education*. London: Routledge and Kegan Paul.

THOULESS, R. H. (1969) *Map of Educational Research*. Slough: NFER.

VERNON, P. E. (1940) *The Measurement of Abilities*. London: University of London Press.

WALL, W. D. (1962) 'Educational research today: IV.—Resistances, organisation and costs', *Brit. J. educ. Psychol.*, **32**, 223–33.

WARD, A. V. (1973) *Resources for Educational Research and Development*. Slough: NFER.

WHIPPLE, G. M. (1912) *Manual of Mental and Physical Tests*, Vol. 1. Baltimore: Warwick and York.

YATES, A. (1971) *The Role of Research in Educational Change*. Palo Alto: Pacific Books.

YOUNG, M. (1965) *Innovation and Research in Education*. London: Routledge and Kegan Paul.

The Contribution of Research to Knowledge and Practice

AMOS, D. (1931) 'Examination and intelligence test forecasts of school achievement', *Br. J. educ. Psychol.*, **1**.

AUSTIN, F. M. (1931) 'An analysis of the motives of adolescents for the choice of the teaching profession', *Br. J. educ. Psychol.*, **1**.

BERLYNE, D. E. (1966) 'The relationship of the social sciences to educational planning, research and development' in *Emerging Strategies and Structures for Educational Change*. Toronto: OISE.

BLOOM, B. (1964) *Stability and Change in Human Characteristics*. New York: Wiley.

BRONFENBRENNER, U. (1974) 'Is early intervention effective?', *Teachers College Record*, **76**, No. 2.

CATTELL, R. B. (1931) 'The assessment of teaching ability', *Br. J. educ. Psychol.*, **1**.

COHEN, D. K. and GARET, M. S. (1975) 'Reforming educational policy with applied research', *Harv. Educ. Rev.*, **45**.

FISHER, R. A. (1937) *The Design of Experiments*. Edinburgh: Oliver and Boyd.

FLOUD, J. E., HALSEY, A. H. and MARTIN, F. M. (1956) *Social Class and Educational Opportunity*. London: Heinemann.

HAGGARD, E. A. (1954) *Social Status and Intelligence: An Experimental Study of Certain Cultural Determinants* (Genetic Psychological Monographs, **XLIX**, No. 2). Provincetown, Mass.: The Journal Press.

HALSEY, A. H. (1972) *Educational Priority Area Publications, Vol. 1: E.P.A. Problems and policies*. London: HMSO.

HESS, R. D. and SHIPMAN, V. C. (1965) 'Early experience and the socialization of cognitive modes in children', *Child Dev.*, **36**.

HUNT, J. MCV. (1961) *Intelligence and Experience*. New York: Ronald Press.

LABOV, W. (1970) 'The logic of non-standard English' in WILLIAMS, F. (ed.) *Language and Poverty*. Chicago: Markham Press.

ROTHSCHILD, LORD (1971) 'The organisation and management of goverment R and D' in *A Framework for Government Research and Development*. London: HMSO.

SMITH, L. M. and GEOFFREY, W. (1968) *The Complexities of an Urban Classroom*. New York: Holt Rinehart and Winston.

START, K. B. and WELLS, B. K. (1972) *The Trend of Reading Standards*. Slough: National Foundation for Educational Research.

SVENNSON, N-E. (1962) *Ability Grouping and Scholastic Achievement*. Report of a five year follow up study. Uppsala: Almqvist & Wiksell.

WESTINGHOUSE LEARNING CORPORATION (1969) *The Impact of Head Start Experience: An Evaluation of the Effects of Head Start on Children's Cognitive and Affective Development*, Vol. 1, *Text and Appendices A–E*. University Report to Office of Educational Opportunity, Clearinghouse for Federal, Scientific and Technical Information, Washington, DC.

WHITEHEAD, A. N. (1932) 'The rhythm of education' in *The Aims of Education*. London: Williams and Norgate (New Edition, 1950).

The Conduct of Educational Case Studies: Ethics, Theory and Procedures

BECKER, H. S. (1958) 'Problems of inference and proof in participant observation', *Am. sociol. Rev.*, **23**, 652–60.

BECKER, H. S. *et al.* (1961) *Boys in White*. Chicago: University of Chicago Press.

BECKER, H. S. (1964) 'Problems in the publication of field studies' in VIDICH, A. J. (ed.) *Reflections on Community Studies*. New York: Wiley.

BECKER, H. S. *et al.* (1968) *Making the Grade*. New York: Wiley.

BEDFORD, S. (1968) *A Compass Error*. London: Collins.

BLYTHE, R. (1969) *Akenfield*. Harmondsworth: Penguin.

BRUGELMANN, H. (1974) 'Towards checks and balances in educational evaluation—on the use of social control in research design'. Unpublished paper, University of East Anglia: Centre for Applied Research in Education.

BRUGELMANN, H. (1976) *The Teachers Centre* (SAFARI case study). University of East Anglia: Centre for Applied Research in Education.

CASE STUDIES IN SCIENCE EDUCATION. Report available from Center for Instructional Research and Curriculum Evaluation, University of Illinois, Champaign, Urbana.

COLLIER, J. (1967) *Visual Anthropology: Photography as a Research Method*. New York: Holt Rinehart and Winston.

CRONBACH, L. (1974) 'Beyond the two disciplines of scientific psychology'. Paper read at American Psychological Association Conference, New Orleans.

DOLLARD, J. (1949) *Caste and Class in a Southern Town*. New York: Harper.

ELLIOTT, J. (1974) 'The Safari Solipsists' in MACDONALD, B. and WALKER, R. (eds) *Innovation, Evaluation, Research and the Problem of Control*, 103–16. (Safari Papers I), University of East Anglia: Centre for Applied Research in Education.

ENTWISTLE, N. (1973) Open University Course E341. *The Nature of Educational Research*. Block 1.

FREUD, S. (1953) *Standard Edition*, Vol. 2. London: Hogarth Press and the Institute of Psychoanalysis.

GRAEF, R. (n.d.) *The Space Between Words—School* (BBC Film) Available from BBC Enterprises, Peterborough.

GUILFORD, J. P. (1954) *Psychometric Methods* (2nd Edition). London: McGraw-Hill.

HAMILTON, D. *et al.* (1977) *Beyond the Numbers Game: A Reader in Alternative Evaluation*. London: Macmillan.

HARGREAVES, D. (1967) *Social Relations in a Secondary School*. London: Routledge and Kegan Paul.

JAMES, W. (1890) *Principles of Psychology* (2 vols). New York: Henry Holt.

KAUFMAN, B. (1964) *Up the Down Staircase*. Englewood Cliffs, New Jersey: Prentice-Hall.

KURCHAK, M. (1974) 'The camera as a surgical instrument', *Take One*, **4**, No. 1.

LABOV, W. (1973) 'The linguist as lame', *Language and Society*, April 1973.

LACEY, C. (1970) *Hightown Grammar: School as a Social System*. Manchester: Manchester University Press.

LEWIS, O. (1959) *Five Families*. New York: Basic Books.

MCCALL, G. J. and SIMMONS, J. L. (1969) *Issues in Participant Observation*. Reading: Mass.: Addison-Wesley.

MACDONALD, B. (1975) 'Evaluation and the control of education'. To be published in TAWNEY, D. (ed.) *Evaluation: The State of the Art*. London: Macmillan (in press).

MACDONALD, B. and WALKER, R. (1975) 'Case study and the social philosophy of educational research', *Cambridge Journal of Education*, **5**, No. 1.

MACDONALD, B. and WALKER, R. (1976) *Changing the Curriculum*. London: Open Books.

MALINOWSKI, B. (1967) *A Diary in the Strict Sense of the Word*. London: Routledge and Kegan Paul.

MEAD, M. (1975) *Blackberry Winter: My Earlier Years*. New York: Pocket Books.

NISBET, J. (1974) 'Educational research: The State of the Art'. Proceedings of the Inaugural Meeting of the British Educational Research Association, 1974, University of Birmingham.

NORRIS, N. (ed.) (1977) *Theory into Practice: SAFARI interim papers 2*. University of East Anglia: Centre for Applied Research in Education.

OETTINGER, A. (1969) *Run Computer Run*. Harvard: Harvard University Press.

PARLETT, M. and HAMILTON, D. (1972) 'Evaluation as illumination: a new approach to the study of innovatory programs', CRES Paper No. 9, University of Edinburgh.

PICK, C. and WALKER, R. (1976) *Other Rooms: Other Voices* (SAFARI case study), University of East Anglia: Centre for Applied Research in Education.

POWDERMAKER, H. (1967) *Stranger and Friend*. London: Secker and Warburg.

RICHARDSON, E. (1973) *The Teacher, the School and the Task of Management*. London: Heinemann.

SCHULTZ, A. (1962–6) *Collected Papers*, 3 vols. The Hague: Nijhof.

SMITH, L. M. (1974) 'An aesthetic education workshop for administrators: some implications for a theory of case studies.' Paper read at AERA, Chicago, 1974.

SMITH, L. M. and GEOFFREY, W. (1968) *Complexities of an Urban Classroom*. New York: Holt Rinehart and Winston.

SPINDLER, G. (ed.) (1970) *Being an Anthropologist: Fieldwork in Eleven Cultures*. New York: Holt Rinehart and Winston.

THOMAS, W. I. (1951) (ed. by E. H. VOLKHART) *Social Behaviour*. New York: Social Science Research Council.

Understanding Computer Assisted Learning. Report available from University of East Anglia: Centre for Applied Research in Education.

WALKER, R. and MACDONALD, B. (1976) Open University Course E203. *Innovation at School Level*. Unit 27.

WALLER, W. (1932) *The Sociology of Teaching*. New York. Wiley.

WOLCOTT, H. (1967) *A Kwakuitl Village and School*. New York: Holt Rinehart and Winston.

YOUNG, M. F. D. (ed.) (1971) *Knowledge and Control*. London: Collier-Macmillan.

Research into Practice

FORD, J. (1969) *Social Class and the Comprehensive School*. London: Routledge and Kegan Paul.

SCHON, D. A. (1971) *Beyond the Stable State*. Harmondsworth: Penguin.

Program Evaluation, particularly Responsive Evaluation

EISNER, E. (1969) 'Instructional and expressive educational objectives: their formulation and use in curriculum', in AERA Monograph Series on Curriculum Evaluation No. 3, 1–31. Chicago: Rand McNally.

ESSLIN, M. (1966) *The Theatre of the Absurd*. London: Eyre and Spottiswoode.

LEVINE, M. (1973) 'Scientific method and the adversary model: some preliminary suggestions', *Evaluation Comment*, **4** No. 2, 1–3.

LINDQUIST, E. F. (ed.) (1951) *Educational Measurement*. Washington: American Council on Education.

MACDONALD, B. (1976) 'Evaluation and the control of education'. To be published in TAWNEY, D. (ed.) *Evaluation: The State of the Art*. London: Macmillan (in press).

PARLETT, M. and HAMILTON, D. (1972) 'Evaluation as illumination: a new approach to the study of innovatory programs', Occasional Paper No. 9. University of Edinburgh: Centre for Research in the Educational Sciences.

PROVUS, M. (1971) *Discrepancy Evaluation*. Berkeley: McCutchan.

RHYNE, R. F. (1972) 'Communicating holistic insights', *Fields Within Fields . . . Within Fields*, **5**, No. 1. New York: World Institute Council.

RIPPEY, R. (ed.) (1973) *Transactional Evaluation*. Berkeley: McCutchan.

SCRIVEN, M. (1967) 'The methodology of evaluation', in AERA Monograph Series on Curriculum Evaluation, No. 1, 39–83. Chicago: Rand McNally.

SCRIVEN, M. (1973) 'Goal-free evaluation' in HOUSE, E. (ed.) *School Evaluation*, 319–28. Berkeley: McCutchan.

SMITH, L. M. and POHLAND, P. A. (1974) 'Educational technology and the Rural Highlands' in AERA Monograph Series on Curriculum Evaluation, No. 7, 5–54. Chicago: Rand McNally.

STAKE, R. E. (1967) 'The countenance of educational evaluation', *Teachers College Record*, **68**, 523–40.

STAKE, R. E. and GJERDE, C. (1974) 'An evaluation of TCITY: the Twin City Institute for Talented Youth, 1971' in AERA Monograph Series on Curriculum Evaluation, No. 7, 99–139. Chicago: Rand McNally.

STUFFLEBEAM, D. L. *et al.* (1971) *Educational Evaluation and Decision Making*. Itasca, Illinois: Peacock.

THORNDIKE, R. L. (ed.) (1971) *Educational Measurement* (2nd Ed.). Washington: American Council on Education.

TYLER, R. W. (1949) *Basic Principles of Curriculum and Instruction*. Chicago: University of Chicago Press.

Schooling as an Agency of Education: Some Implications for Curriculum Theory

ABRAHAMSON, J. H. (1974) 'Classroom constraints and teacher coping strategies.' Ph.D. dissertation, University of Chicago.

ADAMS, R. S. and BIDDLE, B. J. (1970) *Realities of Teaching*. New York: Holt Rinehart and Winston.

AUSUBEL, D. P. (1967) 'Crucial psychological issues in the objectives, organization, and evaluation of curriculum reform movements.' *Psychology in the Schools*, **4**, 111–21.

BARNES, D. (1976) *From Communication to Curriculum*. Harmondsworth: Penguin.

BELLACK, A. A., KLIEBARD, H. M., HYMAN, R. T. and SMITH, F. L. (1966) *The Language of the Classroom*. New York: Teachers College Press.

BEREITER, C. (1973) *Must We Educate?* Englewood Cliffs, NJ: Prentice-Hall.

BERMANN, P. *et al.* (1977) *Federal Programs Supporting Educational Change, Vol. VII: Factors Affecting Implementation and Continuation*. Santa Monica, CA: Rand Corporation.

BERNSTEIN, B. (1973) 'Postscript', *Class, Codes and Control*. St Albans, Herts.: Paladin.

BOURDIEU, P. (1971) 'Systems of education and systems of thought' in YOUNG, M. F. D. (ed.) *Knowledge and Control*. London: Collier-Macmillan.

BRIDGHAM, R. G. (1971) 'Comments on some thoughts on science curriculum development', in EISNER, E. W. (ed.) *Confronting Curriculum Reform*. Boston: Little, Brown and Company.

CALHOUN, D. (1973) *The Intelligence of a People*. Princeton, NJ: Princeton University Press.

CHEVERST, W. J. (1972) 'The role of metaphor in educational thought: an essay in content analysis', *Journal of Curriculum Studies*, **4**, 71–82.

COLEMAN, J. A. (1968) 'Church-sect typology and organizational precariousness', *Sociological Analysis*, **29**, 55–66.

CUSICK, P. A. (1973) *Inside High School*. New York: Holt Rinehart and Winston.

CUSICK, P. A., MARTIN, W. and PALONSKY, S. (1976) 'Organizational Structure and Student Behavior in Secondary School', *Journal of Curriculum Studies*, **8**, 3–14.

DALIN, P. (1973) *Strategies for Innovation in Education. Case Studies of Educational Innovation* (Vol. 4). Paris: Organization for Economic Cooperation and Development.

DEMERATH, N. J. and THIESSEN, V. (1966) 'On spitting against the wind: Organizational precariousness and American religion', *Americal Journal of Sociology*, **71**, 674–87.

DOUGLAS, M. (1970) *Natural Symbols*. London: Barrie and Rockliff.

DOYLE, W. (1978) 'Paradigms for research on teacher effectiveness', in SHULMAN, L. S. (ed.) *Review of Research in Education*, 5. Itasca: F. E. Peacock, Publishers.

DREEBEN, R. (1970) *The Nature of Teaching: Schools and the Work of Teachers*. Glenview, IL.: Scott, Foresman and Company.

DREEBEN, R. (1971) 'American schooling: patterns and processes of stability and change', in BARBER, B. and INKELES, A. (eds) *Stability and Social Change*. Boston: Little, Brown and Co.

DREEBEN, R. (1973) 'The school as a workplace', in TRAVERS, R. M. W. (ed.) *Second Handbook of Research on Teaching*, 450–73. Chicago: Rand McNally and Company

FRIEDMAN, M. (1962) *Capitalism and Freedom*. Chicago: University of Chicago Press

FULLAN, M. and POMFRET, A. (1977) 'Research on curriculum and instruction implementation', *Rev. educ. Res.*, **47**, 335–97.

FURTH, H. G. (1970) *Piaget for Teachers*. Englewood Cliffs, NJ: Prentice-Hall, Inc.

HAMILTON, D. (1977) 'Classroom research and the evolution of the classroom system.' Department of Education, University of Glasgow, unpublished paper.

HODGETTS, A. B. (1968) *What Culture? What Heritage? A Study of Civic Education in Canada*. Toronto: Ontario Institute for Studies in Education.

HOEKTER, J. and AHLBRAND, W. P. (1969) 'The persistence of the recitation', *American Educational Research Journal*, **6**, 145–63.

KALLÓS, D. and LUNDGREN, U. P. (1977) 'Lessons from a comprehensive school system for curriculum theory and research'. *Journal of Curriculum Studies*, **9**, 2–20.

LANDON, J. (1887) *School Management*. Boston: Willard Small.

LAQUEUR, W. (1974) 'The gathering storm'. *Commentary*, **58**, 23–33.

LAYTON, D. (1973) *Science for the People*. London: George Allen and Unwin.

LIPPMAN, W. (1928) *American Inquisitors*. New York: Macmillan.

LORTIE, D. (1975) *Schoolteacher*. Chicago: University of Chicago Press.

MACDONALD, B, and WALKER, R. (1976) *Changing the Curriculum*. London: Open Books.

MCKINNEY, W. L. (1973) 'The Gary, Indiana public school curriculum, 1940–70: A Local History.' Ph.D. dissertation, University of Chicago.

MCKINNEY, W. L. and WESTBURY, I. (1975) 'Stability and change: the public schools of Gary, Indiana, 1940–70', in REID, W. A. and WALKER, D. E. (eds) *Case Studies in Curriculum Change*. London: Routledge and Kegan Paul.

MEYER, J. W. and ROWAN, B. (1978) 'The structure of educational organizations', in MEYER, M. W. (ed.) *Environments and Organizations*. San Francisco: Jossey-Bass.

MONKS, T. G. (1968) *Comprehensive Education in England and Wales*. Slough, Bucks: National Foundation for Educational Research.

NIEBUHR, H. R. (1929) *The Social Sources of Denominationalism*. New York: Henry Holt.

O'DEA, T. F. (1966) *The Sociology of Religion*. Englewood Cliffs, NJ: Prentice-Hall.

OLSON, D. R. and BRUNER, J. S. (1974) 'Learning through experience and learning through media', in OLSON, D. R. (ed.) *Media and Symbols: The Forms of Expression, Communication and Education*. The 73rd Yearbook of the National Society for the Study of Education. Chicago: The Society.

ORGANIZATION FOR ECONOMIC COOPERATION AND DEVELOPMENT (1966) *Curriculum Improvement and Educational Development*. Paris: OECD.

OSTERNDORF, L. C. and HORN, P. J. (1976) *Course Offerings, Enrollments and Curriculum Practices in Public Secondary Schools, 1972–73*. Washington, DC: U.S. Department of Health, Education, and Welfare, National Center for Education Statistics.

PERROW, C. (1970) *Organizational Analysis: A Sociological View*. London: Tavistock Publications.

PINCUS, J. (1974) 'Incentives for innovation in the public schools', *Rev. educ. Res.*, **44**, 113–44.

PRESIDENT'S SCIENCE ADVISORY COMMITTEE, PANEL ON YOUTH (1974) *Youth: Transition to Adulthood*. Chicago: University of Chicago Press.

REID, W. A. (1978) *Thinking About the Curriculum*. London: Routledge and Kegan Paul.

ROSENSHINE, B. (1976) 'Classroom instruction' in GAGE, N. L. (ed.) *The Psychology of Teaching Methods*. The Seventy-fifth Yearbook of the National Society for the Study of Education. Chicago: NSSE.

SEABORNE, M. (1971) *The English School: Its Architecture and Organization*. London: Routledge and Kegan Paul.

SMITH, L. M. and GEOFFREY, W. (1968) *The Complexities of an Urban Classroom*. New York: Holt Rinehart and Winston.

SPADY, W. G. and MITCHELL, D. E. (1977) 'Competency based education: Organizational issues and implications', *Educational Researcher*, **6**, 9–15.

STEBBINS, R. A. (1974) 'The disorderly classroom: Its physical and temporal conditions', *Monographs in Education, No. 12*. St. John's, Nfld: Memorial University of Newfoundland, Faculty of Education.

STINCHCOMBE, A. L. (1965) 'Social structure and organizations' in MARCH, J. G. (ed.) *Handbook of Organizations*. Chicago: Rand McNally and Company.

STINCHCOMBE, A. L. (1968) *Constructing social theories*. New York: Harcourt Brace and World.

STURT, M. (1967) *The Education of the People*. London: Routledge and Kegan Paul.

TAYLOR, P. H. (1973) 'New frontiers in educational research' in *Paedagogica Europaea*, **VIII**, Braunschweig: Georg Westermann Verlag, 17–33.

TAYLOR, P. H., REID, W. A. and HOLLEY, B. J. (1974) *The English Sixth Form: A Case Study in Curriculum Research*. London: Routledge and Kegan Paul.

TROELTSCH, E. (1931) *The Social Teaching of the Christian Churches*. New York: Macmillan.

VOEGE, H. W. (1972) 'The impact of Keynesian Ideas on Secondary School Economics Texts in the United States, 1936–1970', *Social Foundations of Education Monograph Series, No. 3*. Ann Arbor, MI: University of Michigan, School of Education.

VOEGE, H. W. (1975) 'The diffusion of Keynesian Macroeconomics through American High School Textbooks, 1936–1970' in REID, W. A. and WALKER, D. F. (eds) *Case Studies in Curriculum Change*. London: Routledge and Kegan Paul.

WANKOWSKI, J. A. (1974) 'Teaching method and academic success in sixth form and university', *Journal of Curriculum Studies*, **6**, 50–60.

WEST, E. G. (1968) 'Economics, Education and the Politician.' *Hobart Paper 12*. London: Institute of Economic Affairs.

WESTBURY, I. (1973) 'Conventional classrooms, "open" classrooms, and the technology of teaching', *Journal of Curriculum Studies*, **5**, 99–121.

WESTBURY, I. (1977) 'Educational policy-making in new contexts: The contribution of curriculum studies', *Curriculum Inquiry*, **7**, 3–18.

WESTBURY, I. (1978) 'Research into classroom processes: a review of ten years' work', *Journal of Curriculum Studies*, **10**, 283–308.

WESTBURY, I. and GAEDE, O. F. (1975) 'Introducing teachers to a new curriculum: An evaluation of the summer 1975 ECCP implementation program.' (ERIC ED 124–413)

WIRT, J. G. and QUICK, S. K. (1975) 'Research plan and final report outline for a study of the curriculum movement of the 1960s.' Washington, DC: Rand Corporation, unpublished paper.

WISE, A. E. (1976) 'Minimal educational adequacy: Beyond school finance reform', *Journal of Education Finance*, **1**, 468–83.

WISE, A. E. (1977) 'Why educational policies often fail: the hyperrationalization hypothesis', *Journal of Curriculum Studies*, **9**, 43–58.

WOODWARD, J. (1965) *Industrial Organization*, London: Oxford University Press.

Class and Pedagogies: Visible and Invisible

BERNSTEIN, B. (1967) 'Open Schools, Open Society?' *New Society*, 14 September.

BERNSTEIN, B. (1971) *Class, Codes and Control*, Vol. I, Part III. London: Routledge and Kegan Paul.

BERNSTEIN, B., PETERS, R. and ELVIN, L. (1966) 'Ritual in Education', *Phil. Trans. R. Soc.*, Series B, **251**, No. 772.

BOLTANSKI, L. (1969) *Prime Education et Morale de Classe*. Paris—La Haye: Mouton.

BLYTH, W. A. L. (1965) *English Primary Education*, Vols I and II. London: Routledge and Kegan Paul.

BOURDIEU, P. and PASSERON, J. C. (1970) *La Réproduction: éléments pour une théorie du système d'enseignement*. Paris: Les Editions de Minuit.

BRANDIS, W. and BERNSTEIN, B. (1973) *Selection and Control: a study of teachers' ratings of infant school children* (appendix). London: Routledge and Kegan Paul.

CHAMBOREDON, J-C. and PREVOT, J. Y. (1973) 'Le Métier d'Enfant. Définition sociale de la prime enfance et fonctions différentielles de l'école maternelle'. Studies in the learning sciences 3. Paris: CERI/OECD.

CREMIN, L. (1961) *The Transformation of the School*. New York: Knop.

DOUGLAS, M. (1973) *Natural Symbols* (Revised edition). London: Allen Lane.

DURKHEIM, E. (1933) *The Division of Labour in Society*, trans. George Simpson. New York: Macmillan.

DURKHEIM, E. (1938) *L'Evolution Pédagogique en France*. Paris: Alcan.

DURKHEIM, E. (1956) *Education and Sociology*, trans. POCOCK, D. F. (chapters 2 and 3). London: Cohen and West.

GARDNER, B. (1973) *The Public Schools*. London: Hamish Hamilton.

GOLDTHORPE, J. and LOCKWOOD, D. (1968) 'Affluence and the Class Structure', *Sociological Review*.

GREEN, A. G. (1972) 'Theory and Practice in Infant Education, a sociological approach and case study'. M.Sc. dissertation, University of London Institute of Education Library (for discussion of 'busyness').

HALLIDAY, M. A. K. (1973) *Exploration in the Function of Language*. London : Edward Arnold.

HOUDLE, L. (1968) 'An Enquiry into the Social Factors affecting the Orientation of English Infant Education since the early Nineteenth Century'. M.A. dissertation, University of London Institute of Education Library.

PLOWDEN REPORT (1967) *Children and Their Primary Schools*. A report of the Central Advisory Council for Education (England) Vol. I. London: HMSO.

SHULMAN, L. S. and KREISLAR, E. E. (eds) (1966) *Learning by Discovery: a critical appraisal*. Chicago: Rand McNally and Co.

SIMON, B. (ed.) (1972) *The Radical Tradition in Education in Britain*. London: Lawrence and Wishart.

STEWART, W. A. C. and MCCANN (1967) *The Educational Innovators*. London: Macmillan.

ZOLDANY, M. (1935) *Die Entstehungstheorie des Geistes*. Budapest: Donau.

On Educational Phenomena and Educational Research

AHLSTRÖM, K-G. and WALLIN, E. (1976) 'Effects of commissioned research' in ESTMER, B. (ed.) *Educational Research and Development at the NBE*. 83–7. Stockholm: Liber/Läromedel.

ALFF, W. *et al.* (1975) *Plädoyer für eine demokratische Bildungspolitik*. Köln: Pahl-Rugenstein.

ALTHUSSER, L. (1971) 'Ideology and Ideological State Apparatuses', in ALTHUSSER, L. *Lenin and Philosophy and Other Essays*, 127–86. New York: Monthly Review Press.

ALTHUSSER, L. (1977) 'Anmerkungen über die ideologischen Staatsapparate (ISA)' in ALTHUSSER, L. *Ideologie und ideologische Staatsapparate*, 154–68. Hamburg/West-Berlin: Verlag für das Studium der Arbeiterbewegung (VSA).

ALTVATER, E. and HUISKEN, F. (eds) (1971) *Materialien zur politischen Ökonomie der Ausbildungssektors*. Erlangen: Politladen.

BALIBAR, E. (1978) 'Irrationalism and Marxism', *New Left Review*, **107**, 3–18.

BAUDELOT, C. and ESTABLET, R. (1971) *L'Ecole Capitaliste en France*. Paris: Maspero.

BAUDELOT, C. and ESTABLET, R. (1975) *L'Ecole Primaire Divise* . . . Paris: Maspero.

BERNER, B. *et al.* (eds) (1977) *Skola, ideologi och samhälle*. (School, ideology and society. In Swedish.) Malmö: Wahlström & Widstrand.

BERNSTEIN, B. (1975) 'Class and Pedagogies: Visible and Invisible', *Educational Studies*, **1**, 23–41.

BERNSTEIN, B. (1977) 'Aspects of the relations between education and production' in BERNSTEIN, B. *Class, Codes and Control*. Vol. 3 (Second Edition) 174–200. London: Routledge and Kegan Paul.

BOWLES, S. and GINTIS, H. (1976) *Schooling in Capitalist America*. New York: Basic Books.

BROUDY, H. S., ENNIS, R. H. and KRIMERMAN, L. I. (eds) (1973) *Philosophy of Educational Research*. New York: Wiley.

CALLEWAERT, S. and KALLÓS, D. (1976) 'The Rose Coloured Wave in Swedish Pedagogy', *Educational Studies*, **2**, 179–84.

COLLINS, R. (1971) 'Functional and Conflict Theories of Educational Stratification', *Am. sociol. Rev.*, **36**, 1002–1019.

DUNKEL, H. B. (1972) 'Wanted: New Paradigms and a Normative Base for Research' in THOMAS, L. G. (ed.) *Philosophical Redirection of Educational Research*, 77–93. Chicago: University of Chicago Press.

ERBEN, M. and GLEESON, D. (1977) 'Education as Reproduction: A Critical Examination of Some Aspects of the Work of Louis Althusser', in YOUNG and WHITTY (1977), 73–92.

GINTIS, H. (1972) 'Towards a Political Economy of Education: A Radical Critique of Ivan Illich's De Schooling Society', *Harv. Educ. Rev.*, **42** (1), 70–96.

GLEESON, D. (ed.) (1977) *Identity and Structure: Issues in the Sociology of Education*. Chester: Nafferton Books.

GOWIN, D. B. (1972) 'Is Educational Research Distinctive?' in THOMAS, L. G. (ed.) *Philosophical Redirection of Educational Research*, 9–25.

GOWIN, D. B. (1973) 'Artifactual Regularities in Educational Research'. Paper presented at the Annual Meeting of AERA, February 1973, New Orleans, USA. Mimeo.

HEINRICH, R. (1973) *Zur politischen Ökonomie der Schulreform*. Stuttgart: Europäische Verlagsanstalt.

HIRST, P. Q. (1976a) *Problems and Advances in the Theory of Ideology*. Cambridge: Cambridge University Communist Party.

HIRST, P. Q. (1976b) 'Althusser and the Theory of Ideology', *Economy and Society*, **5**, 385–412.

HUISKEN, F. (1972) *Zur Kritik bürgerlicher Didaktik und Bildungsökonomie*. München: List Verlag.

HUNT, A. (ed.) (1977) *Class and Class Structure*. London: Lawrence and Wishart.

KALLÓS, D. (1978) *Den nya pedagogiken*. (The New Pedagogy. In Swedish.) Malmö: Wahlström & Widstrand.

KALLÓS, D. and LUNDGREN, U. P. (1977) 'Lessons from a Comprehensive School System for Curriculum Theory and Research', *Journal of Curriculum Studies*, **9** (1), 3–20.

KALLÓS, D. and LUNDGREN, U. P. (1978) 'Analysen und Modelle am Beispiel von Schweden' in FREY, K., AREGGER, K., KALLÓS, D. and LUNDGREN, U. P.

Curriculumreform unter europäischen Perspektiven. 56–123. Wiesbaden: Diesterweg & Sauerländer.

KLAFKI, W. (1971) 'Erziehungswissenschaft als kritisch-konstruktive Theorie: Hermeneutik-Empirie-Ideologiekritik', *Zeitschrift für Pädagogik*, **17**, 351–85.

KUHN, T. S. (1970) *The Structure of Scientific Revolutions.* (Second Edition) Chicago: University of Chicago Press.

LENIN, V. I. (1918) 'The State and Revolution', *Collected Works*, Vol. 25. Moscow, 1964.

MASUCH, M. (1973) *Politische Ökonomie der Ausbildung. Lernarbeit und Lehrarbeit im Kapitalismus.* Hamburg: Rowohlt.

PAULSTON, R. G. (1976) *Conflicting Theories of Social and Educational Change.* Pittsburgh: University Center for International Studies, University of Pittsburgh, USA.

POULANTZAS, N. (1974) *Fascism and Dictatorship.* London: New Left Books.

POULANTZAS, N. (1975) *Classes in Contemporary Capitalism.* London: New Left Books.

ROLFF, H. G. *et al.* (1974) *Strategisches Lernen in der Gesamtschule. Gesellschaftliche Perspektiven der Schulreform.* Hamburg: Rowohlt.

SCHWARZ, B. (ed.) (1977) *On Ideology. Working Papers in Cultural Studies, 10.* Birmingham: Centre for Contemporary Cultural Studies, University of Birmingham.

SHARP, R. and GREEN, A. (1975) *Education and Social Control: A Study in Progressive Primary Education.* London: Routledge and Kegan Paul.

SHULMAN, L. S. (1970) 'Reconstruction of Educational Research', *Rev. educ. Res.*, **40**, 371–96.

SIMON, J. (1974) '"New Direction" Sociology and Comprehensive Schooling', *Forum for the Discussion of New Trends in Education*, **17** (1), 8–15.

THERBORN, G. (1971) *Klasser och ekonomiska system.* (Classes and Economic Systems. In Swedish.) Kristiansstad: Cavefors.

THERBORN, G. (1973) *Vad är bra värderingar värda?* (What is the Value of Good Values? In Swedish.) Lund: Cavefors.

THERBORN, G. (1976) 'The Swedish Class Structure, 1930–1965: A Marxist Analysis' in SCASE, R. (ed.) *Readings in the Swedish Class Structure*, 151–67.

THIEN, H.-G. (1976) *Klassenlage und Bevusstseinsform der Lehrer im Staatsdienst. Zur Funktion der Lehrer im Reproduktionsprozess der bürgerlichen Gesellschaft.* Giessen: Focus Verlag.

TÖRNEBOHM, H. (1971) *Research as an Example of an Innovative System.* Institute for the Theory of Science, University of Gothenburg, Sweden. Mimeo.

ULICH, D. (1972) 'Probleme und Möglichkeiten erziehungswissenschaftlicher Theorienbildung' in ULICH, D. (ed.) *Theorie und Methode der Erziehungswissenschaft*, 13–87. Weinheim und Basel: Beltz Verlag.

WRIGHT, E. O. (1976) 'Class Boundaries in Advanced Capitalist Societies', *New Left Review*, **98**, 3–41.

YOUNG, M. F. D. (ed.) (1971) *Knowledge and Control. New Directions for the Sociology of Education.* London: Collier-Macmillan.

YOUNG, M. F. D. and WHITTY, G. (eds) (1977) *Society, State and Schooling. Readings on the Possibilities for Radical Education.* Guildford, Surrey: The Falmer Press.

Educational Research and the Shadows of Francis Galton and Ronald Fisher

ALLAN, G. J. B. (1974) 'Simplicity in path analysis', *Sociology*, **8**, 197–212.

BANTOCK, G. H. (1965) 'Educational Research: a criticism' (reprinted in ENTWISTLE, N. J. (1973) *The Nature of Educational Research*, Block 1 of the Open University Course 'Methods of Educational Inquiry', 38–48). Bletchley: Open University Press.

BORING, E. G. (1961) 'The beginning and growth of measurement in psychology' in WOOLF (1961) 108–27.

BREHAUT, W. (1973) 'British research in education: some aspects of its development' in BUTCHER, H. J. and PONT, H. B. (eds) *Educational Research in Britain 3*, 1–18. London: University of London Press.

BURROUGHS, G. E. R. (1974) 'Methods of educational enquiry' (Essay review of Open University course of the same name). *Br. J. educ. Psychol.*, **44**, 184–9.

BURROW, J. W. (1968) *Evolution and Society*. Cambridge: Cambridge University Press.

CAMPBELL, D. T. and STANLEY, J. C. (1966) *Experimental and Quasi-Experimental Designs for Research*. Chicago: Rand McNally.

CATTELL, R. B. (ed.) (1966) *Handbook of Multivariate Experimental Psychology*. Chicago: Rand McNally.

COHEN, J. (1971) 'Multiple regression as a general data-analytic system' in LIEBERMAN (1971) 421–40. (Reprinted from *Psychological Bulletin* (1968) **70**, 426–43.)

COOLEY, W. W. and LOHNES, P. R. (1971) *Multivariate Data Analysis*. New York: Wiley.

CORNISH, E. A. (1970) 'Preface to the fourteenth edition of Fisher's *Statistical Methods for Research Workers*', see FISHER (1925).

CRONBACH, L. J. (1969) 'Validation of education measures' in *Toward a Theory of Achievement Measurement* (Proceedings of the 1969 Invitational Conference on Testing Problems). Princeton: Educational Testing Service.

DARLINGTON, R. B. (1971) 'Multiple regression in psychological research and practice' in LIEBERMAN (1971) 384–407. (Reprinted from *Psychological Bulletin*, 1968, **3**, 161–82.)

DIGMAN, J. M. (1966) 'Interaction and non-linearity in multivariate experiment' in CATTELL (1966) 459–75.

ENTWISTLE, N. J. (1973) 'Complementary paradigms for research and development work in higher education', University of Lancaster Department of Educational Research. (Paper read to the inaugural conference of the European Association for Research and Development in Higher Education, Rotterdam.)

FINNEY, D. J. (1974) 'Problems, data and inference' (Presidential Address), *Jl R. statist Soc.*, Series A, **137**, 1–19.

FISHER, R. A. (1925) *Statistical Methods for Research Workers*. Edinburgh: Oliver & Boyd. (Quotations taken from the fourteenth edition, 1970.)

FISHER, R. A. (1935) *The Design of Experiments*. Edinburgh: Oliver & Boyd. (Quotations taken from the eighth edition, 1966.)

FISHER, R. A. (1959) *Statistical Methods and Scientific Inference*. Edinburgh: Oliver & Boyd. (2nd Edition, originally published in 1956.)

FLANDERS, N. A. (1970) *Analysing Teaching Behaviour*. London: Allison-Wesley.

GALTON, F. (1869) *Hereditary Genius*. London: Macmillan.

GALTON, F. (1883) *Inquiries into Human Faculty and its Development*. London: Macmillan. (Quotations taken from the Everyman edition, London: Dent n.d.)

GALTON, F. (1889) *Natural Inheritance*. London: Macmillan.

GOLDMANN, L. (1969) *The Human Sciences and Philosophy*. London: Cape.

GREENE, J. C. (1962) 'Biological and social theory in the nineteenth century: Auguste Comte and Herbert Spencer' in CLAGETT, M. (ed.) *Critical Problems in the History of Science*. Madison: University of Wisconsin Press.

HAMILTON, D. and DELAMONT, S. (1974) 'Classroom research: a cautionary tale', *Research in Education*, No. 11, 1–15.

HARRÉ, R. and SECORD, P. F. (1972) *The Explanation of Social Behaviour*. Oxford: Basil Blackwell.

HEARNSHAW, L. S. (1964) *A Short History of British Psychology 1840–1940*. London: Methuen.

HERRNSTEIN, R. J. (1973) *IQ in the Meritocracy*. London: Allen Lane.

HOPE, K. (1968) *Methods of Multivariate Analysis*. London: University of London Press.

HOTELLING, H. (1963) 'Different meanings of experimental design' in *Le Plan d'Experiences*, Colloques Internationaux No. 110, 39–49. Paris: Centre National de la Recherche Scientifique.

HUDSON, L. (1966) *Contrary Imaginations*. London: Methuen.

JENCKS, C. *et al.* (1973) *Inequality*. London: Allen Lane.

JENSEN, A. R. (1973) *Educability and Group Differences*. London: Methuen.

KALLÓS, D. (1973) *On Educational Scientific Research*. University of Lund Institute of Education, Report No. 36.

KERLINGER, F. N. and PEDHAZUR, E. J. (1973) *Multiple Regression in Behavioural Research*. New York: Holt Rinehart and Winston.

KOLAKOWSKI, L. (1972) *Positivist Philosophy*. Harmondsworth: Penguin.

LAZARSFELD, P. F. (1961) 'Notes on the history of quantification in sociology—trends, sources and problems' in WOOLF (1961) 147–203.

LIEBERMAN, B. (ed.) (1971) *Contemporary Problems in Statistics*. New York: Oxford University Press.

MURPHY, G. and KOVACH, J. K. (1972) *Historical Introduction to Modern Psychology*. New York: Harcourt Brace Jovanovich.

NEYMAN, J. (1971) 'R. A. Fisher (1890–1962): an appreciation' in STEGER, J. A. (ed.) *Readings in Statistics*, 387–99. New York: Holt Rinehart and Winston. (Reprinted from *Science*, 1967.)

O'NEILL, W. M. (1968) *The Beginnings of Modern Psychology*. Harmondsworth: Penguin.

PARLETT, M. (1972) 'Evaluating innovations in teaching' in BUTCHER, H. J. and RUDD, E. (eds) *Contemporary Problems in Higher Education*, 144–54. London: McGraw-Hill.

PEARSON, E. S. and KENDALL, M. G. (eds) (1970) *Studies in the History of Statistics and Probability*. London: Griffin.

PEARSON, K. (1892) *The Grammar of Science*. London: Walter Scott.

PEARSON, K. (1914) *The Life, Letters and Labours of Francis Galton* (3 volumes published successively in 1914, 1924 and 1930). Cambridge: Cambridge University Press.

PEEL, E. A. (1953) 'The permanent contribution of Francis Galton to psychology', *Br. J. educ. Psychol.*, **24**, 9–16.

PICKENS, D. K. (1968) *Eugenics and the Progressives.* Nashville, Tenn.: Vanderbilt University Press.

PILLINER, A. (1972) 'Testing with educationally disadvantaged children'. Occasional Paper No. 7, University of Edinburgh Centre for Research in the Educational Sciences.

RAO, C. R. (1964) 'Sir Ronald Aylmer Fisher—the architect of multivariate analysis', *Biometrics*, **20**, 286–300.

RAVETZ, J. R. (1971) *Scientific Knowledge and its Social Problems.* Oxford: Oxford University Press.

ROEBUCK, M. (1972) 'Floundering among measurements in educational technology', *Programmed Learning and Educational Technology*, **9**, 87–97.

SHAW, B. (1971) 'Education as an applied science: a critique of theory and research', *Research in Education*, No. 5, 75–87.

SHULMAN, L. S. (1970) 'Reconstruction of educational research', *Rev. educ. Res.*, **40**, 371–96.

SIMON, B. (1953) *Intelligence Testing and the Comprehensive School.* London: Lawrence and Wishart.

SIMON, B. (1956) 'Psychology and Education' reprinted in SIMON, B. (1971) *Intelligence, Psychology and Education*, 125–38. London: Lawrence and Wishart.

SNEATH, P. H. A. and SOKAL, R. R. (1973) *Numerical Taxonomy.* San Francisco: Freeman.

STAKE, R. (1973) 'Measuring what learners learn' in HOUSE, E. (ed.) *School Evaluation*, 193–223. Berkeley: McCutchan.

STANLEY, J. C. (1966) 'The influence of Fisher's "The Design of Experiments" on educational research thirty years later', *Am. educ. Res. Journ.*, **3**, 223–9.

SWIFT, D. F. (1973) 'Sociology and educational research' in TAYLOR, W. (1973) 172–87.

TAYLOR, H. F. (1973) 'Playing the dozens with path analysis: methodological pitfalls in JENCKS *et al., Inequality*', *Sociology of Education*, **46**, 433–50.

TAYLOR, W. (ed.) (1973) *Research Perspectives in Education.* London: Routledge and Kegan Paul.

THOMAS, L. G. (ed.) (1972) *Philosophical Redirection of Educational Research* (71st Yearbook of the National Society for the Study of Education, Part 1). Chicago: University of Chicago Press.

THOULESS, R. H. (1939) 'Scientific method and the use of statistics' in BARTLETT, F., *et al.* (eds) *The Study of Society*, 125–53. London: Routledge and Kegan Paul.

TIBBLE, J. W. (1966) 'The development of the study of education' in TIBBLE (ed.) *The Study of Education*, 1–28. London: Routledge and Kegan Paul.

WEBB, B. (1926) *My Apprenticeship.* London: Longmans, Green. (Quotations from Penguin Books edition, 1971.)

WILKIE, J. S. (1955) 'Galton's contribution to the theory of evolution with special reference to his use of models and metaphors', *Ann. Science*, **11**, 194–205.

WILLER, D. and WILLER, J. (1973) *Systematic Empiricism: Critique of a Pseudoscience.* New Jersey: Prentice-Hall.

WOOLF, H. (ed.) (1961) *Quantification—a History of the Meaning of Measurement in the Natural and Social Sciences.* New York: Bobbs-Merrill.

YATES, F. and MATHER, K. (1963) 'Ronald Aylmer Fisher 1890–1962', *Biographical Memoirs of Fellows of the Royal Society*, **9**, 91–129.

YOUNG, R. M. (1970) *Mind, Brain and Adaption in the Nineteenth Century*. Oxford: Clarendon Press.

YOUNG, R. M. (1973) 'The historiographic and ideological contexts of the nineteenth-century debate on man's place in nature' in YOUNG, R. M. and TEICH, M. (eds) *Changing Perspectives in the History of Science*, 344–438. London: Heinemann.

A Perspective on Nursery Education

AMMAR, H. (1954) *Growing up in an Egyptian village*. London: Routledge and Kegan Paul.

BARATZ, J. (1970) 'Teaching reading in an urban negro school system' in WILLIAMS, F. (ed.) *Language and Poverty*. Chicago: Markham.

BARNES, D. (1969) 'Language in the secondary classroom' in BARNES, D., BRITTON, J. and ROSEN, H., *Language, the learner and the school*. Harmondsworth: Penguin.

BEE, H. L., *et al.* (1969) 'Social class differences in maternal teaching strategies and speech patterns', *Develop. Psychol.*, **1**, 726–34.

BELLACK, A. A., KLIEBARD, M. M., HYMAN, R. T. and SMITH, F. L. (1966) *The language of the classroom*. New York: Teachers' College Press.

BERKO, J. (1958) 'The child's learning of English morphology', *Word*, **14**, 50–177.

BERNSTEIN, B. (1961) 'Social class and linguistic development: a theory of social learning' in HALSEY, A. H., FLOUD, T. and ANDERSON, C. A. (eds) *Education, economy and society*. Glencoe, Illinois: Free Press.

BLOOM, L. M. (1973) *One word at a time: the use of single word utterances before syntax*. The Hague: Mouton.

BRANDIS, W. and HENDERSON, D. (1970) *Social class, language and communication*. London: Routledge and Kegan Paul.

BRINDLEY, C., CLARKE, P., HUTT, C., ROBINSON, I. and WETHLI, E. (1973) 'Sex differences in the activities and social interactions of nursery school children' in MICHAEL, R. P. and CROOK, J. H., *Comparative Ecology and Behaviour of Primates*. London: Academic Press.

BROWN, R. (1973) *A first language*. London: George Allen and Unwin.

CHOMSKY, C. (1969) *The acquisition of syntax in children from five to ten*. Cambridge, Mass.: M.I.T. Press.

CONNOLLY, K. (1971) 'The evolution and ontogeny of behaviour', *Bull. Brit. Psychol. Soc.*, **24**, 93–102.

CONNOLLY, K. (1973) 'Ethological techniques and the direct observation of behaviour' in MITTLER, P. (ed.), *Assessment for learning in the mentally handicapped*. London: Churchill, Livingstone.

CONNOLLY, K. and BRUNER, J. S. (eds) (1974) *The growth of competence*. London: Academic Press.

EIFERMANN, R. (1970) 'Level of children's play as expressed in group size', *Brit. J. educ. Psychol.*, **40**, 161–70.

FEITELSON, D. (1959) 'Some aspects of the social life of Kurdish Jews', *Jewish J. Sociol.*, **1**, 201–16.

FEITELSON, D. (1972) 'Developing imaginative play in preschool children as a possible approach to fostering creativity', *Early Child Development and Care*, **1**, 181–97.

FEITELSON, D. and ROSS, G. S. (1973) 'The neglected factor—, play', *Human Develop.*, **16**, 202–24.

FLANDERS, N. A. (1970) *Analysing Teaching Behaviour*. Reading, Mass.: Addison-Wesley.

FLAVELL, J. M., BOTKIN, P. T., FRY, C. L., WRIGHT, J. N. and JARVIS, P. E. (1968) *The development of role-taking and communication skills in children*. New York: Wiley.

FREYBERG, J. T. (1973) 'Increasing the imaginative play of urban disadvantaged kindergarten children through systematic training' in SINGER, J. L. (ed.) *The child's world of make-believe*. New York: Academic Press.

GEEST, T. VAN DER, GERSTEL, R., APPEL, R., TERVOOT, B. TH. (1973) *The child's communicative competence*. The Hague: Mouton.

GLUCKSBERG, S., KRAUSS, R. and WIESBERG, R. (1966) 'Referential communication in nursery school children: method and some preliminary findings', *J. Exp. Child Psychol.*, **3**, 333–42.

HAWKINS, P. R. (1969) 'Social class, the nominal group and reference', *Language and Speech*, **12**, 125–35.

HESS, R. and SHIPMAN, V. (1965) 'Early experience and the socialisation of cognitive modes in children', *Child Devel.*, **36**, 869–86.

KEENAN, E. O. (1974) 'Conversational competence in children', *J. Ch. Lang.*, **1**, 163–84.

LABOV, W. (1970) 'The logic of non-standard English' in WILLIAMS, F. (ed.) *Language and Poverty*. Chicago: Markham.

LEOPOLD, W. (1939–49) *Speech development of a bilingual child*. 4 Vols. Evanston, Illinois: Northwestern University Press.

LEVINE, R. A. and LEVINE, B. (1963) 'Nyansongo: a Gusii community in Kenya' in WHITING, B. (ed.) *Six Cultures*. New York: Wiley.

MCCARTHY, D. (1954) 'Language development' in CARMICHAEL, L. (ed.) *Manual of Child Development*. (Second edition) New York: Wiley.

MARKEY, F. V. (1935) 'Imaginative behavior of preschool children', *Monog. Soc. Res. Child Devel.*, **18**.

MARSHALL, H. R. and HAHN, S. C. (1967) 'Experimental modification of dramatic play', *J. Pers. Soc. Psychol.*, **5**, 119–22.

MENYUK, P. (1969) *Sentences children use*. Cambridge, Mass.: M.I.T. Press.

MISHLER, E. (1975) 'Studies in dialogue and discourse: an exponential law of successive questioning', *Lang. Soc.*, **4**, 31–51.

PARTEN, M. (1932) 'Social participation among preschool children', *J. Ab. Soc. Psychol.*, **24**, 243–69.

PIAGET, J. (1962) *Play, dreams and imitation in childhood*. London: Routledge and Kegan Paul. (First French edn, 1951.)

ROBINSON, W. P. and RACKSTRAW, S. J. (1972) *A question of answers*. London: Routledge and Kegan Paul.

ROSEN, C. E. (1974) 'The effects of sociodramatic play on problem-solving behavior among culturally disadvantaged preschool children', *Child Devel.*, **45**, 920–27.

SHATZ, M. and GELMAN, R. (1973) 'The development of communication skills: modifications in the speech of young children as a function of the listener', *Monog. Soc. Res. Child Develop.*, **38**.

SINCLAIR, J. MCH. and COULTHARD, R. M. (1975) *Towards an analysis of discourse*. London: Oxford University Press.

SINGER, J. L. (ed.) (1973) *The child's world of make-believe*. New York: Academic Press.

SMILANSKY, S. (1968) *The effects of sociodramatic play on disadvantaged preschool children*. New York: Wiley.

SMITH, P. K. (1974) 'Ethological methods' in FOSS, B. M. (ed.) *New perspectives in child development*. Harmondsworth: Penguin.

SMITH, P. K. (1977) 'Social and fantasy play in young children' in HARVEY, D. and TIZARD, B., *The Biology of Play*. London: Spastics International Medical Publications.

SMITH, P. K. and CONNOLLY, K. (1972) 'Patterns of play and social interaction in pre-school children' in BLURTON JONES, N. (ed.) *Ethological studies of child behaviour*. Cambridge: Cambridge University Press.

SNOW, C. (1972) 'Mother's speech to children learning language', *Child Devel.*, **2**, 549–65.

TAINE, H. (1877) 'Acquisition of language by children', *Mind*, **2**, 252–9.

TOUGH, J. (1974) 'Children's use of language', *Educ. Rev.*, **26**, 166–79.

TULKIN, S. R. (1972) 'An analysis of the concept of cultural deprivation', *Devel. Psychol.*, **8**, 326–39.

General Index

Author Index